SURVEYING CRIME IN THE 21st CENTURY:

Commemorating the 25th Anniversary of the British Crime Survey

Mike Hough

and

Mike Maxfield

editors

Crime Prevention Studies
Volume 22

Criminal Justice Press
Monsey, NY, U.S.A.

Willan Publishing
Cullomptom, Devon, U.K.

Printed in the United States of America. No part of this book may be reproduced in any manner whatsoever without written permission, except for brief quotations embodied in critical articles and reviews. For information, contact Criminal Justice Press, division of Willow Tree Press Inc., P.O. Box 249, Monsey, NY 10952 U.S.A.

ISSN (series): 1065-7029.

ISBN-13 (cloth): 978-1-881798-74-3.

ISBN-10 (cloth): 1-881798-74-7.

ISBN-13 (paper): 978-1-881798-75-0.

ISBN-10 (paper): 1-881798-75-5.

Cover art (paperback edition) by Linda Wade Book Packaging and Design.

Printed on acid-free and recycled paper.

CRIME PREVENTION STUDIES

Ronald V. Clarke, Series Editor

Crime Prevention Studies is an international book series dedicated to research on situational crime prevention and other initiatives to reduce opportunities for crime. Most volumes center on particular topics chosen by expert guest editors. The editors of each volume, in consultation with the series editor, commission the papers to be published and select peer reviewers.

*   *   *

Volume 1, edited by Ronald V. Clarke, 1993.

Volume 2, edited by Ronald V. Clarke, 1994.

Volume 3, edited by Ronald V. Clarke, 1994 (out of print).

Volume 4, *Crime and Place*, edited by John E. Eck and David Weisburd, 1995.

Volume 5, *The Politics and Practice of Situational Crime Prevention*, edited by Ross Homel, 1996.

Volume 6, *Preventing Mass Transit Crime*, edited by Ronald V. Clarke, 1996.

Volume 7, *Policing for Prevention: Reducing Crime, Public Intoxication and Injury*, edited by Ross Homel, 1997.

Volume 8, *Crime Mapping and Crime Prevention*, edited by David Weisburd and J. Thomas McEwen, 1997.

Volume 9, *Civil Remedies and Crime Prevention*, edited by Lorraine Green Mazerolle and Jan Roehl, 1998.

Volume 10, *Surveillance of Public Space: CCTV, Street Lighting and Crime Prevention*, edited by Kate Painter and Nick Tilley, 1999.

Volume 11, *Illegal Drug Markets: From Research to Prevention Policy*, edited by Mangai Natarajan and Mike Hough, 2000.

continued

Contents

Contents

Acknowledgments

This volume is the product of a conference held at Cumberland Lodge, Windsor, in October 2006. Various thanks are due to those who made the conference possible, and to those who helped turn a collection of conference articles into a book.

We are very grateful to the Home Office and to Rutgers University for providing financial support for the conference and for the editorial work in producing the book. The British Crime Survey team was a pleasure to work with, and we are particularly grateful to Sian Nicholas, Maya Kara, and Alison Walker for their efforts in organizing the conference and for their helpful comments in the editorial process. Special thanks are also due to Ron Clarke for his consistently helpful advice and support throughout the process of planning the conference and editing the book.

We would like to thank Lesley Jenkins and Sian Turner of ICPR for their administrative support in organizing the conference and the staff of Cumberland Lodge for their hospitality throughout the conference.

Mike Hough
Mike Maxfield

London and Newark
April 2007

Foreword

Towards the end of the 1970s, several of us in the Home Office Research Unit, including Pat Mayhew and Mike Hough, began to make the case for the British Crime Survey, a national survey of crime victimization similar to one that started in America. Speaking at least for myself, I thought the survey would be a corrective to crime policy by focusing more attention on crime victims. I also thought it would help sell the concept of crime prevention by showing that much crime experienced by the public never comes to the notice of the criminal justice system and is therefore beyond its influence. Finally, I believed that by providing a new and improved index of crime, the survey would raise the Research Unit's profile within the Home Office, and it would do the same in the broader field of criminology by making a rich new source of crime data available to researchers. (As regards the latter, Pat and Mike were in fact for many years the most cited British criminologists because of their British Crime Survey work.)

There were powerful objections to mounting the survey, however, which included the costs of interviewing the necessary large sample of the public, and the anticipated political fallout from revealing that much more crime occurred than was reported in the annual Criminal Statistics. So we knew it was going to be hard to get the survey off the ground. I clearly remember the many hours spent agonizing with Pat and Mike about ways of getting reluctant Home Office officials on board, particularly in the Criminal and the Statistical departments. We were fortunate, however, to secure the active support of Bob Morris in the Crime Policy Planning Unit. This alliance between the two departments was critical in finally getting agreement for the survey.

The process of securing this agreement was tortuous, however. We took great pains in drafting position papers and proposals and carefully planned our approach to every critical meeting, trying to anticipate the objections and difficulties that might be raised by those likely to be present. We carefully scrutinized the minutes of meetings with ministers and senior officials where we were not present, and we questioned the more accessible participants in order to divine unfavorable nuances of attitude that might later damage the enterprise. We also had to appease Research Unit colleagues who foresaw their own work being overshadowed. I can particularly remember the acute anxiety with which I faced the prospect of pitching our plan for funding the survey with John Croft, the head of the Research Unit. The plan involved taking a large portion of the budget reserved for funding university research to pay for the interviewing work. This would likely raise the hackles of universities, but to my relief, John Croft agreed readily to the idea and became a staunch advocate of the survey.

The intensity of this experience over many months, and the elation when the survey was approved by ministers, has always remained with me. I was therefore surprised to learn (see chapter 2) that the official files suggest it was the Crime Policy Planning Unit, not the Research Unit, that had led the effort to get the British Crime Survey approved. This chastening fact is perhaps an example of one law of human nature, which holds that all parties to a joint enterprise overestimate the importance of their individual contributions. It might also reflect the fact that most of the official record was produced by the Crime Policy Planning Unit, not the Research Unit, and "he who writes the minutes sets the agenda." Another part of the explanation, however, is that the plotting and strategizing that Pat, Mike, and I had engaged in was deliberately concealed from view and unrecorded in the files because there is nothing as deadly to a civil service initiative as the appearance of unrestrained partiality! Last, we had probably underestimated the compelling case for the survey, though this was recognized by the Crime Policy Planning Unit, perhaps because it was somewhat removed from the day-to-day policy concerns of the rest of the Home Office.

Indeed, if we had failed to get the survey started when we did, it would probably not have been long before someone else would have got it off the ground. It was an idea whose time had come and we were in the fortunate position of giving it form because of our place in government. At the time, however, it did not feel like that. We really did see ourselves as outsiders arguing an unpopular case. In fact, this was how Home Office researchers often thought of themselves because they so frequently found that they were advocating positions or producing research that seemed inconvenient or irritating to their official superiors and political masters. These feelings were rooted, on the one hand, in junior status and youthful insecurity and, on the other, in a general suspicion of social science and disdain for specialists amongst senior civil servants of the day. The relationship certainly had little resemblance to the role of "administrative criminologists" as portrayed by their academic critics outside government. Home Office researchers generally did not think their job was to conduct work that would support official policy. They did not see themselves as handmaidens of administrators and politicians, or even as working hand in glove with them. Instead, many saw themselves as working for the general public and saw their role as producing knowledge to inform more rational policy making, even if the resultant policies were in flat contradiction to those of the government of the day. This attitude inevitably brought them into conflict with the administrators whose lives were made more difficult by research. It explains why so few researchers remained comfortable with their positions in the Home Office and why so few stayed in the civil service for their entire careers but instead departed for the more congenial environments of university departments. In fact, the very availability of this ready escape route created by the expansion of universities was an important factor contributing to the quality and independence of Home Office criminology.

If the time was ripe in the early 1980s for a national crime survey, it appears from chapters in this volume that if an omnibus national survey is to continue, it has to adapt and evolve to meet new circumstances. The successive sweeps of the British Crime Survey have taught us a great deal about the experience of crime in this country and that knowledge has been fed into crime policy and criminological theory. Each sweep of the survey has also helped to expose our ignorance about many other aspects of crime and about the performance of the police and criminal justice system. Indeed, it has been continually modified to help fill the gaps in our knowledge. It is these achievements that are celebrated in this volume, published in the British Crime Survey's 25th year. Although the survey is likely to continue, it may be time now to devote more energy to new kinds of surveys and research instruments to monitor more directly the performance of local police forces and to measure new manifestations of crime resulting from globalization, changing technology, and changed social arrangements. It is in these ways that we can best build upon the successes of the British Crime Survey.

Ronald V. Clarke
Rutgers University, Newark

Introduction

by

Mike Hough
Institute for Criminal Policy Research
King's College London

and

Mike Maxfield
School of Criminal Justice
Rutgers University, Newark

This book marks the 25th anniversary of the British Crime Survey (BCS), which first went into the field in 1982. It has its origins in a conference held at Cumberland Lodge, Windsor, in October 2006. This event, funded by Rutgers University and the British Home Office, brought together many of those who have contributed to the survey in various ways over its life, as well as others with expertise in crime surveys in Britain and elsewhere.

The conference was co-organised by the editors of this book, by Ron Clarke, and by the current BCS team. We and the team thought that the survey's 25th birthday should not go unmarked. We all felt that the BCS has proved to be a significant phenomenon, both in terms of public administration and of criminological knowledge, and that some sort of stocktaking would be sensible at this juncture. We decided to combine forces, and organise an event that would bring together academic and government researchers, past and present, to reflect on the past and to consider the future.

Crime Prevention Studies, volume 22 (2007), pp. 1–6.

Whilst it is obviously pleasant to look back with satisfaction on past achievements, the more important purpose of the event was to think about the future of crime surveys. The BCS – and its various cousins in other countries – have been subject only to small changes over the last quarter of a century. The genre is still largely unchanged. Whether it can and should continue well into the 21st century are important questions to ask. The answers partly turn on practical issues – whether, for example, a high enough proportion of the public will continue to take part in social surveys of this sort to guarantee reliable findings. In part, however, the survival of large national crime surveys depends on the changing informational needs of government. The 14 substantive chapters in this book all address these issues in various ways.

Chapter 2 traces the development of the BCS, noting its origins in the policy and research community of the day. The authors describe the most important contributions to research and practice that can be traced to the BCS. This includes methodological innovations in how basic counts of victimization can be combined with special-purpose groups of questions. Some thoughts about alternative futures for the BCS are expressed, themes picked up in the last chapter and applied to crime surveys generally.

Identifying the significance of multiple victimization is one of the major contributions of the BCS. Chapter 3 tells many tales, first tracing the discovery of repeat victimization to almost 30 years ago. Graham Farrell and Ken Pease then once again highlight the imbalance between the number of crime victims and the number of victimization incidents. The authors conclude that the BCS decision rule to cap incidents at five in a series seriously underestimates the incidence of both household and personal victimization. Further, truncating the distribution in this way systematically undercounts crimes targeting those most often victimized.

Recognition that victims and offenders are often the same people is an idea that predates victim surveys, traced in chapter 4 by Janet Lauritsen and John Laub to Marvin Wolfgang's study of a birth cohort. Most research in this area is based on either specialized samples, small numbers of individuals, or specific offenses. The BCS has been an important source of information from a general population sample, including selected self-report offending questions in a large victim survey. Nevertheless, Lauritsen and Laub argue that the existence of the overlap is now so well documented that further research with large-scale general surveys is not likely to produce much new information. The chapter concludes by describing more-focused research strategies that are more promising for understanding the mechanisms of victimization and offending.

Only a limited number of self-reported offending items can be included in a general-purpose crime survey. In chapter 5, David Matz describes the development of a remarkable survey that focuses on self-reported offending among the population at large, aged 10 to 65, and then from a subsample of respondents in younger age groups where offending is more common. Those aged 10 to 25 were interviewed in the second wave of the survey to reveal information about sequences of offending and victimizations. Matz presents brief results from the 2003 and 2004 waves of the OCJS, and describes how the survey articulates with other efforts to collect victimization and offending data from different target populations.

The ability to link individual and household characteristics to types of areas and neighborhoods has been a key feature of the BCS since the 1984 sweep. In chapter 6, Tim Hope takes advantage of this to examine dimensions of victimization in community context, finding covariation between burglary and a composite measure of community deprivation. The social environment of high-crime communities is different from that of low-crime areas. One important element of this, Hope argues, is differential ability to adopt personal crime prevention, something he calls "reflexive securitization." Hope concludes by observing that the shift in sampling strategies introduced in 2000 has reduced the relative sample sizes of inner city areas, undermining the potential for subsequent research questions such as reflexive securitization.

Since its first wave in 1989, the International Crime Victims Survey has been conducted in dozens of countries, making it possible to compare crime rates, police reporting, and a variety of other basic indicators of crime and justice. Jan van Dijk begins chapter 7 with an overview of the ICVS. Because different countries and different regions often face varying crime problems, surveys in individual countries are partly tailored to meet more specific needs. Country-specific items supplement measures of traditional volume crimes. van Dijk discusses how indirect measures of crimes such as corruption or organized crime activity can complement survey measures of other crime types. This chapter also highlights key dimensions of crime that are not well measured by crime surveys and their focus on victims.

The NCVS is the only national crime survey that has provided annual data for an extended period. The U.S. survey has also been the model for other national crime surveys. Chapter 8, by Michael Rand, traces the evolution of the NCVS, highlighting its contribution to research. Conducted by the U.S. Census Bureau, the U.S. survey includes certain distinctive features: large samples, bounded interviews, and a six-month recall period. Each of these adds to the cost of conducting the NCVS. Rand describes how pressures to economize have mostly reduced sample sizes. Considering the future of the NCVS, Rand believes the survey will become leaner and more flexible, resembling early sweeps of the BCS.

Crime surveys provide information about police as well as about crime. In chapter 9, Wesley Skogan examines how surveys meet the growing interest in measures of police performance, concluding "not very well." Memories of bad encounters are more long-lived and contagious than recall of positive experiences. Skogan also shows that citizen perceptions of police performance do not covary with measures of policing quality collected by direct observation. Given a range of problems with validity and reliability of survey-based measures, Skogan calls for a program of research aimed at learning more about patterns of error in perceptions of police. In the meantime, it appears that measuring change in attitudes is more reasonable than measuring variation across neighborhoods or jurisdictions.

Since its earliest sweeps in the 1980s, the BCS has incorporated many batteries of questions about police performance. Now, following heightened government interest in performance measures, the BCS sample has been redesigned to obtain at least 700 completed interviews in each of 42 police force areas nationwide. Jonathan Allen describes these efforts in chapter 10, explaining how they link up with different performance assessment initiatives.

Different sweeps of the BCS have included a variety of measures of public attitudes toward various elements of crime and justice. Chapter 11, by Mike Hough and Julian Roberts, discusses different attempts to gauge attitudes toward crime and punishment, culminating in a comprehensive bundle of questions in the 1996 BCS. Like Skogan's analysis of attitudes toward police, Hough and Roberts' findings show sharp discrepancies between public beliefs and other measures of such things as change in crime rates or criminal sentences. Disparities between opinion and purported fact are not limited to the BCS, as similar gaps in public knowledge have emerged from surveys in other countries. The authors conclude with a range of proposals for better understanding what survey data on public opinion do and do not measure.

Fear of crime has been of interest since the first sweep of the BCS. In chapter 12, Jason Ditton and Stephen Farrall briefly summarize what has been learned about fear over the past 25 years, concluding that despite a lengthy body of research a great deal of conceptual ambiguity still limits what we can claim to know. This is especially interesting, since few attitudes in criminology have received as much attention in efforts to improve measurement. The authors conclude that fear is best viewed as a multi-dimensional construct that should be measured by multiple items together with experiments in scaling.

Mike Sutton, in chapter 13, argues that crime surveys yield little information about a growing variety of crimes and related problems. Frauds targeting individuals or businesses, together with an expanding range of computer-facilitated offenses, are the most well known of these. Sutton considers these problems broadly. Traditional crime types operate in realms of traditional physical and social behavior that form the basis of crime surveys. Individual behavior and economic transactions are increasingly framed by the Internet, and traditional conceptions of crime have not yet caught up. The chapter describes examples of basic research that would begin to address these shortcomings. Sutton offers suggestions on how to take advantage of changes in communications technology to measure victimization by fraud and other offenses.

The BCS and selected spin-offs have begun to accumulate knowledge about fraud, as described by Jacqueline Hoare in chapter 14. Questions in the BCS asked about individual experiences of fraud, though this assumes individuals are aware they have been victimized. Two surveys that sampled businesses included questions about fraud victimization. The Offending Crime and Justice Surveys contain items about fraud offenses committed by respondents. Hoare also describes a range of administrative and private sources of data on fraud, concluding with an analysis of what is needed to understand better this complex family of offenses.

David Cantor and James Lynch begin chapter 15 by describing how changes in the social environment of surveys have reduced response rates, presented new challenges in sampling, and generally made it more difficult to conduct large-scale crime surveys. At the same time, changes in telecommunications and other technologies offer opportunities for improving measurement and reaching target populations otherwise difficult to contact. Cantor and Lynch also discuss the changing role of crime surveys as part of a system of statistical indicators of crime. Just as many clusters of indicators monitor health and economic conditions, evolving crime problems should be measured through a statistical system.

The final chapter centers on the future of crime surveys, pulling together topics raised mostly in other chapters. In much the same spirit that surveys of victims were proposed as measures of unreported and unrecorded crime over 40 years ago, chapters in this volume describe new directions for crime surveys.

✦

Address correspondence to: mike.hough@kcl.ac.uk or maxfield@rutgers.edu

The British Crime Survey Over 25 Years: Progress, Problems, and Prospects

by

Mike Hough
Institute for Criminal Policy Research
King's College London

Mike Maxfield
School of Criminal Justice
Rutgers University, Newark

Bob Morris
Former Assistant Under Secretary of State
U.K. Home Office

and

Jon Simmons
Research Development and Statistics Directorate
U.K. Home Office

Abstract: *Since its first sweep in 1982, the British Crime Survey has become an invaluable source of data for research and policy development. Whilst it has served its purpose in yielding a measure of crime that includes unreported crime, it also has incorporated a number of innovative features in its 25 years. This chapter reflects on the evolution of the BCS, on its notable achievements and how these have*

Crime Prevention Studies, volume 22 (2007), pp. 7–31.

contributed to the development of crime surveys generally. Revealing the key role of repeat victimization is especially significant. We also examine linked surveys of victimisation and offending, such as the Youth Lifestyle Survey, the Offending Crime and Justice Survey, and surveys of nonhousehold victimisation, which have expanded the scope of survey-based tools for policy and research.

Over a quarter of century, the BCS has achieved considerable institutional status. Media "opinion formers" know about it and understand it – at least in broad outline. It is recognised by most informed commentators as one of the key indicators of crime. More recently, it has evolved as an important technology for performance management through the use of quantitative targets to an extent that its originators never envisaged or foresaw. Ironically, this process of institutionalisation has occurred at a time when weakening trust in government generally has contributed to some problems over the credibility of *any and all* government crime statistics.[1] Over the course of most of the life of the BCS, the integrity of both the survey itself and of other government-generated crime statistics was largely unquestioned, yet over the last 5 years the meaning and validity of crime statistics have become politically contested, and subject to increasing misrepresentation.[2]

With political claims and counterclaims multiplying, many people have understandably concluded that there are "lies, damned lies and criminal statistics." This view may have appeared to have received an official endorsement when the then Home Secretary announced early in 2006 that he was setting up a review of the arrangements for producing crime figures to sit beside the one that had been set up the year before by the Statistics Commission (2006).[3] Thus, the BCS celebrates its 25th birthday at a time of uneasy tension between its credibility and its visibility as a government-sponsored survey.

We have envisaged this chapter as a stocktaking exercise. It starts with an account of the survey's origins in the early 1980s, examining how the idea of a crime survey was "sold" within the Home Office and to the politicians of the day. To many at that time, a crime survey seemed a risky and expensive venture, but the investment also promised considerable political and criminological benefits. We describe how the balance sheet looked prospectively in 1981.

We then summarise the key design features of the survey and the key messages that have emerged over its life. Some of these relate to crime trends, of course, but we shall also consider some of the central findings on repeat victimisation, on "fear of crime," on attitudes to the police and to sentencers, on drug use, and so on. We do not claim to have provided a comprehensive account, but if the reader is to understand the contribution that the BCS has made to policy and to academic criminology, an overview of this sort is a necessary first step.

Next, we offer our assessment of the extent to which the BCS has delivered on its promises. This stocktaking can hardly be regarded as an impartial exercise. Two of the authors were involved in getting the survey off the ground, a third currently carries responsibility for the survey within the Home Office, and the fourth has worked on various BCS datasets and on similar North American surveys. Nevertheless, we hope that we can muster enough objectivity to offer an account of the BCS's strengths and of its weaknesses. Our assessment is partly based on "domestic" knowledge, drawing on a close familiarity with the uses that the survey has been put to, and partly on comparative knowledge, examining the BCS relative to national surveys conducted in other jurisdictions.

The chapter ends by looking to the future. We consider what sort of future there may be for large-scale government sample surveys of any sort, and whether public compliance in exercises of this sort will at some stage fall below a critical level of viability. We discuss whether the tensions are reconcilable between surveys mounted as research exercises and those conducted primarily for the purpose of performance management. We conclude with our own recommendations for the survey's next quarter decade.

ORIGINS OF THE BCS

This section describes how the decision to initiate crime surveys was reached within the policy-making structures of the Home Office of the day. The viewpoints expressed are those of the two coauthors of this chapter who were involved in the process. One of us (Bob Morris) was a "generalist" Home Office official, and was at the time director of the Home Office's Crime Policy Planning Unit (CPPU).[4] The other (Mike Hough) was one of the initial BCS research team in the Home Office Research Unit (HORU).[5] The core BCS team was small, the other members being Pat Mayhew and Ron Clarke, who at the time was Deputy Director of the Unit. The Director, John Croft, also played an important role in supporting the concept of a national survey, and – crucially – in being able to commit the necessary finance to the project.

We have relied partly on our memories, and partly on the files that we were able to retrieve from the Home Office archives. Sifting through these papers, any independent historian would conclude that the initiative was very largely initiated and led by the CPPU, and that HORU filled an almost entirely subordinate role. As we shall describe, the reality was more complex: the BCS never would have got off the ground without the active promotion of the idea by the RPU and the equally active sponsorship of the CPPU. The intellectual interest in crime surveys and the impetus for getting one off the ground came originally from HORU; so too did the necessary technical expertise. The CPPU, however, was quick to see the opportunities that a survey presented, in terms of revitalising criminal statistics and in contributing to policy development within the Home Office. Equally important, CPPU played a crucial facilitative role, in that it had access to the levers necessary for steering the proposal through an initially sceptical department – and HORU did not.

There were various reasons why none of us within HORU or CPPU thought that the former could or should effectively front the proposal for a national crime survey: to avoid the appearance of self-interest; to avoid inflaming the rivalry that already existed between the research and the statistical units; and because sponsorship by a policy division was essential if internal and ministerial support were to be secured. Equally, as will be described below, a national crime survey fitted well with the CPPU agendas for holding the police to account for their effectiveness and for reforming the production of criminal statistics.[6]

The Context

HORU had commissioned the first crime survey of any significance in Britain in the early 1970s, published as *Surveying Victims* (Sparks, Genn, & Dodd, 1977).[7] This study was conducted in London on a scale that was very modest by current standards, but it addressed all of the key conceptual and methodological issues relating to crime surveys, and the British Crime Survey (BCS) certainly owes a debt to this work. The results of the survey, however, were presented very much in the tradition of academic criminology – and, indeed, some considerable time after the work had been commissioned. It failed to fire Home Office enthusiasm for a national survey.

Crime surveys came tentatively back on to the Home Office policy agenda in the late 1970s. By this time, HORU and CPPU had discussed the possibility of mounting a national survey, both recognising the possibilities that this represented. Early discussion took account of the United

States experience, the HORU sponsorship of the Sparks et al. survey, the outcome of the few questions inserted twice in the General Household Survey (GHS), and some early forays into local crime surveys.[8] A CPPU review in 1978 had touched without enthusiasm on crime surveys in the context of a more general review. It was not until later in 1979 that the CPPU began to look at the prospect in more depth, when the 1979 general election resulted in a change of government.

The new government was committed to a strong law and order agenda. Not only was there the penology of the "short, sharp shock," but immediate payment of the second instalment of the Edmund Davies pay award to the police as part of a commitment to fight crime. In another part of the new woods, a "Quango cull"[9] swept away the Advisory Council on the Penal System (ACPS), the standing, independent body that had brought together academics and criminal justice practitioners and acted as a continuing source of policy advice. On the face of it, this might not have seemed like a government that would welcome novel depictions of crime levels (for example, calibrating the "dark figure") that might be thought to call the success of their policies into question or to make them more difficult to achieve.

There were also likely to be presentational difficulties – to put it mildly – in responding to the expected report of the Royal Commission on Criminal Procedure (HMSO, 1981) This had been set up by the previous government as a result of serious miscarriages of justice generally attributed to defects in police investigative procedure and powers. In the event, such handling difficulties as the Royal Commission Report created[10] were significantly eclipsed by the severe civil disorders that occurred in a number of urban areas in the early summer of 1981.

In addition, there was in no sense a single mind amongst the officials on the Crime Policy Planning Committee (CPPC), which supervised the CPPU. Some generalists were deeply sceptical of an expensive proposal that could not promise any evident operational or policy payoffs. Further, there were professional issues. HORU was one thing but the separate Statistical Department (SD) was another, with different management constraints. Whereas HORU looked largely to the Criminal Department as its sponsor, SD – dealing with the whole range of Home Office statistical requirements – answered to the Chief Scientist and partly to the head of the Government Statistical service rather than to the head of the Criminal Department. Thus, a defective organisation structure amplified normal and understandable differences of view. Relations between the two specialist departments were characterised by considerable competitiveness, verging at times on well-mannered hostility.[11]

The relationship of the CPPU with SD was complicated at the time by the fact that the head of the CPPU had been the Rayner reviewer of SD as part of a government-wide efficiency review of government statistics.[12] The reviewer, as many others have done, called into question whether continuing remorselessly and exclusively with ancient, immemorial tasks was the best policy:

> The drive to refine and elaborate what is already collected can overlook the desirability of balancing reduced effort in some traditional areas against more effort in fresh ones equally as important could be trying to chart by survey the hinterland of unreported crime, the extent and character of victimisation, and the incidence of fear of crime.[13]

This was in July 1980. Plainly, the CPPU had by then got the bit between their teeth. Why?

In the Criminal Department, there had long been dissatisfaction with the reliance on police recorded crime. The defects were well understood of a disaggregated system reliant on the vagaries of police administrative processes. Experience with attempts to "reform" the system – of which the Perks Committee in 1967[14] had been only the latest in a series from the 1890s – had merely continued to expose what were in fact irremediable defects. There was also unease about a system inevitably dominated by police service interests in the outcomes. Whereas in the early days – perhaps now surprisingly – the bias had been towards *under*-recording offences, the balance was thought to have swung decisively the other way.[15] In the CPPU, these long-term dissatisfactions began to see in survey approaches something that would not only open up new sources of data but also lessen reliance on old ones.

By themselves, however, such considerations were not enough: four other factors came also into play. First, the Police Department were open to fresh approaches. Not only were they not captured by the service for which they were responsible, but they were also keen to take hold of measures that could elucidate questions of police effectiveness. Second, whilst the new government had a strong law and order agenda, it was at the same time not hostile to the consumer point of view in its supply-side approaches to policy making. It followed that targeted social surveying – asking the public directly about their views and experiences – was not wholly without appeal. Third, convinced that the criminological value of the enterprise would be extensive, HORU itself was determined to get a national crime survey off the ground. Fourth, judiciously reallocating funds already available to it, HORU had the necessary resources to embark on a new venture in principle. This fact was cardinal in persuading the CPPU that it would be worth making a run for crime surveys in practice.

Making the Case for a National Crime Survey

Throughout 1979, HORU and CPPU had been collaborating in working up a case for a crime survey. The CPPU was ready make its case to the Crime Policy Planning Committee in February 1980.[16] The case that was made placed less importance on the "dark" figure of unreported crime than on obtaining more intelligence in respect of crime prevention, fear of crime, and for informing enforcement responses. Because nothing was to be gained from offering an unbalanced account, the CPPU paper was also frank about the drawbacks of expense and uncertainty of impact. Discussion revealed the battle lines to be as indicated above. In addition, SD was concerned about the proposed methodology and, assuming that the Office of Population, Census and Surveys (OPCS) would be the right body to undertake any survey, pointed out that recent Rayner manpower cuts had reduced its capacity for doing so. After a further airing of the issues at a New Options seminar initiated by the Permanent Under Secretary in June 1980, the CPPC agreed – not unanimously – in October that there should be a spring workshop in 1981 to ventilate the issues as thoroughly as possible.[17]

Chaired by the head of the Criminal Department, this was a crucial initiative, co-organised by CPPU and HORU and funded by the latter. It involved a much wider group than hitherto, together with strong academic and official representation, including in the former case from North America[18] and Europe. Also present were researchers who had much practical experience of surveys on the scale being contemplated. Articles from the CPPU and HORU looked at the policy and practical issues, respectively. The former assessed the likely benefits and risks of the enterprise; the latter included fairly well fleshed-out proposals for the first survey, including sampling methods, questionnaire content, timing, and costs.[19] Workshop discussion groups teased out a wide range of questions relating to both. The record shows a balanced collective appraisal devoid of evangelistic fervour, and notably sceptical at some points, for example about the likely effects on public perceptions of crime (Home Office, 1981).

The seminar allayed some opposition, but did not end it. There were extensive discussions about the nature of the survey. Was it a research initiative – in which case it properly fell to HORU? Or was it an exercise in the collation of statistics – in which case the statisticians could claim it for their own? Should it be taken over by the Office for Population Censuses and Surveys? Could a single-tender contract to another organisation be justified? HORU and CPPU managed to steer the proposal through what seemed at the time very choppy waters. In May, the CPPC discussed the seminar record and a CPPU recommendation that the survey should go ahead. The exchanges were not helped by a *Times Higher Education Supplement* (THES)[20] story that a decision in favour had already been made. In the event, however, the chairperson of the CPPC summed up in favour of proceeding. Remarking that, like others, he had felt misgivings about the advantages of a crime survey, the workshop had persuaded him that one would be worthwhile. He did not stop there: "He wondered, indeed, if survey techniques could not prove an aid in other areas of policy where some kind of public perspective was necessary; it had been felt, for example, at the time of the abolition of the ACPS that a source of external opinion was still needed."[21]

The chairperson thereupon put the proposal to ministers, explaining in moderate tones that officials remained sceptical of the largest claims made for surveys:

> On the other hand, with varying degrees of reservation, we think surveys are a sensible investment: they will improve our intelligence on crime and inform more effective action. In the end, the case for them is that they make a more rational, because better informed, crime policy possible.
>
> However, it would be wrong to oversell them. Whilst it is true for many years we have been concerned about the limitations of the recorded crime figures, survey data have their own blemishes. Careful presentation will be necessary to explain the limitations on the accuracy and reliability of survey methods, just as with any other piece of research.[22]

In putting the articles to the Home Secretary, the Minister of State drew attention to the high costs and, separately, the possible downsides of including the self-report offending component. The issues were discussed at a meeting with the then Home Secretary in July, attended by the Minister of State, the Permanent Under Secretary, the chairman of the CPPC, the Chief Scientist, and the heads of SD and the re-badged Research and Planning Unit (RPU). Also present was the head of the former CPPU, an outfit whose role but not its personnel had by then been folded into the RPU. Much beleaguered at the time, the Home Secretary could have easily postponed or simply rejected a proposal that was likely to complicate rather than directly assist his tasks. He did not, however, take the easy route:

> The Home Secretary said that he was inclined to think the project should go ahead, despite the reservations that had been expressed (some of which he shared) since it would be desirable for the Home Office to show its willingness to contribute to the public debate about crime, which would inevitably follow the recent urban disorders.[23]

And that was that – except that the RPU then, of course, had to shoulder the considerable amount of work involved in establishing the new venture. The RPU awarded a contract to Social and Community Planning Research (now the National Centre for Social Research). A crime survey team was set up under the direction of Ron Clarke, and work began on the survey immediately. The sampling strategy and the questionnaire were devised by Douglas Wood of SCPR, Pat Mayhew, and Mike Hough, with the academic advice of Hazel Genn, David Farrington, and Wes Skogan. The first survey went into the field in January 1982. This could genuinely claim to be a *British* crime survey, in that the Scottish Office decided to conduct a parallel survey using a near-identical questionnaire.[24]

The first BCS report (Hough & Mayhew, 1983) was published a year later. Although it may not appear unusual now, it was in many ways a groundbreaking piece of work. It was produced very rapidly by the standards of the time, at low cost. It was written in a style that was less formal and more accessible than conventional Home Office research reports. We were also careful to ensure that the results could withstand methodological criticism – partly by ensuring that it was technically competent, and partly by being as open as possible about the limitations of the survey method. The research team were also heavily involved in the preparation of press notices, and more broadly in the development of media handling strategies. This contrasts with what subsequently became the norm, with increasingly less involvement by research professionals with media contact. The first survey was largely well received. Whilst its findings attracted a great deal of attention, press coverage largely avoided the sort of sensationalism that had always been recognised as a risk inherent in revealing a "dark figure" of crime.

The second BCS was mounted in 1984, followed by sweeps in 1988, 1992, and biennially thereafter until 2001, when it was changed into a continuous survey, with interviews running throughout the year. It is now one of the largest and most visible government surveys, with a sample of around 45,000 people interviewed each year.

Key Contributions Since 1982

This part of the chapter centres on what the BCS has become and what elements of it have been especially influential in criminological research. It is neither an exhaustive chronicle nor a technical description of the survey's execution. Those are important topics dealt with elsewhere in this chapter and in other parts of the book. The perspective represented here is that of researchers fortunate to have worked with BCS data along with members of the Research and Planning Unit. Some of us also have experience of other crime surveys and other ways to measure crime.

The idea for the BCS originated in the United States in the form of the National Crime Victimization Survey (NCVS), which predates the British version and provided the main model for the BCS to adapt to its own local purpose. Serving as an alternate count for police statistics has always been the most important goal of the American NCVS. This was among the objectives of the BCS – although reports always took care to present the survey as a complementary measure of crime, rather than as a substitute. The BCS always had a broader range of objectives to the NCVS, benefiting from the lessons that could be drawn from this earlier exercise. It has always been very much less expensive. Under its sample design that was in place until 2001, the BCS leaned as much toward efficiency as precision of victimization estimates. From the first sweeps, a variety of questionnaire items supplemented victimization questions. Many supplementary items varied from one sweep to the next.

Being freed somewhat of precision and consistency as absolute requirements for crime issues that stretched beyond the main crime measures, the BCS became a flexible tool for criminological research and policy development; it was "nimble," in the words of Dave Cantor and Jim Lynch in their chapter of this book. The policy development uses of the BCS have been subtle, but wide-ranging. This is distinct from policy evaluation, something that requires more deliberate longitudinal designs. Rather than looking only at today's issues, the BCS has been adept at looking forward at tomorrow's concerns, providing a bedrock of knowledge on some of the key issues that only subsequently became a matter of widespread political or public concern.

Serial surveys are well suited for such purposes. As knowledge is acquired and funnelled into policy development, new topics can be added to the next sweep. From its outset, the BCS combined a set of core items to monitor levels of victimisation, reporting to police, and concern about crime. Periodic supplements gathered information on special topics of particular interest to public officials and researchers. Results were presented in Home Office reports and academic publications. The scope of basic and applied research produced with BCS data is much broader than that from any other single source of data on crime, its correlates and impact. This influence is a product of the survey's design.

Design Elements

Several design elements have contributed to the survey's utility as a research and policy instrument, which in combination give the BCS its distinctive shape.

Research Platform

As a product of an agency engaged in research (the Home Office Research and Planning Unit, later to be absorbed into the Research and Statistics Directorate), the BCS was designed to accommodate varying clusters of questions that would supplement its core crime-counting function. This made it possible to add questions as needed to meet emerging interests, while maintaining a standard series to monitor victimisation consistently over time. It is especially important that the BCS was designed to incorporate standard, rotating, and purpose-built questionnaire modules.

Independent and Dependent Variables

As a research platform, each sweep of the BCS included bundles of items that are antecedents or consequences of victimisation. These have largely been developed from criminological theories, and their inclusion has supported basic research. Measures based on opportunity-related ideas have been prominent. The first sweep asked about routine behaviour thought to be linked with victimisation risk. Among these were items on self-reported offending. Later sweeps expanded on the latter, as research documented how the same factors were associated with higher victimisation and offending, within different population groups, and more importantly how victimisation was linked to offending at the individual level.

Policy Development

The BCS has also supported applied research to develop and clarify justice policies. Various sweeps of the BCS have centred on special topics such as contacts with police, domestic violence, drug misuse, fraud and technology offences, and attitudes toward criminal justice agencies. Selected survey results have been presented in special publications that target the criminal justice community. Reducing repeat victimisation is one especially well-known example of a policy initiative rooted in findings from the BCS. Just as locally targeted surveys are tools for local police forces, national surveys are well suited to exploring general features of social problems that can subsequently inform broader policy initiatives.

Contextual Analysis

In collaboration with the research firm CACI, neighbourhood-level data from the decennial census were appended to each BCS interview record from the 1984 sweep onward. This innovation played an important role in supporting multilevel contextual analysis of crime and disorder problems. The specific area identifiers have been changed, and the BCS is now stratified by police force area.

Sampling

Until the 2000 revisions, the BCS was based on a core sample of moderately large size, supplemented by booster samples that targeted groups and areas of particular interest. This approach yielded sufficient numbers of cases for analysis of most crimes and topics, while avoiding the expense of interviewing very large numbers of people as is done in the U.S. Booster samples yield victims in higher-risk areas, or they are used to oversample groups of particular interest, as in boosters for ethnic minority respondents or young people. This was innovative, offering a good example of adaptive sampling. In its current configuration, the BCS has moved toward the U.S. model, with concomitant increases in cost. This is appropriate for developing more precise estimates of infrequent crimes and for obtaining representative samples within police force areas. Yet, larger sample sizes are not necessary for the broader uses supported by former sampling practices. The final chapter returns to this point.

Asking Sensitive Questions

Asking respondents about their experiences of victimisation is at the core of crime survey methodology. Yet some types of victimisation seemed to demand a more anonymous approach than direct questions put by interviewers. This led to the adoption in the BCS in 1994 of computer-assisted self-interviewing (CASI) – where the respondent inputs responses to the interviewer's laptop computer themselves – to look at family violence and sexual victimisation. Moreover, although self-reported offending questions have been included in the BCS since its first sweep, there was also a shift to the use of CASI to try and elicit more honest responses – for instance, in relation to drug-taking, stalking, being offered and buying goods known to be stolen, fraud, and technology crimes.

Influence on Criminological Research and Justice Policy

Tracing the influence of a survey such as the BCS is inevitably a subjective process. Here we offer simply one version of the impact that it has had on criminal policy and on criminological thinking.

Various lists of publications using BCS data have been produced over the last 20 years or so. One included in a guide to BCS analysis (Budd & Mattinson, 2001) lists more than 20 topics covered by hundreds of publications. With the combination of RDS published overviews of annual findings, RDS publications on particular topics rotated through different sweeps, and publications in academic journals, results from the BCS have been widely disseminated. A Google search of Web references located around 300,000 references to the phrase "British Crime Survey." The survey's influence has been particularly important in certain areas, most of which are represented by other chapters in this volume.

Multiple Victimisation

This is arguably the body of research that can be linked most closely and most exclusively to the BCS. It is especially interesting because BCS data have been used to identify multiple victimisation as a problem, while serial victimisation has not received much attention in U.S. crime surveys. Victimisation data also prompted researchers to begin to seek out measures of repeat crimes in police data. This revealed links between area-level measures of crime concentration (hot spots) and repeat victimisation. Repeat victimisation is perhaps the best available illustration of the progression from exploratory research findings through further research, crafting interventions, and ultimately the measurement of the impact of crime reduction policies.

Experience and Attitudes to Police

Although victim surveys emerged to measure the crimes not reported to police, they are also well suited to measuring respondent experiences with police. Like unreported crime, such experiences may not be included in police records. The specific police-contact modules added to follow-up forms are good examples of how the survey has been supplemented to assess emerging issues in crime and justice. Special attention was first devoted to police contacts in the 1984 survey. Special Home Office research studies on police contacts were published in 1984, 1990, and 1995. With police force areas as primary sampling units, the BCS is currently able to monitor police/public contacts routinely in geographic context. As with data on repeat victimisation, BCS data were first used to understand better police/public contacts, which have now become a central focus of the survey. Perhaps reflecting its centrality as a specific policy issue, BCS-based research on policing has been published infrequently in journals. On the other hand, the BCS interest in this topic spread to the U.S., where a supplement to the NCVS now gathers information on police/public contacts.

Crime and Communities

This stems from the multilevel analysis supported by area identifiers in the BCS. Research published in the U.S. is widely recognized for demonstrating how community-level measures of social disorganisation are related to crime and its perceptions. Further studies by U.K. researchers have expanded our knowledge of the role macro-level community characteristics play in criminal victimisation.

Fear of Crime

"Fear of crime" is what psychometricians call an indirect observable. One may want to argue whether "fear" is the right term for the phenomenon, but it is clear that worries or anxieties about crime are, in principle, well suited for measurement by surveys. Parts of the BCS have tackled this topic since the first wave for two related reasons. First, despite its attitudinal content, fear has been difficult to measure in ways that researchers and policy makers can agree on. Second is the persisting gap between subjective measures such as fear and more objective measures of crime risks. Research has established, after a fashion, that fear is a complex, multidimensional construct – and one that would be better labelled as anxiety. The topic has attracted quite a lot of interest from researchers and public officials. Officials view fear as a policy problem at least partly independent of crime and linked to confidence in the criminal justice system. Researchers have long been engaged in attempts to better measure fear and model it with resulting data. Though not alone in covering fear, the BCS has offered much more detailed measures of the concept than surveys in the U.S. and most other nations. As a result, more has been learned about fear from analysis of BCS data than from any other national crime survey.

Attitudes Toward Justice Issues

This is another topic that has been viewed as an important policy issue. Again, surveys are best at measuring attitudes, since they are subjective concepts elicited through questioning. The BCS has covered attitudes almost as a social indicator, seeking public views of punishment as a rough gauge for lawmaking. Because attitudes to punishment and other criminal justice processes do not travel well internationally, most BCS research on this topic has appeared in the U.K. To the extent that democratic nations should benchmark policy against the preferences of citizens, however, the BCS serves as something of a model for periodically assessing public views, and several other countries have adopted or adapted the approach taken from the 1996 BCS onwards.

Risks of Crime

The body of BCS-based research on risks of crime encompasses policy relevance and criminological theory. Two influential publications in the late 1970s laid out lifestyle and routine activity theories of crime and victimization (Cohen & Felson, 1979; Hindelang, Gottfredson, & Garofalo, 1978). Lifestyle theories of crime had a significant impact especially on early sweeps of the survey.[25] The first sweep included a variety of items to measure directly certain dimensions of behaviour that had only been inferred from previous crime surveys. Research on this topic has continued with subsequent sweeps, published in highly regarded journals in the U.S. and Europe. Research on crime risks has also contributed to crime prevention initiatives. As with data on fear, the BCS has been the single most fruitful source of data on crime risks.

Drug use

From the 1992 sweep, the BCS incorporated detailed self-report drug use items collected through computer-assisted interviewing. Results from that and subsequent sweeps have been reported in the continuing series of *Drug misuse declared* Home Office publications (most recently, Roe & Man, 2006). This segment of the BCS is important for four related reasons. First, as a national crime survey it provides regular data for monitoring the scope of drug use among the general population. Second, occasional booster samples make it possible to assess drug use among targeted populations. Third, drug use can be examined against the variety of other variables measuring behaviour and experiences. Finally, the use of CASI (computer-assisted self-interviewing) produces better estimates than those obtained through other means – although no one would claim that the survey provides reliable information on dependent or problematic use of drugs such as crack or heroin.

THE BCS - TAKING STOCK

In assessing the impact of the BCS, it is useful to distinguish between its contribution to technical knowledge about crime and its control, and its impact on the political environment within which crime policy is shaped.

Technical Knowledge

We use this term to encompass the knowledge of academic criminologists as well as that of government officials and researchers working in the field. It is hard to convey to those with no direct experience of criminology prior to 1980 the severely limited nature of the evidence base about crime at that time. The scale of the dark figure of unrecorded crime was a matter largely of speculation; so too was the degree of variability in public reporting to the police (over time, and by crime), and the degree of variability in police recording practice. The demographic profile of victims of different sorts of crime was largely unknown, as were the factors that determined the risk of victimisation. No one would want to claim that this informational void would have remained unfilled without the BCS.

There would have been the piecemeal results of smaller surveys, extrapolation from national surveys in other countries, more fine-grained analysis of police statistics. Yet a large amount of the knowledge taken for granted about crime that is routinely deployed by criminological theoreticians and in the better informed public discourse derives from the BCS. The point has been well made by Rod Morgan, talking more generally about the empirical work of RDS:

> It can never be stressed too often that those authors who engage in more abstract theorizing about the social construction of crime and the different reactions to it are dependent for most of their insights on the wealth of empirical data that the RDS has largely been responsible for amassing. These data, collected through processes too often derided, are the clay and straw that produce the bricks which both make for an accountable criminal justice system and permit it to be effectively challenged and analysed. (Morgan & Hough, 2007)

The limitations of the BCS are routinely rediscovered by successive generations of critics: it covers only a subset of crime; it is imprecise, as any sample survey must be; there are some potential systematic biases through its omissions; it omits important groups of at-risk populations, and so on. All of these things are true, of course, but BCS analysts always have been properly restrained about the claims that are made for the survey, and clear in their descriptions of what can be validly reported from its findings.

RDS's programme of survey development work over the last decade is also significant here. Partly to address some of the criticisms of the BCS, but more pertinently to add to the evidence base in some less commonly researched areas, the Home Office has run two important new crime surveys in recent years. The Offending Crime and Justice Survey (OCJS) measured self-reported offending by a representative sample of the general public, but importantly also covered those aged 12 to 15 (as well as the 16 and over age group), which the BCS did not. Although the methodology was not the same, the OCJS estimates do provide a picture of offending and victimisation amongst those under 16, and a comparison between that younger age group and the victims covered by the BCS. In 2002, the Home Office also ran a Commercial Victimisation Survey (CVS), similar to the CVS it had run 10 years previously. This filled the other significant omission in the general household BCS. In addition to these surveys, the Home Office has also run other surveys from time to time, aimed at illuminating those dimly lit corners of knowledge that the BCS fails to reach – such as surveys of offenders in prison or of problematic drug users.

Impact on Crime Policy

What contribution has the BCS made to the development of crime control technologies? As mentioned earlier, there are some examples of approaches to crime prevention that are very closely associated with the BCS, notably the targeting of repeat victims of domestic violence. More generally, its contribution has probably been greatest in the field of situational crime prevention, one of the prerequisites of which is detailed, crime-specific analysis of the circumstances and characteristics of offending. To date, policy has drawn less on a different strand of BCS analysis that we associate with Rob Sampson initially and more recently with Tim Hope and colleagues on the role of communities in crime control. Whatever the reasons for the steep falls in crime shown by the BCS, one consequence has been to accentuate the interest in the problems of those most disadvantaged communities with fewest resources to take action.

If the particularity or granularity of much BCS analysis has pointed policy and practice towards specificity in methods of crime control, other BCS findings have helped to remind policy that there are broader issues that also need attention, such as the legitimacy accorded to the institutions of justice and the trust they are able to command. As discussed by Hough and Roberts, the emergence of the Home Office's "confidence agenda" is at least in part a consequence of BCS findings on low public trust in the judiciary and declining support for the police.

One has to be more sceptical about the claims originally made for crime surveys that they might help engender a better informed and calmer climate of debate about crime. In its early years skilful media handling – or the professionalism of journalists in "reporting the facts" – meant that documenting the dark figure of crime did not lead to alarmist coverage in the media. By the early 1990s, media restraint had been abandoned, and – to give but one lurid example – BCS estimates of crime were translated into worrisome statistics on "crimes per minute." Since crime started falling in the mid-1990s, we know (thanks to the BCS) that majorities of the population have continued to believe that crime is on the increase. Optimists might argue that things would have been worse were it not for the calming effects of BCS statistics. Those with a more pessimistic outlook might argue that the less information populist politicians and news-hungry journalists have about crime, the better. Whatever the case, the fact is unavoidable that public confidence in crime statistics of any sort is currently at an all-time low.

The reasons are not to be found in the technical quality of RDS's work on crime statistics, of course. The last 15 years have seen an unprecedented climate of penal populism that was an inevitable consequence of the greater politicisation of crime politics. In Britain, this change can be traced back to that period in the early 1990s, when for the first time, Labour mounted an effective challenge to the Conservatives as the party of law and order. Whatever the consequences for penal policy – and for public concern about crime – Tony Blair's famous promise to be "tough on crime, tough on the causes of crime" must be judged a huge success in electoral terms. At the same time, there were various tragic and high-profile crimes such as the murder of the toddler James Bulger, which caused a step change in public and media concern over crime from which the country has not yet recovered.[26]

PROSPECT FOR THE NEXT 25 YEARS

From their initial development 40 years ago, victim surveys have assumed a variety of forms and addressed many different purposes. U.S. surveys have been most attentive to producing alternative measures of crime. A related goal is to align survey figures with police measures by classifying victimization as reported or not. Large samples, more precise estimates, bounding, short reference periods, and consistency have been important toward that end. The long series of NCVS data now offers useful comparisons against trends in police records, showing a steady convergence of comparable offences. But this precision is increasingly difficult and costly. As Michael Rand's chapter explains, changes to the NCVS now look likely.

The International Crime Victimization Survey (ICVS) has operated on a different front to provide broad estimates of victimisation risks cross-nationally, based on modest samples, without much heed to the picture from the alternative – albeit problematic in comparative terms – source of police statistics. What the ICVS provides is a variety of fascinating comparisons, mostly at the national level. This is illustrated by the fact that country rankings on different offences and perceptions are the most common way ICVS results are reported. The prospects for the future of the ICVS are currently unclear, although appetite for information on how different countries fare in relation to victimization is likely to remain keen.[27]

At its outset, the BCS took a different tack from the NCVS and the ICVS. It produced alternate counts of crime to match more precisely with those from police records. Yet, apart from the HORS summary report on each sweep of the survey, most publications by researchers and Home Office staff have pursued other topics. As described earlier, many of those topics turned out to be major contributions to criminological research and practice. Since its redesign in 2000, the BCS is becoming more of a performance management system, producing national and subnational estimates of victimisation and related perceptual measures of organisational competence. It is now a key "national statistic," routinely reporting on trends and key issues in crime. It is also currently an integral part of the police performance framework, and indeed that was a key reason for its redesign – the very significant increase in sample size (and therefore cost) being a requirement of the demand to provide crime and confidence measures for each of the 43 police forces in England and Wales.

Its importance as a generator of National Statistics has led to calls for the Office of National Statistics to take it over.[28] There are, of course, counterbalancing arguments for leaving the survey within the government department that is its primary user. It is to be hoped that if there is to be a change of direction, it will avoid the dysfunctional separation that existed in the Home Office in the late 1970s between statistics on the one hand, and research on the other, to which we referred in our account of the origins of the BCS. No reorganisation that divorces the policy responsibility from the statistical function to the extent now proposed will by itself increase public confidence. The remedy for that malaise is primarily behavioural rather than structural.

Leaving to one side issues of public trust in statistics, there are other potential consequences of the institutionalisation of the BCS within the government's performance management framework. One problem is partly a matter simply of questionnaire space, and partly with the focussing of limited analytic resources: once policy customers have come to expect trend data on a particular issue, the pressure to retain the relevant items in the survey can be very strong. This comes at the expense of new insights and the added value in exploring alternative areas of either current or probable future policy interest. And it is hard for the BCS team in RDS simultaneously to run a timely performance-management machine and to exploit the survey's capacity for innovative criminological research. The more the BCS becomes embedded in the current administrative needs of the Home Office, the less its capacity to look to the future and prompt new ideas and new ways of thinking about crime.

So many questions in criminology are exploratory and descriptive, centering on fundamental questions of measurement. Most of the advances in knowledge produced by the BCS have been through these more modest purposes. Modest sample sizes, adaptive sampling, rotating banks of follow-up questions, and other features of a multipurpose survey have enabled policy makers and researchers to learn a great deal about crime and its impact. Historically the NCVS has been bound by tradition and slow to adapt to new problems and technologies. The BCS has been better suited to recognize emerging research interests and questions, and then adapt the survey accordingly. Shifting to the more narrow purpose of measuring victimisation and police accountability is, over time, likely to reduce further contributions to policy and research.

Consider that victim surveys offer an alternate perspective on crime, not just an alternative way to count. Asking people about their experiences in victimisation and offending, their attitudes to police and other justice institutions, their behaviours and routines, implies broader thinking about crime and disorder as public policy problems. This is still a critical issue for policing and crime reduction policy in the current period where neighbourhood policing is being rolled out nationally, and the debate on how best to engage with the public on their attitudes to policing their communities is of utmost importance. If we accept that crime and disorder affect people and communities in a variety of ways not always best met with police action, then we should better understand the scope of those problems so we can devise reasonable interventions. The BCS provides an opportunity to explore national issues robustly in a way that would enhance and inform the local debate on how to address crime and disorder.

As other articles suggest, perhaps it is time to reconsider the focus on victims in a crime survey. Have crime surveys reified "victim" in such a way to divert attention from other kinds of offences, or from victims that cannot be measured with household-based samples? Together with the Offending Crime and Justice Survey and the 2002 Commercial Victimization Survey, the evolution of the BCS into something more like a victimisation survey signals more specialized data collection efforts. These efforts might better reflect the broad scope of crime problems and have been designed to measure the specific issues presented by the often quite different social problems that can be summarised under the generic heading of crime.

Address correspondence to: mike.hough@kcl.ac.uk or
maxfield@rutgers.edu

NOTES

1. See Kelly (2005).
2. Perhaps the most outrageous example of this is to be found in the Conservative Party's 2005 election campaign, which included advertisements portraying the steep growth in recorded violent crime over Labour's tenure as an unproblematic fact, when the tendentious nature of this claim should have been clear.
3. Both reports were published in late 2006: see Statistics Commission (2006) and Smith (2006).
4. This was a small, freestanding outfit in the Criminal Department headed by an Assistant Secretary assisted by a Principal and, crucially, also by a Principal Research Officer. Its work has been described in Train (1977) and Morris (1980a). It involved wholly intra-Home Office coordination. "Tripartism" – coordination between the Home Office, the then Lord Chancellor's Department and the Law Officers' Department – emerged in rather different circumstances later.
5. HORU was reorganised and re-badged as the Home Office Research and Planning Unit in 1981, and much later incorporated into a larger Research Statistics and Development department.
6. There is clearly a lesson for archival historians here: that the footprint left by an initiative in bureaucratic files may not closely match its original shape. The one thing that clearly emerged from the papers was the intensely dysfunctional rivalry and bickering that characterised the relationship between researchers and statisticians.
7. From 1972 the General Household Survey had include a question on burglary, which suggested that much of the increase in this offence over the course of the 1970s was due to increased recording by the police rather than any increase in public propensity to report or any real increase in offences. This was reported in a Home Office Statistical Bulletin around the time the BCS was launched (see Home Office, 1982, for details).
8. Two local surveys predated the first BCS: in Sheffield (Bottoms, Mawby, & Walker, 1987), and a Home Office survey in Mosside comparing black and white residents (Tuck & Southgate, 1981).

9. Quangos were "Quasi-autonomous nongovernmental organisations" – essentially, governmental organisations set up at arm's length from government departments. Their proliferation was a source of political concern at the time.

10. The handling difficulty was to explain how proposals that the police thought restrictive were going to help the fight against crime.

11. The convention was that all significant exchanges were in writing; and memoranda between the two units would do as much as possible, as politely as possible, to demolish the arguments and credibility of the other, ending without fail with the sentence, "I hope these comments are helpful."

12. Morris (1980b).

13. Ibid. p. 20.

14. Perks (1967).

15. When pressed in the 1920s to explain why Birmingham had proportionately much less crime than similar cities, the Chief Constable (Rafter) exclaimed: "To get anywhere near those figures you would have to report every dog that was lost in Birmingham – 6,000 crimes a year in Birmingham, the thing is absolutely ridiculous." TNA HO 329/109, 29 July 1929. In the 1920s, a large number of recorded offences betokened police *preventative* shortcomings. By the 1970s, when relevant to resource allocation, large numbers had come to evidence the *burdens* on the service.

16. RES 80 0508/001/12/078, CPP(80)3 "Public Surveys of Crime" and CPP(M)58.

17. Meeting of 13 October 1980, CPP(M)61.

18. It was significant that Al Biderman, Al Reiss, and Wes Skogan all attended the workshop.

19. This proposal was implemented with only minor amendments.

20. THES 8 May 1981.

21. Meeting of 15 May 1981, CPP(81)64.

22. RES 81 0661/0008/004 submission of 15 June 1981 on.

23. Ibid. Note of meeting on 22 July 1981.

24. There have been six published sweeps of the Scottish Crime Survey, with varying degrees of comparability to the BCS. The 2005 sweep involved an unhappy experience with telephone interviews.

25. With a degree of obsession that now seems misplaced, we designed the first questionnaire to grill respondents not only on the mode of transport they used when going out in the evening, but also about

their mode of return. The small subsample who used different modes of transport to go out and to return never led to any significant criminological breakthrough!

26. MORI has asked the public about the most important issue facing Britain today since the mid1970s and routinely since 1982. There was a spike in concern in 1988 and an upward step change in 1993 following the murder of Jamie Bulger. See http://www.ipsos-mori. com/polls/trends/issues_files/image002.gif

27. A fifth round of ICVS surveys took place in about 18 European Union countries in 2004-2005, with the European Commission funding the surveys in EU countries. There were some changes to the questionnaire used in previous sweeps, probably an inevitable result of new sponsors feeling they needed to ring changes.

28. "Home Office cannot be trusted on crime figures, says watchdog" *Times* 5 September 2006. The recommendation included in the Statistics Commission report – for there to be a fully costed feasibility study – was also supported by the *Economist* the following day.

REFERENCES

Bottoms, A. E., Mawby, R. I., & Walker, M. (1987). Localised crime survey in contrasting areas of a city. *British Journal of Criminology, 27*, 125-154.

Budd, T., & Mattinson, J. (2001). *British Crime Survey training notes* [Unpublished technical Report.]. London: Home Office, Crime Surveys Section, Crime and Criminal Justice Unit, Research, Development and Statistics Directorate. Available at http://www.ndad.nationalarchives.gov.uk/CRDA/2/DD/detail.html

Cohen, L. E., & Felson, M. (1979). Social change and crime rate trends: A routine activity approach. *American Sociological Review, 44*, 588-608.

Hindelang, M. J., Gottfredson, M. R., Cohen, L. E., & Garofalo, J. (1978.) *Victims of personal crime: An empirical foundation for a theory of personal victimization.* Cambridge, MA: Ballinger.

Her Majesty's Stationery Office. (1981) *Royal Commission on Criminal Procedure, Cmnd 8092.* London: Her majesty's Stationery Office.

Home Office. (1981). *Public surveys of crime: Report of a workshop held at Sidney Sussex College Cambridge, 6-8 April 1981.* London: Home Office.

Home Office. (1982). *Unrecorded offences of burglary and theft in a dwelling in England and Wales: Estimates from the general household survey.* Statistical Bulletin 11/82. London: Home Office.

Hough, M., & Mayhew, P. (1983). *The British Crime Survey: First report.* Home Office Research Study No. 76. London: Her majesty's Stationery Office.

Kelly, M. (2005). *Public confidence in British official statistics.* London: Office of National Statistics.

Modood, T., Berthoud, R., Lakey, J., Smith, P., Virdee, S., & Beishon, S. (1997). *Ethnic minorities in Britain: Diversity and disadvantage.* London: Policy Studies Institute.

Morgan, R., & Hough, M. (2007). The politics of criminological research. In R. King & E. Wincup (Eds.), *Doing research on crime and justice* (2e). Oxford: Oxford University Press.

Morris, R. M. (1980a). Home office crime policy planning: Six years on. *Howard Journal*, 135-141.

Morris, R.M. (1980b). *Review of home office statistical services.* London: Home Office.

Perks, W. (1967). *Report of the departmental committee on criminal statistics*, Cmnd 3448. London: Her Majesty's Stationery Office.

Roe, S., & Man, L. (2006). *Drug misuse declared: Findings from the 2005/06 British crime survey, England and Wales. Statistic Bulletin 15/06.* London: Home Office.

Smith, A. (2006). *Crime statistics: An independent review.* (Carried out by the Crime Statistics Review Group for the Secretary of State for the Home Department, November 2006). London: Home Office. Available at http://www.homeoffice. gov.uk/rds/pdfs06/crime-statistics-independent-review-06.pdf

Sparks, R., Genn, H., & Dodd, D. (1977). *Surveying victims.* London: Wiley.

Statistics Commission. (2006). *Crime statistics: User perspectives.* Statistics Commission Report No.30. London: Statistics Commission. Available at www.stats com.org.uk/uploads/files/reports/Crime_Statistics_Review-final.pdf

Train, C. J. (1977). The development of criminal policy planning in the home office. *Public Administration, 55*, 373-384.

Tuck, M., & Southgate, P. (1981). *Ethnic minorities, crime and policing.* Home Office Research Study 70. London: Her Majesty's Stationery Office.

The Sting in the Tail of the British Crime Survey: Multiple Victimisations

by

Graham Farrell

and

Ken Pease

Midlands Centre for Criminology and Criminal Justice
Loughborough University

Abstract: *The British Crime Survey (BCS) has made a major contribution to the understanding of repeat and chronic victimisation. BCS evidence on repeats has led to a range of theoretical and methodological developments capable of informing crime control and victim services. The present paper shows that BCS counting conventions mask the extent of chronic victimisation in most official BCS reports. Crucially, where a victim reports multiple linked and similar events, the series is capped at an arbitrary maximum of five incidents. By thus truncating the long statistical "tail" of victimisation, the incidence of personal crime was reduced by at least a third in every BCS sweep since 2001-2002, and by 52% in the 2005-2006 BCS. The incidence of property crime is reduced by up to a quarter, and by 15% in the 2005-2006 BCS. The contribution of harms against those frequently victimised to total crime suffered is thus revealed as even more important than hitherto acknowledged, and personal crime is revealed as constituting a higher proportion of all crime suffered.*

Crime Prevention Studies, volume 22 (2007), pp. 33–53.

I'm bound to tell, for better or for worse
All of their stories, or else falsify
My subject matter as you have it here.

—"The Miller's Prologue"[1]

Over its quarter century of existence, the British Crime Survey (BCS) has made a major contribution to the understanding of crime and its prevention. The survey's reputation has grown as its evidence has informed theory and practice. It now forms a cornerstone of how the U.K. government routinely represents its crime problem.

The elder transatlantic sister to BCS was the U.S. National Crime Survey (NCS). This was underpinned by a series of pioneering methodological studies. Driven by the Department of Justice's Bureau of Justice Statistics, these remain important. Among these, two collections edited by Lehnen and Skogan (1981, 1984) contain 32 articles that develop or document critical issues. Early studies with particular relevance to series of victimisations against the same target include those of Biderman (1980), Dodge (1975, 1977, 1987), Dodge and Lentzner (1978), Reiss (1977, 1980), and Fienberg (1980). A jewel in the methodological crown is Wes Skogan's review (see Skogan, 1981, 1986), which instills in the reader an appreciation of the fragility of crime measures, and continues to warrant study by anyone working with victim surveys, recorded crime statistics, or victim ethnographies. More recent studies help maintain methodological rigour (see, for example, Rand & Rennison, 2005; Cantor & Lynch, 2000, 2006, and in this volume; Rand, 2006, and in this volume). Seemingly mundane methodological issues – the way a question is phrased, when a question is asked, the manner of the interviewer, the memory of respondents, what is counted as crime and what is not – can significantly influence crime counts. Because what gets counted carries weight in informing policy and practice, this makes methodological probity crucial. Of course, this is not evidence for the greater robustness of police statistics of crime, where, aside from the invisibility of unrecorded crime, apparently trivial counting practices have no less disproportionate consequences (see, for example, Farrington & Dowds, 1985).

A key aim of crime victim surveys was to reveal the nature and distribution of unrecorded crime. Much crime is not reported to the police. When it comes to multiple victimisation, the problem is compounded. For example, let us assume there to be a 50% chance (0.5 probability) that a household burglary is recorded by the police. For a household burgled twice, there is only a 25% chance that, *ceteris paribus*, both burglaries will be reported to the police (0.5 × 0.5 = 0.25). Fifty percent of two-time victims will appear as one-off victims, and 25% as unvictimised. Dissatisfaction with police performance and other factors will mean that, in practice, victim decisions to report successive crimes will not be independent. It was demonstrated by Mukherjee and Carcach (1998) that repeat crimes are less likely to be recorded by the police.

The tail referred to in the title of this chapter is the statistical tail of the frequency distribution showing the number of times that respondents are victimised. The tail is the signature of repeat victimisation. Each chronic victim's tale is hidden in the tail of the distribution. In Geoffrey Chaucer's *Canterbury Tales*, the Wife of Bath was one of English literature's first recorded victims (and perpetrators) of domestic violence. Her husband had "beaten me on every bone" and "once gave my ear such a box . . . that from the blow my ear became quite deaf." The tail/tale pun acts as a reminder that the tales within the tail represent the suffering of those unfortunates for whom crime is a recurrent blight on life rather than a regrettable episode. The distinctive experience and plight of the chronic victim should not be overlooked. Mandy Shaw's (2001) analogy with bereavement is not fanciful. In her account, the process of coming to terms with a loss or harm is never completed, being disrupted by new victimisation.

THE SCHOLARS' TALES

Various counsellors made various
suggestions; they debated up and down
Many a subtle argument was brought forth.

(From "The Sergeant-at-Arms' Tale")

Sparks and Hindelang

In the late 1970s, two classics in victimology appeared. *Surveying Victims* by Richard Sparks, Hazel Genn, and David Dodd was published in 1977. This was a British study of three areas of London. It informed the development of the British Crime Survey. One year later, a U.S. study based on a survey of eight cities, *Victims of Personal Crime: An Empirical Foundation for a Theory of Personal Victimization* by Michael Hindelang, Michael Gottfredson, and James Garafalo, was published. Both books included a chapter on multiple victimisation.[2] Both books noted the highly skewed distribution of victimisation, with a small proportion of multiple victims experiencing a disproportionately large proportion of total crime. Several of the authors went on to further work on repeat victimisation.

Biderman and Reiss

The origins of the U.S. National Crime Survey (NCS) lay in the President's Commission on Law Enforcement and Administration of Justice (1967). Albert D. Biderman and Albert J. Reiss, both involved in that commission's work, wrote some of the earliest work on repeat victimisation. Biderman introduced the notion of a "once bitten, twice shy" immunization to subsequent victimisation, noting the following:

> [W]hile there are many plausible post hoc interpretations in terms of both phenomena and method for the distributions of multiple victimizations that are observed, nonetheless, the problem invites consideration of a possible immunizing effect of victimization. (Biderman, 1980, p. 31)[3]

In a volume edited with Stephen Fienberg, Reiss demonstrated that repetition by the same type of crime was more likely (Reiss, 1980), findings echoed by Fienberg (Fienberg, 1980). Biderman and Reiss both recognized the effect that excluding series crimes has on the officially reported crime rate in the U.S. Reiss wrote the following:

> Adding estimates of the number of incidents in series victimization to those for nonseries victimization would increase the number of victim incidents by 18 percent. Series victimization generally makes a greater contribution to the victimization rate of crime that involve contact with persons that those without contact. (Reiss, 1980, p. 16)

Biderman (1975) also suggested that series victimisations were separate phenomena to other crimes and should be viewed as processes or enduring conditions. Although series crimes have some ongoing elements (such as the fear they may induce), the criminal events can still be counted even when they are frequent violent incidents in a continuing relationship. There was at least one modest NCS attempt to incorporate series when considering the cost of crime (Miller, Cohen, & Wiersema, 1996), though this seems to be the exception to NCS practice. It is likely that the NCS decision to exclude series crimes influenced the BCS decision to adopt a similar approach.

Michael Gottfredson

Hindelang's coauthor Gottfredson (Hindelang, Gottfredson, & Garafalo, 1978) crossed the Atlantic to spend time working on BCS data. The resulting report, *Victims of Crime: The Dimensions of Risk* (Gottfredson, 1984), assessed the lifestyle theory of crime proposed in the earlier U.S. book, using data from the first BCS sweep of 1981-2002. Gottfredson's theory-driven approach leads him to a plea for policy development based on the prevention of multiple victimisation:

> For a few individuals, victimisation is not a rare occurrence, but happens with some regularity along with a number of other of life's misfortunes. . . . Victims of one form of crime are more likely than others to be victims of another form of crime, as well as to be more likely to suffer a variety of misfortunes, such as household fires and accidents. . . . These findings suggest that economies might be gained from focusing prevention resources on those most at risk. It might also be prudent to make high risk groups the subject of broad-based prevention measures (e.g., which attended to, say, both household crime and motor vehicle crime). By being tailored to those most in need, crime prevention schemes would not only enjoy some economy but would avoid unnecessarily inconveniencing other people.
> . . . The BCS lifestyle findings suggest that victimisation research needs to focus its attention increasingly on the small portion who suffer repeated victimisation and who thus bear a disproportion of the burden from crime. (Gottfredson, 1984, pp. 30-33)

Gottfredson's 1984 study retains a remarkable relevance and heuristic value more than two decades after publication.

Hazel Genn

From the team that published *Surveying Victims* in 1977, Sparks and Genn went on to publish separate contributions focused on multiple victimisation. Richard Sparks (1981) extended theoretical thinking relating to repeat victimisation and inspired work on the time-course of repeat victimisation. Hazel Genn, in the article "Multiple Victimisation" (1988), argued that "to devote less attention to those people who for some reason are repeatedly victimized, than to those who suffer an isolated incident in an otherwise 'normal' crime-free life, results in a blinkered view of social reality" (Genn, 1988, p. 92).

Genn spent months observing the lifestyle and environment of a woman who reported six personal and seven property crimes, many quite serious, to the victim survey. Genn found that the 13 incidents were probably a conservative estimate of the number of crimes being experienced, and echoed Skogan's word in criticising the practice of imposing an upper limit upon a series of crimes:

> The difficulties involved in quantifying the volume of multiple victimization and in adequately reflecting the experiences of multiple victims do not justify their exclusion from survey data, neither do they justify denying their experiences of crime by imposing arbitrary upper limits. (Genn, 1988, p. 100)

The Scholars' Theoretical Home

Although the present study is primarily about methodology, a brief note is warranted lest it be felt that empirical study has outpaced theoretical or policy-related developments. The existence of multiple victimisation is demonstrated by a wide range of studies using diverse data sets and methods. The theoretical issue concerns why it happens, and why it is widespread. Lynch, Berbaum, and Planty (1998) note that studies of repeat victimisation "have also led to the development of theories of crime that emphasize the direct role of entering into the victimization state as the source of subsequent victimization (Osborn et al., 1995; Pease, 1998; Sparks, 1981)" (Lynch et al., 1998, p. 2).

Repeat victimisation may be understood within the theoretical frameworks of rational choice theory (see, e.g., Cornish & Clarke, 2001) and routine activity and/or lifestyle theory (see, e.g., Felson, 2006). Repetition is a "rational" choice for an offender who learns from a first victimisation that the target can be victimised again with low risk, little effort, or a high reward. Repeat victimsation can also occur if particularly attractive targets are repeatedly victimised by different offenders. The theories of event dependence or "boost" (one crime increases the likelihood of another) and state heterogeneity (some potential targets are consistently more attractive) have been variously explored (see, e.g., Lauritsen & Davis-Quinet, 1995; Tseloni & Pease, 2003, 2004), drawing upon parallel theories developed in criminal career research and optimal foraging theory in ecology. It has also been hypothesised that the prevention of repeat victimisation is less likely to result in displacement (see Chenery, Holt, & Pease, 1997; Bouloukos & Farrell, 1997) because offenders are less familiar with alternative targets, drawing upon the theory of familiarity decay as described by Eck (1993). Repeat victimisation has (in patchy fashion) informed crime prevention and policing practice relating to the allocation of scarce resources, as well as the provision of services to victims. This literature is reviewed by Farrell (2005). In the U.K., the manner in which it did this was facilitated by a series of hypothesis-testing research efforts (see Laycock, 2001). A full understanding of the contributions of flag and boost accounts of repeat victimisation by offence type will greatly enhance the precision of crime reductive practice. Boost explanations of chronic domestic violence are especially intriguing to the writers.

THE TALE OF THE SCHIZOID STATISTICIAN

> As for my eyes, they water from the wool
> Pulled over them.
>
> (From "The Canon's Assistant's Tale")

The present authors have argued that the NCS and NCVS should include series crimes in the official crime counts. Victimisation surveys were introduced with the presumption that people will pretty much tell the truth about what they recall has happened to them. If one asks people what happened to them and then disregards the response on the basis of disbelief or because it is deemed too costly to extend the interview to the degree that would flow from accepting their veracity, then the result is schizoid at best and hypocritical at worst.

We have described the neglect of series events variously as a travesty of justice, seriously flawed, and have suggested (not entirely lightheartedly) that a class action suit might be needed to overturn the routine distortion of U.S. national crime statistics, which constitutes the systematic suppression of the tales within the tail (Farrell & Pease, 2002; Farrell, Tseloni, & Pease, 2005). It is despite the survey redesign that much of Skogan's 1981 critique is as relevant now as then:

> The current treatment of series is indefensible. By definition series offenses occurred at least three times, and the description of the latest of them must be clear enough to classify it as falling within the purview of the National Crime Survey. Not to count them at all when generating estimates of victimization rates is difficult to justify. . . . The inadequate representation of series offenses in the data used for estimation purposes partially explains the apparent paucity of multiple victimization in the population. (Skogan, 1981, pp. 31-32)

Mike Planty and Kevin Strom conducted a definitive analysis to estimate the U.S. crime rate if we only believed what respondents were telling us. They concluded that

> The findings suggest that these high-volume repeat victims can have a significant impact on the magnitude and distribution of violent victimization. Current government counting rules that exclude series incidents do not include about three out of every five violent victimizations and distort the characterization and risk of violence in the United States. . . . The dramatic change occurs when series incidents are counted by the estimated number of victimizations reported by the respondent. Here the increase ranged from a high of 174% in 1996 to a low of 62% in 2000. For 1993, this means that the annual victimization count would rise from about 11,365,000 to about 27,375,186 . . . If the number of victimizations reported by the respondents is accurate, the current government counting rules do not include about 58% of all violent victimizations; in other words, three out of five victimizations reported by respondents were excluded in 1993. (Planty & Strom, 2007)

THE CANTERBURY (NZ) TALE

I know best where my shoe pinches me.

(From "The Merchant's Tale")

From the mid-1990s, analysis of repeat victimisation was often incorporated in the main BCS reports from the Home Office, under the guidance of Pat Mayhew and Mike Hough. There were many revealing analyses of patterns and trends in repeat victimisation for different crime types (see Mayhew, Aye-Maung, & Mirrlees-Black, 1993). The most recent BCS report at the time of writing includes a section on repeat victimisation (Walker, Kershaw, & Nicholas, 2006). There was a period of neglect in the early years of the new century, but perhaps now repeat victimisation is becoming integrated into mainstream thinking about crime in the U.K. (see Laycock, 2001, for the policy "story" of repeat victimisation). Pat Mayhew, the "onlybegetter" of much of the relevant literature, now works in New Zealand. At the meeting from which this volume derives, it was heartening that she recognized the importance of conventions about series in assessing the dimensions of the presenting problem of crime and victimisation. In the most recent survey of victimisation in New Zealand, a ceiling of 30 crimes in a series was used, rather than 5 (Mayhew, personal communication, 2006), a development that sits well with the present analysis and the evolution of thinking about the central importance of repeat victimisation in the profile of crime.

THE REVISIONISTS' TALE

What is amiss, I pray you to amend.

(From the prologue to "The Second Nun's Tale")

As a pilgrim's journey begins with a single step, so too a series of crimes begins with a single criminal act. The journey and the crime series are composed of repeated nonindependent events. Most journeys are short but a small number are far longer. It would be statistically simpler to count all long journeys as having a length equal to 5 steps, but it would be a grossly inaccurate way of estimating distance travelled. Yet when it comes to series crimes, official BCS reports count the criminological equivalent of only the first 5 steps. There is a counting convention that means nobody in the U.K. is allowed to experience more than five crimes in any one series, however many they recall having suffered. The BCS first report appropriately applied the adjective "arbitrary" to this practice:

> In calculating offence rates for 1981, series incidents were given a score equal to the number of incidents in the series occurring in 1981, with an arbitrary top limit of five. (Hough & Mayhew, 1983, p. 40)

With some variation in the number of incidents in a series, the practice has been influential in crime survey research, and the arbitrary limit has remained for BCS main reports of the nation's crime rates. Some exceptional analyses have used different conventions. Walby and Allen (2004) analysed repeated domestic violence, sexual assault, and stalking using the 2001 BCS. They capped series at 51 incidents. When there were too many incidents for a respondent to recall, they used a value of 60 (Walby & Allen, 2004, p. 24), the convention adopted for the analysis herein.[4] For the most part, however, the arbitrary severance of series incidents, with its implicit silencing of the most victimised members of society, has gone largely unchallenged.

The BCS Training Notes (Budd & Mattinson, 2000) provides the principal reference point for the analysis that follows. Pages 59 to 65 of those notes contain the exact SPSS syntax (the statistical analysis software instructions) used to generate prevalence and incidence rates from BCS victim forms. A crime series, in BCS terms, is a number of very similar crimes against the same victim judged by that victim to be at least probably the work of the same perpetrator. The syntax on page 60 of the Training Notes contains the line:

If (number *gt* 5) number = 5.

Which means: *If the number of crimes in a series is greater than "gt" five, then set that number as equal to five.*

The BCS Training Guide explains capping as follows:

> For "series" incidents the number of incidents is capped at 5. Therefore if someone reports 10 incidents in a "series", only 5 are counted. The limit is to avoid extreme cases distorting the rates. (Budd & Mattinson, 2000, p. 32)

Of course, if the people who say they suffered 10 incidents really did, it is capping the series at 5 that distorts the rate. It is truly bizarre that the victimisation survey, based as it is on the assumption that people will by and large tell the truth about what happened within the limits of their memory, suddenly withdraws its credulity when victim testimony becomes inconvenient. Part of the problem lies with the hegemony of central tendency over dispersion in crime statistics. One is reminded of the joke that if one's feet are on fire and one's head is frozen, the statistician judges one to be comfortable on average. Measures of inequality that are widely used in geography and economics, such as the Gini coefficient, have failed to permeate criminology (see Barr & Pease, 1990; Tseloni & Pease, 2005).

The practice of capping series crimes has been consistently applied in Home Office BCS analyses for 25 years. To asses the impact of this practice upon the official U.K. crime rate, the analysis in Table 1 and Table 2 calculates crime rates with, and then without, an arbitrary cap of 5 incidents.

Analysis for this chapter was conducted on five sweeps of the BCS covering 2001-2002 to 2005-2006, the latter being the most recent publicly available at the time of writing. A summary of findings for personal and household crime is shown in Tables 1 and 2. Prevalence rates (victims/ targets per 100 capita) and incidence rates (crimes per 100 capita) are shown. The difference between prevalence and incidence is due to repeat victimisation because there are more crimes than targets. Two incidence

Table 1: BCS Personal Crime Rates

BCS Sweep	Prevalence	Capped Incidence	Actual Incidence	% Difference in Incidence
2001-2	7.3	11.3	15.5	37.2
2002-3	7.5	11.3	15.0	33.1
2003-4	7.3	10.7	14.3	33.1
2004-5	6.5	9.5	12.9	35.2
2005-6	6.4	9.6	14.5	51.9

Table 2: BCS Household Crime Rates

BCS Sweep	Prevalence	Capped Incidence	Actual Incidence	% Difference in Incidence
2001-2	21.6	35.9	41.8	16.6
2002-3	21.0	34.3	43.4	26.6
2003-4	20.0	32.2	38.8	20.7
2004-5	18.4	29.8	35.3	18.4
2005-6	18.1	29.4	33.9	15.4

rates are shown, one calculated with series capped at five incidents, and one calculated using what victims actually reported to the survey. The final column of each table shows the percentage difference between capped and uncapped incidence rates. The prevalence rates and the capped incidence rates correspond exactly with those shown in the most recent main Home Office BCS report available at the time of writing (Walker et al., 2006, pp. 24-25).[5]

When the limit of five crimes in a series is removed

- the actual number of personal crimes reported by victims is always at least a third more than the "official" rate, and 52% more in 2005-2006;

- the number of household property crimes reported by victims has been as much as a quarter more than the official rate, and was 15% more in 2005-2006.

Another way of interpreting the Percentage of Difference in Incidence columns in Tables 1 and 2 is that they show the percentage of household and personal crime excluded from the nation's crime count by the practice of capping series incidents.

Figure 1 shows the percentage of crimes, personal and household, that were repeat crimes against the same targets. Here, a repeat does not include the first incident against a target that year, so the proportion of crime experienced by targets that were repeatedly victimized would be greater than shown. Two lines are shown in Figure 1 for each of personal and household crime, the higher one in each case representing the extent of repeats as actually reported by victims rather than using the arbitrary cap. It is evident that around half of crime is that which is being repeated against targets victimized already in any given year.

It is important to clarify the issue of the clustering of incident within the statistical tail of frequency distributions. Frequency distributions by crime, showing percentage of respondents, victims, incidents, and repeats, often reveal significant variation in the tail. When frequency distributions are examined for particular types of crime, the frequency of crimes can cluster around easy decimal system reference points: 10, 20, 30, 40 incidents, and so on, a phenomenon found elsewhere (Rand & Rennison,

Figure 1: Multiple victimisation as percentage of personal and household crime.

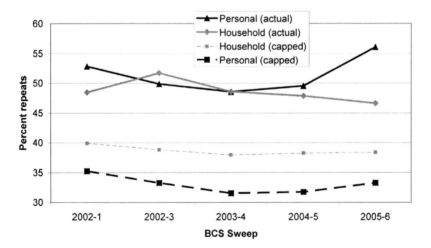

2005). There is also some indication of clustering around monthly reference points: 12, 24, and 36. These patterns are to be expected. If a pizza-loving reader were asked how many times she had sent out to Pizza Express over the previous year, the answer would have two characteristics. First, it would be a multiple of a preferred number base (usually 5 or 10) or, given a mental strategy that concentrated on the year as a unit of 12 months, as a multiple of 3 (or perhaps 6 or 12 among the most victimised). Second, the gaps between typically given answers increase in size. If the number of pizzas ordered is more than 10, the answer will be 15. If it is more than 30, the answer will more likely be 40 than 35. This reflects what is known in psychophysics as a just noticeable difference (JND). The JND increases as the initial quantity increases. These two aspects of quantity estimation – number preference and psychophysical scaling – have long been understood. Number preferences were first looked at in a penal context by Francis Galton (1895). The classic work on psychophysical scaling (Stevens, 1975) identifies a range of applications of his power law in real-life applications. Fitzmaurice and Pease (1986) apply these principles to the assessment of offence seriousness, offence severity, and sentence length. This is illustrated for BCS data in Table 3, which shows the frequency distribution for all motor vehicle crime in the 2005-2006 BCS. That offence category is chosen only for the convenience of its presentational simplicity, and many statistical tails extend beyond 30 incidents. Although there are relatively few cases in the tail of Table 3, they are at the expected cluster points of 10, 12, 15, and 30 incidents. The distribution is offered as an exemplar of just noticeable difference. The clustering of reported number of victimisations around preferred numbers does not devalue these estimates. It is how people behave when the numbers they have to handle become large. The important point is that some people are victimised so often that they are reduced to estimation. The issue is of methodological importance because Rand and Rennison (2006) have suggested that such clustering indicates tail-ender data is faulty and misleading, which is not the case. The patterns are precisely what would be expected due to JND.

The present analysis examined the capping of incidents within a series. It did not account for the practice of capping the number of series that a respondent is allowed to report to the survey (the number of victim forms that the interviewer will complete). Although the number of victim forms has increased to six in recent BCS sweeps, this type of capping would also act disproportionately upon the rate of multiple victimisation and, to our

Table 3: Motor Vehicle Crimes in 2005-2006 BCS, Illustrating Just Noticeable Difference (JND) in the Tail

Times Victimised	% Respondents	% Victims	% Incidents	% Repeats
0	94.01	0.00	0.00	0.00
1	4.85	80.97	61.18	0.00
2	0.71	11.92	18.01	36.84
3	0.28	4.65	10.54	28.74
4	0.08	1.37	4.14	12.69
5	0.03	0.42	1.59	5.19
6	0.02	0.25	1.15	3.93
7	0.01	0.15	0.81	2.82
8	0.004	0.07	0.41	1.48
10	0.002	0.03	0.26	0.95
12	0.051	0.09	0.78	2.93
15	0.002	0.04	0.45	1.71
30	0.002	0.03	0.69	2.72
Total	100.00	100.00	100.00	100.00

knowledge, remains to be assessed in terms of its impact upon the crime incidence rate.

THE MURDERER'S TALE

> This world is but a thoroughfare of woe
> And we are pilgrims, travelling to and fro
> All earthly troubles have an end in death.

> (From "The Knight's Tale")

In the classroom, the insensitive lecturer can get a cheap laugh with the remark that murder appears to be the only offence immune from multiple victimisation. This is misleading, as well as crass. Personal experience in repeat victimisation studies showed that lesser offences often anticipate murder. Close reading of the files from murder enquiries reveal the tangled relationships, often involving numerous calls for police service, whose final resolution is achieved by murder. By relationships in this case, we mean not just domestic links, but all circumstances where the victim and murderer already know each other, as is currently the case in some 80% of detected murders in England and Wales (Coleman, Hird, & Povey, 2006). Even press accounts of murders make the point clearly. Two recent cases can be cited to illustrate the point.

On January 12, 2006, petrol was poured through the letterbox of a house in Wythenshawe, Manchester, and ignited. The two adults in the home, Mr. and Mrs. Cochrane, died, and their daughter Lucy was burned. It emerged that a hostile other family, the Connors, were responsible.

> The 18-month feud began after schoolgirl Natalie Connor developed an obsessive hatred of her classmate because of an apparent slight. The dispute between the two families, in which Natalie falsely claimed she had been bullied by Lucy, came to a head when Michael bought two litres of petrol and poured it through the Cochranes' letterbox. A heavy drinker, he was goaded by his wife, who plied him with alcohol before the attack early on January 12 this year. Five days earlier, Mrs Cochrane discovered what appeared to be a flammable liquid on her front door and found that someone had tried to uproot a tree from the garden. She called the police but no sample of the liquid was taken. Connor and his wife were convicted last week on two counts of murder. Their daughter was found guilty of manslaughter and attempting to cause grievous bodily harm to Lucy. Alistair Webster QC, prosecuting, had told the jury during the six-week trial that Natalie had developed an obsessive enmity towards her classmate that eventually led to her and her mother inciting Connor to start the fire. (*Guardian*, December 21, 2006, p. 15)

The second case concerns the murder of Tania Moore by Mark Dyche.

> The pair had met at a Young Farmers' ball and were soon engaged. But in February 2003 Miss Moore, fed-up over Dyche's jealous and threatening behaviour, ended the relationship. For a year he waged a hate campaign against her, which included repeated threats to kill her. In June 2003 he even paid three men armed with baseball bats . . . to rob and beat her at her family's farmhouse home in Alkmonton, near Ashbourne, Derbys. Nottingham Crown Court heard that Dyche, who has a history of terrorising women, "wanted her hurting, wanted her legs breaking, wanted her eyes gouging out, wanted to be in control". He offered criminal associates £50,000 to kill her but, when no one came forward, did it himself, lying in wait

on a country road in March 2004 and blasting her in the face with a shotgun. A few days before she was murdered, Miss Moore presented officers with a bundle of threatening text messages from Dyche. (*Daily Telegraph*, November 2, 2006, p. 12)

The criminologist reader will at this point be screaming "false positives." Thankfully only a minuscule proportion of troubled relationships end in murder. Thus, throwing resources at troubled relationships is immensely wasteful if the purpose is the prevention of murder, because most such cases will be false positives as a harbinger of murder (see, for example, Brookman & Maguire, 2003). But what if the purpose is the resolution of troubled or oppressive relationships? Since we know that the probability of an $n + 1$ call for police service increases with n, increased resourcing of a response as the number of calls for service increases is justifiable on the grounds of prevention of future calls, with the not inconsiderable bonus of an occasional prevented murder. Inspection of police calls for service could yield minimum numbers of preventable assault crimes, including murder. We have elsewhere bemoaned the police tendency to "premature evacuation," that is, the too ready termination of involvement where repetition is likely. It seems otiose to remark that premature evacuation sometimes leads to murder.

EPILOGUE

I only want to put right what's amiss.
This tale is not directed just at you
But lots of other people.

(From "The Canon's Assistant's Tale")

The foregoing analysis demonstrates that the seemingly mundane administrative practice of restricting series incidents has a significant impact upon the amount of crime the BCS estimates to have occurred. The effect is most pronounced for personal crime, where the sundering of series repeat victimisations has, for 25 years, excluded around 40% of personal crime suffered. The effect of the sundering of series household crimes is less pronounced but still excludes around 20% on average and in some years over a quarter of household crimes.

There are, in summary, three conclusions to be drawn from the analysis undertaken.

1. The amount of crime suffered is substantially higher than BCS publications have hitherto allowed. This is dramatically true from personal crimes, that is, crimes of violence, threat, and sexual crime. This changes the proper balance of concern as between property and personal crime. It has been conventional to say that violent crime is only a small proportion of all crime. It emerges that this is not as true as was thought.

2. The proper inclusion of series events shows that victimisation is even more concentrated on particular people and households than was hitherto evident.

3. Because of the extent to which victims of personal crime in particular know their offender, policing properly should be more concerned to recognise the centrality in crime causation of troubled ongoing relationships.

Address correspondence to: Graham Farrell (g.farrell@lboro.ac.uk) or Ken Pease (k.pease@lboro.ac.uk).

Acknowledgements: This is a revised version of an article presented at the conference to mark Twenty Five-Years of the British Crime Survey, held at Cumberland Lodge in Windsor Great Part in England on the 16th and 17th of October, 2006. Particular thanks are due to Michael Maxfield, Michael Hough, Ron Clarke, and to Alison Walker and Katharine Thorpe of the British Crime Survey team at the Home Office, for the invitation, and for advice upon aspects of this chapter.

NOTES

1. This and all extracts from Chaucer's *Canterbury Tales* are taken from the David Wright translation (1986).
2. Hindelang et al. drew primarily on surveys in 8 cities, but the chapter on multiple victimisation drew on surveys in 26 cities in order to increase the sample (see Hindelang et al., 1978, p. 127).

3. Cantor and Lynch (2000) also cite earlier works by Biderman (1967, 1975) as relevant to the development of the study of repeat victimisation.
4. Specifically, when there are too many incidents for a respondent to recall, they are assigned the value 97 in the BCS datasets, which we recoded to value 60 in line with Walby and Allen (2004).
5. In Walker, Kershaw, and Nicholas (2006), incidence rates are shown per 10,000 adults or households, whereas they are shown here as rates per 100 adults or households.

REFERENCES

Barr, R., & Pease, K. (1990). Crime placement, displacement and deflection. In M. Tonry & N. Morris (Eds.), *Crime and justice: An annual review of research*. Chicago: University of Chicago Press.

Biderman, A. (1967, November). Surveys of population samples for estimating crime incidence. *Annals of the American Academy of Social and Political Science, 374*, 16-34.

Biderman, A. (1975). *Notes on the significance of measurements of events and of conditions by criminal victimization surveys.* BSSR 0003-58. Washington, DC: Bureau of Social Science Research.

Biderman, A. (1980). Notes on measurement by crime victimization surveys. In S. E. Fienberg & A. J. Reiss (Eds.), *Indicators of crime and criminal justice: Quantitative studies* (pp. 29-32). Washington, DC: U.S. Bureau of Statistics.

Bouloukos, A. C., & Farrell, G. (1997). On the displacement of repeat victimisation. In G. Newman, R. V. Clarke, & S. G. Shoham (Eds.), *Rational choice and situational crime prevention*. Aldershot, England: Dartmouth Press.

Brookman, F., & Maguire, M. (2003). *Reducing homicide: Summary of a review of the possibilities.* RDS Occasional Paper 84. London: Home Office.

Budd, T., & Mattinson, J. (2000). *British Crime Survey training notes.* Crime Surveys Section, Crime and Criminal Justice Unit, Research and Development Statistics Directorate. London: Home Office.

Cantor, D., & Lynch, J. (2000). Self-report surveys as measures of crime and criminal victimization. In *Measurement and analysis of crime and justice* (Vol. 4.). Washington, DC: Bureau of Justice Statistics.

Chaucer, G. (1986, trans. D. Wright). *The Canterbury tales.* Oxford: Oxford University Press.

Chenery, S., Holt, J., & Pease, K. (1997). *Biting back II: Preventing repeat victimisation in Huddersfield.* Crime Detection and Prevention Paper 82. London: Home Office.

Coleman, K., Hird, C., & Povey, D. (2006). *Violent crime overview: Homicide and gun crime 2004/5.* Home Office Statistical Bulletin 02/06. London: Home Office.

Cornish, D., & Clarke, R. V. (2001). Rational Choice Theory. In R. Paternoster & R. Backman (Eds.), *Explaining criminals and crime.* Los Angeles: Roxbury.

Dodge, R. W. (1975). Series victimizations – what is to be done? Reprinted in R. G. Lehnen & W. G. Skogan (Eds.). (1984), *The national crime survey: Working papers. Vol. II: Methodological studies* (pp. 2-3). Washington, DC: U.S. Department of Justice Bureau of Justice Statistics.

Dodge, R. W. (1977). A preliminary inquiry into series victimizations. Reprinted in R. G. Lehnen & W. G. Skogan (Eds.). (1984). *The national crime survey: Working papers. Vol. II: Methodological studies* (pp. 4-7). Washington, DC: U.S. Department of Justice Bureau of Justice Statistics.

Dodge, R. W. (1987). *Series crimes: Report of a field test bureau of justice statistics* technical report. Washington, DC: U.S. Department of Justice Bureau of Justice Statistics.

Dodge, R. W., & Lentzner, H. R. (1978). Patterns of personal series incidents in the National Crime Survey. Reprinted in R. G. Lehnen & W. G. Skogan (Eds.). (1984), *The national crime survey: Working papers. Vol. 2: Methodological studies* (pp. 8-15). Washington, DC: U.S. Department of Justice Bureau of Justice Statistics.

Eck, J. E. (1993). The threat of crime displacement. *Criminal Justice Abstracts, 25,* 527-546.

Farrell, G. (1992). Multiple victimisation: Its extent and significance. *International Review of Victimology, 2,* 85-102.

Farrell, G. (2005). Progress and prospects in the prevention of repeat victimisation. In N. Tilley (Ed.), *Handbook of crime prevention and community safety.* Cullompton, England: Willan.

Farrell, G., & Pease, K. (2002). Repeat victimization. In D. Levinson (Ed.), *Encyclopedia of crime and punishment.* Thousand Oaks, CA: Sage.

Farrell, G., Tseloni, A., & Pease, K. (2005). Repeat victimization in the ICVS and NCVS. *Crime Prevention and Community Safety, 7,* 7-18.

Farrington, D. P., & Dowds, L. (1985). Disentangling criminal behaviour and police reaction. In D. P. Farrington & J. Gunn (Eds.), *Reactions to crime.* Chichester, England: Wiley.

Fienberg, S. E. (1980). Statistical modelling in the analysis of repeat victimisation. In S. E. Fienberg & A. J. Reiss (Eds.), *Indicators of crime and criminal justice: Quantitative studies.* Washington, DC: U.S. Bureau of Statistics.

Fienberg, S. E., & Reiss, A. J. (Eds.). (1980). *Indicators of crime and criminal justice: Quantitative studies.* Washington, DC: U.S. Bureau of Statistics.

Felson, M. (2006). *Crime and nature.* London: Sage.

Fitzmaurice, C., & Pease, K. (1986). *The psychology of judicial sentencing.* Manchester University Press.

Galton, F. (1895). Terms of imprisonment. *Nature, 52,* 174-176.

Genn, H. (1988). Multiple victimisation. In M. Maguire & J. Pointing (Eds.), *Victims of crime: A new deal?* Berkshire, UK: Open University Press.

Gottfredson, M. (1984). *Victims of crime: The dimensions of risk.* Home Office Research Study 81. London: Home Office. Also available at www.homeoffice.gov.uk/rds/pdfs05/hors81.pdf

Hindelang, M. J., Gottfredson, M. R., & Garafalo, J. (1978). *Victims of personal crime: An empirical foundation for a theory of personal victimisation.* Cambridge, MA: Ballinger.

Hough, M., & Mayhew, P. (1983). *The British crime survey: First report*. London Home Office Research Study no. 76. London: Her Majesty's Stationery Office.

Hough, M., & Mayhew, P. (1985). *Taking account of crime: Key findings from the 1984 British crime survey*. Home Office Research Study no. 85. London: Her Majesty's Stationery Office.

Lauritsen, J. L., & Davis-Quinet, K. F. (1995). Repeat victimization among adolescents and young adults. *Journal of Quantitative Criminology, 11*, 143-166.

Laycock, G. L. (2001). Hypothesis-based research: The repeat victimisation story. *Criminal Justice: The International Journal of Policy and Practice, 1*, 59-82.

Lehnen, R. G., & Skogan, W. (Eds.). (1981). *The national crime survey: Working papers. Vol. 1: Current and historical perspectives*. Washington, DC: U.S. Department of Justice Bureau of Justice Statistics.

Lehnen, R. G., & Skogan, W. G. (Eds.). (1984). *The national crime survey: Working papers. Vol. II: Methodological studies*. Washington, DC: U.S. Department of Justice Bureau of Justice Statistics.

Lynch, J. P. (2006). Problems and promise of victimization surveys for cross-national research. In M. Tonry (Ed.), *Crime and justice: A review of research* (p. 34). Chicago: University of Chicago Press.

Lynch, J. P., Berbaum, M., & Planty, M. (1998). *Investigating repeat victimization with the NCVS, Executive Summary*. U.S. Department of Justice document no. 193414. Washington, DC: U.S. Department of Justice.

Mayhew, P., Aye-Maung, N., & Mirrlees-Black, C. (1993). *The 1992 British crime survey*. London: HMSO.

Mukherjee, S., & Carcach, C. (1998). *Repeat victimisation in Australia*. Canberra: Australian Institute of Criminology.

Miller, T. R., Cohen, M. A., & Wiersema, B. (1996). *Victim costs and consequences: A new look*. Washington, DC: National Institute of Justice.

Office of National Statistics. (2005). *Households*. Retrieved 27 October 2006 from http://www.statistics.gov.uk/CCI/nugget.asp?ID=1162

Osborn, D., Ellingworth, D., Hope, T., & Trickett, A. (1995). *The puzzle of victimization: Are multiple victims different?* School of Economic Studies, University of Manchester. Discussion Paper 95 12.

Pease, K. (1998). *Repeat victimisation: Taking stock*. Crime Detection and Prevention Series, Paper 90, Police Research Group. London: Home Office. Also available at www.homeoffice.gov.uk/rds/prgpdfs/fcdps90.pdf

Planty, M., & Strom, K. J. (2007). Understanding the role of repeat victims in the production of annual victimization rates. *Journal of Quantitative Criminology, 23*, 179-200.

Rand, M. (2006). Telescoping effects and survey nonresponse in the national crime *victimization survey*. Statistical Commission and UN Economic Commission for Europe, Conference of European Statisticians, Joint UNECE-UNODC Meeting on Crime Statistics, Vienna, 25-27 January 2006, Working Paper No. 4, 20 January 2006. Vienna: United Nations Office on Drugs and Crime.

Rand, M., & Rennison, C. M. (2005). Bigger is not necessarily better: An analysis of violence against women. Estimates from the national crime victimization survey and the national violence against women survey. *Journal of Quantitative Criminology, 21*, 267-291.

Reiss, A. J. (1977). Summary of series and nonseries incident reporting, 1972-1975. Reprinted in R. G. Lehnen & W. G. Skogan (Eds.). (1984). *The national crime survey: Working papers. Vol. II: Methodological studies* (pp. 16-17). Washington, DC: U.S. Department of Justice Bureau of Justice Statistics.

Reiss, A. J. (1980). Victim proneness in repeat victimisation by type of crime. In S. E. Fienberg & A. J. Reiss (Eds.), *Indicators of crime and criminal justice: Quantitative studies*. Washington, DC: U.S. Bureau of Justice Statistics.

Skogan, W. G. (1981). *Issues in the measurement of victimization*. Washington, DC: U.S. Department of Justice, Bureau of Justice Statistics.

Skogan, W. G. (1986). Methodological issues in the measurement of victimization. In E. A. Fattah (Ed.), *From crime policy to victim policy: Reorienting the justice system*. London: Macmillan.

Sparks, R. F. (1981). Multiple victimization: Evidence, theory and future research. *Journal of Criminal Law and Criminology, 72*, 762-778.

Stevens, S. S. (1975). *Psychophysics: Introduction to its perceptual, neural and social aspects*. Chichester, England: Wiley.

Tseloni, A., & Pease, K. (2003). Repeat personal victimisation: "Boosts" or "flags"? *British Journal of Criminology, 43*, 196-212.

Tseloni, A., & Pease, K. (2004). Repeat personal victimisation: Random effects, event dependence and unexplained heterogeneity. *British Journal of Criminology, 44*, 931-935.

Tseloni, A., & Pease, K. (2005). Population inequality: The case of repeat victimisation. *International Review of Victimology, 12*, 75-90.

Walby, S., & Allen, J. (2004). *Domestic violence, sexual assault and stalking: Findings from the British crime survey*. Home Office Research Study 276. London: Home Office Available at http://www.homeoffice.gov.uk/rds/pdfs04/hors276.pdf

Walker, A., Kershaw, C., & Nicholas, S. (2006). *Crime in England and Wales 2006*. Home Office Statistical Bulletin 12/06. London: Home Office.

Understanding the Link Between Victimization and Offending: New Reflections on an Old Idea

by

Janet L. Lauritsen

Department of Criminology and Criminal Justice
University of Missouri, St. Louis

and

John H. Laub

Department of Criminology and Criminal Justice
University of Maryland

Abstract: *One of the best predictors of an individual's risk for criminal victimization is the extent to which that person is involved in criminal offending. Frequently referred to as the "victim–offender overlap," this relationship has been found to exist in numerous countries, across various time periods, among adults as well as youths, and for many types of crime ranging from homicide to bicycle theft. Research has found that this relationship cannot be accounted for by shared individual and contextual characteristics or earlier victimization experiences. In this chapter, we summarize and evaluate existing research on the victim–offender overlap. We devote particular attention to quantitative and qualitative efforts to sort out the causal mechanisms underlying these associations. To understand better the importance of this*

Crime Prevention Studies, volume 22 (2007), pp. 55–75.

relationship, we recommend that future research use mixed methodologies that systematically combine rigorous quantitative analyses with detailed analyses of narrative data or focused interviews with offenders and victims. In addition, we speculate on why criminological theorists and policy makers have failed to take seriously the overlap between victims and offenders. Finally, we offer a modest research agenda to integrate more fully a focus on the victim-offender overlap into criminology and criminal justice.

More than 50 years ago, Hans von Hentig introduced criminologists to the notion that victims play a critical role in understanding the criminal event. In a chapter entitled "The Contribution of the Victim to the Genesis of Crime" (von Hentig, 1948), he argued that "the relationships between perpetrator and victim are much more intricate than the rough distinctions of criminal law" (p. 383). These relationships also are linked more closely than the distinctions made in mainstream criminology and victimology. Indeed, it is telling that the study of offenders and victims consists of two distinct areas of inquiry and specialization.

In this chapter, we summarize and evaluate existing research on the victim-offender overlap and argue, as others have, that neither victimization nor offending can be understood without full consideration of the other. We devote particular attention to quantitative and qualitative efforts to sort out causal mechanisms underlying these relationships. In addition, we speculate on why criminologists and policy makers have been relatively disinterested in the overlap between victims and offenders. We conclude with a discussion of how future studies of offending and victimization can benefit from an explicit focus on this issue.

EMPIRICAL RESEARCH ON THE LINK BETWEEN VICTIMIZATION AND OFFENDING

Research on the relationship between victimization and offending has consistently found that one of the strongest correlates of victimization is involvement in deviant or criminal behavior and, alternatively, that victimization is one of the strongest correlates of offending. These findings have been confirmed using various data sources and methodologies. Studies of official records have included the examination of homicide narratives (e.g., Wolfgang, 1958), criminal history records (e.g., Singer, 1981, 1986), and medical records (e.g., Moscovitz et al., 1997; Broidy et al., 2006).

Research using nonofficial data has relied on cross-sectional (e.g., Jensen & Brownfield, 1986; Fagan et al., 1987 and longitudinal self-report surveys of youth (e.g., Esbensen & Huizinga, 1991; Lauritsen et al., 1991, 1992; Lattimore et al., 1997; Loeber et al., 2001; Shaffer & Ruback, 2002; Smith, 2004; Stewart et al., 2006); retrospective and prospective data from cohort studies (e.g., Singer, 1981, 1986); cross-sectional victimization surveys of adults (e.g., Hough & Mayhew, 1983; Gottfredson, 1984; Sampson & Wooldredge, 1987; Sampson & Lauritsen, 1990; Wittebrood & Nieuw-beerta, 1999, 2000); samples of high school students (Peterson et al., 2004) and college students (e.g., Mustaine & Tewksbury, 2000); interviews with homeless youth (Whitbeck et al., 2001; McCarthy et al., 2002), and data from prisoners and offenders (Wooldredge, 1994; Fattah, no date). Qualitative and ethnographic data from serious offenders located in high-crime neighborhoods have shed important insight on this issue as well (e.g., Decker & Van Winkle, 1996; Miller, 1998; Anderson, 1999; Jacobs & Wright, 2006). It is impossible to review the full body of research in the space available.[1] Instead, our overview highlights some of the key insights that have been drawn from this research.

The earliest American studies to draw attention to the "victim–offender overlap" analyzed homicide records. In his classic study of homicide in the city of Philadelphia, Wolfgang (1958) highlighted two important facts: (1) that "victim-precipitation" was a fairly common occurrence in homicide, and (2) that a large proportion of both offenders and victims had arrest records. It is difficult to overstate the importance of these findings for establishing the direction of subsequent homicide research.

In particular, many of the findings from Wolfgang's comparison of victim-precipitated and other types of homicides continue to be replicated in contemporary research. For instance, he found that victim-precipitation was more common in homicides in which women kill men and in which alcohol was used by the victim. Fifty years later, these findings remain true and inquiries on the role of gender and substance use continue to permeate contemporary studies of homicide.

Yet it was Wolfgang's discovery that a large proportion of offenders and victims had arrest records that set in motion the systematic consideration of how individual characteristics and social processes might influence risk for both violent victimization and offending. If many homicide victims had an offending history, then it might be the case that these two groups are similar to one another in ways that also distinguish them from the broader population. The stability of his findings over time and places in the U.S. is worth highlighting. Wolfgang (1958) found that roughly 64% of homicide offenders and nearly half of the victims in Philadelphia in 1948-1952 had previous arrest records. Nearly 50 years later, in the very different city of Albuquerque, New Mexico, Broidy and her colleagues (2006) report that 57% of the offenders and 50% of recent homicide victims had prior arrest records.

Although a wide variety of homicide studies would show that there were important similarities between victims and offenders, it was unclear whether similar conclusions would be drawn if the investigation were extended to other forms of crime. Certainly, there were theoretical reasons to expect that the pattern would be similar for other types of violence. Subcultural theories, for instance, hypothesized that violence was concentrated among groups that hold norms supportive of the use of force to resolve conflicts (e.g., Wolfgang & Ferracuti, 1967). These limitations would be addressed in the late 1970s and early 1980s when survey research methods were catapulted to the forefront of criminological research.

One of the first American studies that permitted further investigation of the "homogeneity" of victims and offenders was a follow-up survey administered to Wolfgang's birth cohort data from Philadelphia (Wolfgang, Figlio, & Sellin, 1972). Using a random sample of 26-year-old males from the birth cohort, Singer (1981) examined how retrospective self-reports of victimization during three periods of the life-course were related to self-reported serious adult offending and arrests. He found that victimization during childhood, adolescence, and young adulthood were highly correlated with adult offending, even when other correlates of adult offending were controlled. Singer acknowledged that these significant correlations were insufficient for establishing the existence of a violent subculture. However, he contended that these patterns could not be solely a function of opportunity or exposure to offenders as competing hypotheses had suggested, and he recommended that additional research be conducted to understand the effect that victimization has on "an individual's sense of justice and propensity to obey the law" (1981, p. 787).

Broader developments in population-based surveys made it possible to study the relationship between victimization and offending on a much larger scale, and it was British data that initially permitted such analyses. To our knowledge, the first population-based study was done by Sparks and his colleagues (1977), who noted a significant association between assault victimization and offending, using survey data from London. In our view though, it was the research based on the British Crime Survey

(BCS) that solidified the importance of the victim-offender overlap (Hough & Mayhew, 1983; Gottfredson, 1984, 1986; Sampson & Wooldredge, 1987; Mayhew & Elliott, 1990; and Sampson & Lauritsen, 1990). Analyses of the BCS showed that involvement in deviant activities was associated with the risk for victimization, and that this relationship remained significant despite controls for sociodemographic factors and proxies for neighborhood crime rates. In fact, involvement in deviant activities helped account for some of the bivariate demographic differences in victimization. By uncovering the victim-offender overlap with a broader, population-based sample, it became clear that the phenomenon was not limited to the most serious forms of violence.

The development of lifestyle and routine activities frameworks for studying crime encouraged researchers to use survey data to identify factors and behaviors that were associated with individual's risk for victimization. In the United States, however, the National Crime Survey (NCS) lacked the requisite behavioral measures for parsing out the relative contributions of crime prevention and lifestyle activities that were important to researchers. The NCS and its later version, the National Crime Victimization Survey (NCVS), would never contain measures about involvement in deviant or criminal behavior. The NC(V)S data collection is funded by the U.S. Department of Justice and it was believed that if this sponsor were to ask such questions, participation in the survey would be jeopardized and its main purpose – to provide reliable estimates of victimization independent of the police – would be undermined (personal communication, Klaus & Rand, 2006).

Throughout the 1980s and 1990s, researchers continued to search for behavioral antecedents of victimization, and in the U.S. they relied primarily on cross-sectional surveys of adolescents and young adults. The findings from these studies were consistent: delinquent behavior was associated with increased risk of personal victimization. Even those behaviors that did not involve the use of violence, but instead represented more common forms of delinquency, were associated with victimization (e.g., Jensen & Brownfield, 1986; Lauritsen, Laub, & Sampson, 1992). The main challenges to these findings centered on the interpretation of the relationship between victimization and offending. More specifically, it was believed that the relationship might be spurious because victims and offenders disproportionately live in areas that are socioeconomically disadvantaged. Concerns about causal ordering were also raised. Subcultural theories of violence and Black's (1983) notion of crime as social control suggested that victimization was an important source of offending behavior, as did interactionist analyses (e.g., Felson & Steadman, 1983). However, most of the extant literature that linked the two phenomena focused on modeling the influence of offending on victimization risk using the frameworks offered by routine activities and lifestyle theories (see, e.g., Cohen, Kluegel, & Land, 1981; Hindelang, Gottfredson, & Garofalo, 1978).

As longitudinal survey data became available, researchers were able to consider whether the relationship between victimization and offending might have been misspecified. Using self-report panel data from the National Youth Survey in the U.S., Lauritsen and colleagues (1991) found significant reciprocal effects even when sociodemographic and neighborhood factors were controlled. Equally important, they demonstrated that the effects of delinquency on victimization and victimization on delinquency were larger than the effects of any other factors in the model including demographic characteristics and prior levels of victimization or offending. They also noted that the coefficients appear to be larger for violent victimization and offending than for nonviolent incidents.

Research on the relationship between offending and victimization has been especially ambitious in Great Britain and the Netherlands where data sources are not limited to samples of youths. Like American research, the majority of these studies focus on understanding variation in victimization risk and use past or present offending or deviant behavior as predictors of various forms of victimization (e.g., Wittebrood & Nieuwbeerta, 1999, 2000; Smith, 2004; Matz, 2007). What is clear from this broader set of findings is that the relationship between victimization and offending is robust and does not appear to be limited to one or two countries (e.g., Bjarnason, Sigurdottir, & Thorlindsson, 1999; Klevens, Duque, & Ramiriz, 2002).

In fact, we are unaware of any research that has examined the link between offending and victimization and failed to find a strong relationship. The relationship has been found across time, place, and for various subgroups (e.g., adolescents and adults, males as well as females). It is significant regardless of the type of data used or the type of offending and deviance (e.g., homicide, nonlethal violence, property offending, road rage, alcohol use) or victimization (e.g., bicycle theft, vandalism, violence, and homicide) under consideration. It persists despite controls for demographic correlates and lifestyle characteristics such as drug or alcohol use, time spent with delinquent peers, gang involvement, or other measures of activities. Indeed, even the correlations within an institutional setting as regulated as a prison are significant (Wooldredge, 1994).

CAUSAL MECHANISMS UNDERLYING THE VICTIM-OFFENDER OVERLAP

Although the research findings are unequivocal, the meaning of the relationship is less clear. Hypotheses about the causal mechanisms can be categorized into two broad types: "individual heterogeneity" and "state-dependent" processes.[2] Explanations consistent with heterogeneity arguments are those that assert that individuals differ according to some generally stable characteristics that are correlated with both offending and victimization (see, e.g., Nagin & Paternoster, 1991, 2000; Lauritsen & Davis-Quinet, 1995; Tseloni & Pease, 2003, 2004). Garofalo (1987) pointed out this possibility years ago when he noted that "variations in risk cannot be accounted for entirely at the sociological level of explanation; psychological and even biological variables may be relevant" (p. 39). Heterogeneity may reflect time-stable traits such as the propensity for risk taking, impulsivity, or low self-control (Gottfredson & Hirschi, 1990; Schreck, 1999); or biological characteristics that are associated with one's capacity to detect danger signals in the environment or one's facility to resolve conflicts. Moreover, heterogeneity may also reflect shared social conditions. For instance, living in a disadvantaged and socially isolated neighborhood or subscribing to subcultural values supportive of the use of violence may account for the shared heterogeneity between victimization and offending if those social conditions remain fairly constant for the individual during the period under investigation. Hence, stability does not necessarily imply causal forces operating solely at the level of the individual (see Sampson & Laub, 1992, p. 78).

State-dependent hypotheses suggest that experiences operate in such a way as to alter an individual's future risk of the event. For example, under certain conditions victimization encourages retaliation which, in turn, prompts revictimization (see Lauritsen & Davis-Quinet, 1995). State-dependent hypotheses also include those that assert that offending increases future victimization because it increases one's proximity to offenders or reduces one's access to formal mechanisms of social control. Examples of the latter include the notion that offenders may be victimized with impunity because they are unable or unwilling to use the law to resolve disputes or obtain justice (e.g., Sparks, 1982; Kubrin & Weitzer, 2003; Jacobs & Wright, 2006). Similarly, if offending leads to a reduction in social ties that are a source of capable guardianship or broader connections to social institutions of informal social control, then subsequent victimization and offending will be more likely to occur (see Gottfredson, 1981).

A wide body of research can be drawn upon to help think about the causal processes underlying the victim-offender overlap. One example is a recent study by Stewart and his colleagues (2006) who find, like other researchers, that prior offending is the strongest predictor of future victimization risk among adolescents, even when sociodemographic characteristics, contextual factors, and prior victimization are taken into account. The key finding highlighted in this study is that "street code" norms did not protect youth from victimization; in fact, adherence to these norms was associated with elevated risk in the most disadvantaged neighborhoods. Although hypothesized as a source of the overlap, this research found that street code norms had little effect on the relationship between offending and victimization.

Other research has also found little change in the relationship despite the inclusion of a wide variety of additional variables such as family, peer, and neighborhood characteristics (e.g., Lauritsen et al., 1991; Lauritsen & Davis-Quinet, 1995; Wittebrood & Nieuwbeerta, 1999). For example, in a recent study of how gang membership might influence victimization, Peterson and her colleagues (2004) used panel data to compare victimization self-reports of gang members before, during, and after their involvement in gangs to reports from nongang members during the same periods. Contrary to youths' perceptions about how gangs might protect them, victimization increased during periods of gang membership. Moreover, violent offending remained the strongest predictor of victimization even when gang membership was taken into account (see also Singer, 1981).

It appears that the persistent effect of offending on victimization most likely reflects both forms of individual heterogeneity not considered in existing research, as well as unmeasured state-dependent processes. Yet the relative contribution of the two types of influences is unknown. To date, we know much more about the factors that do *not* account for the relationship between offending and victimization than we do about those that might be responsible. If we want to identify the mechanisms underlying the relationship between victimization and offending, researchers must examine types of heterogeneity that are not captured by demographic characteristics, family and peer factors, neighborhood characteristics, various lifestyle activities, or subcultural norms. We must consider various biological and psychological measures that capture aspects of personality and decision-making capacities and assess how these individual differences in tandem with specific types of social environments may be linked to differential proneness in victimization. Moreover, as is the case for offending, much more needs to be learned about the specific factors underlying state-dependent processes of victimization. Are the factors that alter trajectories of criminal offending the same factors that alter victimization trajectories over time?

Although studies have shown that both state-dependent and heterogeneity processes are involved in patterns of offending over time (e.g., Sampson & Laub, 1993), we are unaware of any research that has tried to model these processes in offending while controlling for victimization over time. In an assessment of these processes in victimization using random-effects panel modeling with longitudinal data from the National Youth Survey, Lauritsen and Davis-Quinet (1995) found that both heterogeneity and state-dependent processes were involved in patterns of repeat victimization over time and that those processes maintained despite controlling for involvement in delinquency.

Much of what is known about the overlap among the adult population has been obtained from self-report surveys where offending and victimization incidents are predominantly of a less serious nature (e.g., simple assaults). It appears that research using adult population-based samples has reached something of an impasse partly because the methodology has not been able to capture the detail necessary for sorting out various heterogeneity and state-dependence hypotheses that would provide new insight into the underlying mechanisms. Yet even if such measures were included, levels and trends in survey participation suggest that it may be unreasonable to assume that persons with the highest levels of serious victimization or offending will be represented (see, e.g., Ybarra & Lohr, 2002).

In our view, some of the most helpful insights come from detailed quantitative studies of homicide narratives and qualitative, ethnographic research on street offending. For instance, Kubrin and Weitzer (2003) examined homicides in St. Louis, Missouri, using quantitative data on homicide in conjunction with detailed narrative accounts of homicide incidents. "Cultural retaliatory homicides" were found to be more common in neighborhoods characterized by economic disadvantage, cultural norms tolerant of violence, and problematic policing. As a result, residents within these neighborhoods took matters into their own hands and resolved disputes informally yet with lethal violence. Kubrin and Weitzer (2003) identify four conditions associated with retaliatory killings in disadvantaged areas: "retribution for disrespect, insults toward female significant others, a policing vacuum, and community and family support for retaliation" (p.

171). This study points to the role of both structural factors and cultural norms in accounting for violence at the neighborhood level and suggests how the roles of victim and offender are often interchangeable. Perhaps most striking, Kubrin and Weitzer point out that "far from being an isolated, individual affair, the narrative data show that retaliatory violence can be collectively tolerated, endorsed, and rewarded by other residents" (p. 178).

Along similar lines, qualitative studies of street offenders have focused on gangs, robbery, homicide, and drug sales, and what is apparent throughout is the constant presence of retaliation as a response to various forms of victimization (see, e.g., Decker & Van Winkle, 1996; Jacobs, 2000; Jacobs & Wright, 2006). Street offenders use retaliation as a way of handling a variety of affronts ranging from disrespectful insults to violent acts committed against the street offender or someone in their social network. Many, but not all, of these actions take place because street offenders do not have access to the formal legal system for resolving disputes or exacting more civilized forms of revenge. Many also appear, however, to result from the desire to discharge emotion and to maintain an invulnerable persona on the street. According to Jacobs and Wright, many criminal victims choose to retaliate even if they can report their victimization to the police without fear of self-incrimination because they believe that reporting would not lead to a satisfactory outcome: "Violations cut to the core of who street offenders are and how they perceive themselves. Criminal victims want violators to pay. They want them to hurt. They want them to think about the strike long after it happens" (2006, pp. 25-26).

These studies suggest that reporting victimization to the police threatens the persona that most street offenders want to maintain, by conveying that they are cowards who are incapable of handling their own business. In fact, talking to the police about any incident identifies one as a snitch or an informer and puts one in great jeopardy from other offenders, including those who might not have been involved in a specific incident. In a study of snitching among street offenders, Rosenfeld and his colleagues (2003) found that none of the offenders they interviewed reported they had snitched, yet they all stated that the streets were filled with such offenders. The authors concluded that snitching led to increases in violent offending and victimization by escalating the spiral of retaliation and counterretaliation. These interviews also remind us of another difficulty common when obtaining information from serious offenders: establishing the reliability and validity of their information. The methodological adaptations that are necessary for studying these groups make it difficult to see how a single approach can be used to study both victim-offenders involved in serious crime, especially violence, as well as less serious forms of victimization and offending experiences.

WHY DON'T WE KNOW MORE ABOUT THE VICTIM-OFFENDER OVERLAP?

There are several reasons why the field of criminology has failed to take seriously the overlap between victims and offenders. Here we identify five reasons for this unfortunate outcome. First, part of the answer lies in the historical origins of the subfields of study. It is the case that studies of offending preceded studies of victimization by many decades, hence victimization has been traditionally thought of as a minor subfield of criminology. Even more significant is the fact that the study of victims in the U.S. has been dominated by practical concerns regarding the treatment of victims in the criminal justice system and the lack of available services for victims of crimes. In general, there has been little exchange between victimization research and more traditional criminological approaches.

Second, there is a strong tendency within criminology to focus on crime exclusively and not to link crime to other forms of deviance and problem behavior. Gottfredson and Hirschi (1990) have argued that "crime is only part of a much larger set of deviant acts, acts that include accidents, victimizations, truancies from home, school, and work, substance abuse, family problems, and disease" (1990, p. xiv). In a different domain, Black (1983) makes a similar point when he states "crime often expresses a grievance. This implies that many crimes belong to the same family as gossip, ridicule, vengeance, punishment, and law itself" (p. 42). Thinking of crime as social control or as a form of self-help forces one to consider commonalities in behavior and less about offender–victim designations.

Third, one cannot discount the lack of data in this area of inquiry. For the most part, data for criminal victimization research lacks information on offending and vice versa. Initial formulations of lifestyle and routine activity theories contained limited discussions of how offending might be linked to victimization, and those links were largely focused on proximity or exposure to offenders rather than on population heterogeneity or state-dependent processes. It is also fair to say that most large-scale studies lack the kinds of dynamic measures that are necessary for studying interrelationships between victims and offenders.

Fourth, there is a legitimate concern with the appearance of "blaming the victim" (Ryan, 1971). Academics are acutely aware that by raising the question of victim-offender overlap or investigating the behavior of victims in the interaction with offenders that their work can be perceived as victim-blaming. We wish to be clear on this point as well. We are not saying that all victims of crime are offenders or that all offenders are victims. However, we are saying that victims and offenders are disproportionately drawn from the same population and ecological setting. For serious crimes of violence, the victim-offender overlap is strong and cannot be ignored.

Fifth, it must be recognized that there is political reticence to tackle the victim-offender issue. Social values and public attitudes influence how Americans think of offenders and victims. In current popular discourse about crime, offenders are perceived as bad and victims are perceived as good (see Tonry, 2004). Lab (2004) has contended that certain topics in the study of crime are not discussed because "it is not politically expedient" to do so (p. 684). Although writing about the politics regarding crime prevention policies, Lab's argument applies to the study of victims and offenders as well. Specifically, Lab argues that in the U.S. (and increasingly in the United Kingdom and Europe as well), politicians look for immediate results, seek to achieve outcomes that can be easily counted (like new laws, increased jail and prison counts, longer sentences), emphasize policies that play well in the media, and respond to issues of the moment with knee-jerk responses (see Lab, 2004). Under these conditions, policy makers who recognize the victim–offender overlap are likely to be accused of being too sympathetic toward some offenders. Politicians would find it more difficult to exploit a "pro-victim" position if they recognized that some victim behavior is relevant to crime. As Garland (2001) has noted, "the new political imperative is that victims must be protected, their voices must be heard, their memory honoured, their anger expressed, their fears addressed" and "a zero-sum policy game is assumed wherein the offender's gain is the victim's loss, and being 'for' victims automatically means being tough on offenders" (p. 11).

WHAT TYPES OF RESEARCH WOULD BE MOST USEFUL?

Despite the scientific, political, and ideological challenges, we offer a modest research agenda to encourage criminologists to take seriously the victim-offender overlap. We believe that research in this area can be advanced best by using mixed methods that systematically combine sound quantitative analyses with detailed analyses of narrative data drawn from official records or large-scale surveys or from focused interviews with offenders and victims (for a general discussion of strategies to bridge the quantitative and qualitative divide see Laub & Sampson, 2004). With regard to victim-offender overlap, the study by Kubrin and Weitzer (2003) serves as a model for the kind of mixed method research that is needed. Here we identify three broad-based areas of research that we think hold the most promise.

Crime and the Life Course

We find it curious that the victim–offender overlap is not seriously considered in any of the major longitudinal studies on crime over the life course. Although studies of criminal trajectories have become the staple of life-course research, few studies attend to parallel trajectories of victimization. Moreover, to our knowledge, there have been no efforts to include victimization as a time-varying covariate in longitudinal studies of crime. It is not readily apparent why this is the case, although we suspect that the lack of sufficient measures of victimization and offending are part of the difficulty (Lauritsen, 1998). Nonetheless, we believe that the study of continuity and change in offending would benefit from an explicit focus on the victim–offender overlap issue.

In one of the few research efforts that we are aware of in existing life-course research, Farrall and Calverley (2006) examine victimization in conjunction with desistance from crime. They ask, does one desist from offending *and* victimization? Farrall and Calverley expect that this would be the case because desisting offenders would "cease to become exposed to situations or relationships in which they would be victimized" (p. 157). They find, however, that desisters in their sample did not have significantly lower rates of victimization compared with offenders who persisted in crime. The explanation offered for this result is that desisting offenders are still residing in marginalized and impoverished areas (e.g., housing estates) (pp. 159-162).

The findings from the Farrall and Calverley study need to be replicated on a larger sample with better measures and more adequate control variables to determine how victimization might affect desistance. Recently, Laub and Sampson (2003) have focused attention on the role of social ties that result from marriage and work in the process of desistance from crime.

A key question is whether similar processes are at work in desistance from victimization. Perhaps an important component in the process of desistance from victimization is the "knifing off" from one's immediate environment as well as one's former social networks; especially other offenders (see Laub & Sampson, 2003). Thus, we encourage researchers examining desistance from crime to consider the victim-offender overlap issue in their future studies.

We also need to learn more about heterogeneity and state-dependence processes in victimization and offending. One topic that calls for an explicit victim–offender overlap focus is the ongoing work on gene/environment interactions with respect to antisocial behavior (see Wikstrom & Sampson, 2006). Unique about this research effort is the linkage of three important concepts in the understanding of crime – social context, mechanisms (processes), and individual development. It is intriguing to add the victim–offender overlap issue into the mix.

Crime Trends

Over the last decade, criminologists have offered a wide range of explanations for the so-called "crime drop" in the United States (see Blumstein & Wallman, 2006 for a general overview). These studies are dominated by offender-based orientations and examine the effects of a variety of structural factors and/or criminal justice policies, especially police practices and incapacitation on changing crime rates. There is virtually no consideration of the victim–offender overlap in this small but growing body of research.[3] We believe that future research on crime trends would benefit from an explicit focus on the victim-offender overlap phenomenon.

Drawing on the research we reviewed above, the lack of access to formal mechanisms of social control is a salient feature in high-crime neighborhoods in the United States. Sampson and Jeglum Bartusch (1998) refer to this as "legal cynicism" – the feeling among residents that access to law, police protection, and ultimately, a sense of fairness and justice are not viable. Legal cynicism and retaliatory violence are a deadly tandem in certain neighborhoods in American cities and research is needed to understand better and possibly circumvent the spiral of retaliation and counterretaliation that occurs on the streets. In fact, these actions by victims and offenders may well account for the heretofore unexplained sudden spikes and rapid declines we see in crime trends, especially over the short term.

We would also like to see studies that examine whether expanding access to law following victimization among less serious offenders (e.g., prostitutes or drug users) helps lower their future risk of victimization. Zero-tolerance policing makes this difficult, and according to Rosenfeld and his colleagues (2003), may make the streets worse because it often decreases the perceived legitimacy of police and the legal process, thus encouraging victims-offenders to solve problems on their own. Regarding snitching, these authors state that the "police must begin to treat the victimization of criminals by fellow law breakers as the serious problem that it is, and not as something to be tolerated or even encouraged by pitting offenders against one another" (Rosenfeld et al., 2003, p. 307).

The Prevention of Victimization and Offending

Policies originally designed to prevent victimization need to be explicitly connected to policies regarding offending in order to provide a more effective reduction in both rates of victimization and offending. We believe that a key component in the prevention of adolescent crime, especially violence, is delinquency prevention. Not only would delinquency prevention reduce the risk of violence among delinquent-prone subgroups, but the risk of violence for other groups in proximity to delinquents should also be reduced as well. This is likely to occur because efforts to reduce delinquent involvement among youth will influence the very same factors that affect victimization risk. With the current emphasis on "what works" and "evidence-based" strategies, the victim-offender overlap issue should be at the center of future research in crime prevention. We need more studies that seek to find ways to minimize and contain the harm from victimization, both by preventing the onset of victimization as well as reducing repeat victimization.

Understanding the conditions under which victimization programs are likely to succeed or fail is also critical to effective prevention. Using a quasi-experimental design, Davis and Smith (1994) introduced a subgroup of victims to various crime prevention strategies in an effort to teach them how to lower their risk of future victimization. The crime prevention training did achieve some of its goals: victims who took the course knew more about crime prevention and took more precautionary measures than victims who were not exposed to the training. However, the training did not have a significant effect on revictimization. The authors contend that this finding was not the result of the lack of potency of the intervention.

Instead, they state that "the assumptions behind the experiment appear to have been wrong" (Davis & Smith, 1994, p. 66). Perhaps this result occurred because the program did not take directly into account the victim-offender overlap. Yet even if this is not the case, thinking critically about the source of programmatic failure is key to designing successful prevention efforts.

CONCLUSION

In 2003, Farrall and Maltby threw down the gauntlet to those who study victims of crime. They wrote: "Because an accurate victimology is desirable . . . we, as scholars, need to tackle one of the most common findings of victimology, namely that victims and offenders are often drawn from the same population pool" (p. 50). We wholeheartedly agree with their assessment and wish to expand the challenge they made to the field of victimology to all those who study crime and its consequences. On this occasion, it is important to mark and celebrate how much we have learned from surveys like the British Crime Survey over the last 25 years. At the same time, it is an opportunity for honest reflection regarding the limitations of our knowledge with respect to the victim–offender overlap issue and to convey our hope that the scientific, political, and ideological challenges that face this important line of inquiry can be overcome.

◆

Address correspondence to: Janet L. Lauritsen, Department of Criminology and Criminal Justice, University of Missouri-St. Louis, St. Louis, MO, U.S.A. 63121, or e-mail Janet_Lauritsen@umsl.edu

Acknowledgments: We would like to thank Michael Maxfield and Michael Hough for their invitation to write this chapter and for their helpful comments throughout the process. The chapter also benefited from the many discussions at the October 2006 conference to mark the 25th anniversary of the British Crime Survey. We are grateful to all of the participants at that meeting.

NOTES

1. Although they are clearly relevant to the topic, space limitations preclude a review of the important literature on the effects of child maltreatment, abuse, and domestic violence on later involvement in offending that has appeared in the fields of psychology and social work and more recently, criminology (see, e.g., Widom, 1989a, 1989b; Fagan & Browne, 1994; Moffitt el al., 2000).
2. The term "event dependence" has been used synonymously with "state dependence" (e.g., Tseloni & Pease, 2003, 2004). We use the latter term here to be consistent with language used in earlier studies (see Nagin & Paternoster, 1991, 2000; Lauritsen & Davis-Quinet, 1995).
3. The exception to this is the research on intimate partner homicide. It appears that male rates of intimate partner homicide decreased in part because females had more options than using defensive lethal violence (see Dugan et al., 1999, for details).

REFERENCES

Anderson, E. (1999). *Code of the street*. New York: W.W. Norton.

Bjarnason, T., Sigurdottir, T., & Thorlindsson, T. (1999). Human agency, capable guardians, and structural constraints: A lifestyle approach to the study of violent victimization. *Journal of Youth and Adolescence, 2,* 105-119.

Black, D. (1983). Crime as social control. *American Sociological Review, 48,* 34-45.

Blumstein, A., & Wallman, J. (Eds.). (2006). *The crime drop in America* (rev. ed.). New York: Cambridge University Press.

Broidy, L., Dady, J., Crandall, C., Sklar, D., & Jost, P. (2006). Exploring demographic, structural, and behavioral overlap among homicide offenders and victims. *Homicide Studies, 10,* 155-180.

Cohen, L., Kluegel, J., & Land, K. (1981). Social inequality and predatory criminal victimization: An exposition and test of a formal theory. *American Sociological Review, 46,* 505-524.

Davis, R., & Smith, B. (1994). Teaching victims crime prevention skills: Can individuals lower their risk of crime? *Criminal Justice Review, 19,* 56-68.

Decker, S., & Van Winkle, B. (1996). *Life in the gang.* New York: Cambridge University Press.

Dugan, L., Nagin, D., & Rosenfeld, R. (1999). Explaining the decline in intimate partner homicide: The effects of changing domesticity, women's status, and domestic violence resources. *Homicide Studies, 3,* 187-214.

Esbensen, F., & Huizinga, D. (1991). Juvenile victimization and delinquency. *Youth & Society, 23,* 202-228.

Fagan, J., & Browne, A. (1994). Violence between spouses and intimates: Physical aggression between men and women in intimate relationships. In A. Reiss, Jr. &

J. Roth (Eds.), *Understanding and preventing violence, Vol. 3, Social influences* (pp. 115-292). Washington, DC: National Academy Sciences Press.

Fagan, J., Piper, E., & Cheng, Y. (1987). Contributions of victimization to delinquency in inner cities. *Journal of Criminal Law and Criminology, 78,* 586-613.

Farrall, S., & Calverley, A. (2006). *Understanding desistance from crime: Theoretical directions in resettlement and rehabilitation.* Berkshire, England: Open University Press.

Farrall, S., & Maltby, S. (2003). The victimisation of probationers. *Howard Journal of Criminal Justice, 42,* 32-54.

Fattah, E. (no date). The vital role of victimology in the rehabilitation of offenders and their reintegration into society. In *Resource material series no. 56, United Nations Asia and Far East Institute 112th training course,* Tokyo, Japan (pp. 71-86).

Felson, R., & Steadman, H. (1983). Situational factors in disputes leading to criminal violence. *Criminology, 21,* 59-74.

Garland, D. (2001). *The culture of control: Crime and social order in contemporary society.* University of Chicago Press.

Garofalo, J. (1987). Reassessing the lifestyle model of criminal victimization. In M. Gottfredson & T. Hirschi (Eds.), *Positive criminology* (pp. 23-42). Beverly Hills, CA: Sage.

Gottfredson, M. (1981). On the etiology of criminal victimization. *Journal of Criminal Law and Criminology, 72,* 714-726.

Gottfredson, M. (1984). *Victims of crime: The dimensions of risk.* Home Office Research Study No. 81. London: Her Majesty's Stationery Office.

Gottfredson, M. (1986). Substantive contributions of victimization surveys. In M. Tonry & N. Morris (Eds.), *Crime and justice: A review of research* (Vol. 7, pp. 251-287). Chicago: University of Chicago Press.

Gottfredson, M., & Hirschi, T. (1990). *A general theory of crime.* Stanford, CA: Stanford University Press.

Hindelang, M., Gottfredson, M., & Garofalo, J. (1978). *Victims of personal crime: An empirical foundation for a theory of personal victimization.* Cambridge, MA: Ballinger.

Hough, M., & Mayhew, P. (1983). *The British Crime Survey: First report.* Home Office Research Study No. 76. London: Her Majesty's Stationery Office.

Jacobs, B. (2000). *Robbing drug dealers: Violence beyond the law.* New York: Aldine de Gruyter.

Jacobs, B., & Wright, R. (2006). *Street justice: Retaliation in the criminal underworld.* New York: Cambridge University Press.

Jensen, G., & Brownfield, D. (1986). Gender, lifestyles, and victimization: Beyond routine activity theory. *Violence and Victims, 1,* 85-99.

Klaus, P., & Rand, M. Personal communication, September 5, 2006. Bureau of Justice Statistics.

Klevens, J., Duque, L., & Ramirez, C. (2002). The victim-offender overlap and routine activities: Results from a cross-sectional study in Bogota, Columbia. *Journal of Interpersonal Violence, 17,* 206-216.

Kubrin, C., & Weitzer, R. (2003). Retaliatory homicide: Concentrated disadvantage and neighborhood culture. *Social Problems, 50,* 157-180.

Lab, S. (2004). Crime prevention, politics, and the art of going nowhere fast. *Justice Quarterly, 21*, 681-692.

Lattimore, P., Linster, R., & MacDonald, J. (1997). Risk of death among serious young offenders. *Journal of Research in Crime and Delinquency, 34*, 187-209.

Laub, J., & Sampson, R. (2003). *Shared beginnings, divergent lives: Delinquent boys to age 70*. Cambridge, MA: Harvard University Press.

Laub, J., & Sampson, R. (2004). Strategies for bridging the quantitative and qualitative divide: Studying crime over the life course. *Research in Human Development, 1*, 81-99.

Lauritsen, J. (1998). The age-crime debate: Assessing the limits of longitudinal self-report data, *Social Forces, 77*, 127-155.

Lauritsen, J., Sampson, R., & Laub, J. (1991). The link between offending and victimization among adolescents. *Criminology, 29*, 265-291.

Lauritsen, J., Laub, J., & Sampson, R. (1992). Conventional and delinquent activities: Implications for the prevention of violent victimization among adolescents. *Violence and Victims, 7*, 91-108.

Lauritsen, J., & Davis-Quinet, K. (1995). Patterns of repeat victimization among adolescents and young adults. *Journal of Quantitative Criminology, 11*, 143-166.

Loeber, R., Kalb, L., & Huizinga, D. (2001). *Juvenile delinquency and serious injury victimization*. Washington, DC: Office of Juvenile Justice and Delinquency Prevention.

Matz, D. (2007). Development and key results from the first two waves of the Offending Crime and Justice Survey. In M. Hough & M. Maxfield (Eds.), *Surveying crime in the 21st century*. Monsey, NY: Criminal Justice Press; Cullomptom, England: Willan.

Mayhew, P., & Elliott, D. (1990). Self-reported offending, victimization, and the British Crime Survey. *Violence and Victims, 5*, 83-96.

McCarthy, B., Hagan, J., & Martin, M. (2002). In and out of harm's way: Violent victimization and the social capital of fictive street families. *Criminology, 40*, 831-866.

Miller, J. (1998). Up it up: Gender and the accomplishment of street robbery. *Criminology, 36*, 37-66.

Moffitt, T., Krueger, R., Caspi, A., & Fagan, J. (2000). Partner abuse and general crime: How are they the same? How are they different? *Criminology, 38*, 199-232.

Moscovitz, H., Degutis, L., Bruno, G., & Schriver, J. (1997). Emergency department patients with assault injuries: Previous injury and assault convictions. *Annals of Emergency Medicine, 29*, 770-775.

Mustaine, E., & Tewksbury, R. (2000). Comparing the lifestyles of victims, offenders, and victim-offenders: A routine activity theory assessment of similarities and differences for criminal incident participation. *Sociological Focus, 33*, 339-362.

Nagin, D., & Paternoster, R. (1991). On the relationship of past to future participation in delinquency. *Criminology, 29*, 163-189.

Nagin, D., & Paternoster, R. (2000). Population heterogeneity and state dependence: State of the evidence and directions for future research. *Journal of Quantitative Criminology, 16*, 117-144.

Peterson, D., Taylor, T., & Esbensen, F. (2004). Gang membership and violent victimization. *Justice Quarterly, 21*, 793-815.

Rosenfeld, R., Jacobs, B., & Wright, R. (2003). Snitching and the code of the street. *British Journal of Criminology, 43,* 291-309.

Ryan, W. (1971). *Blaming the victim.* New York: Vintage Books.

Sampson, R., & Jeglum Bartusch, D. (1998). Legal cynicism and (subcultural?) tolerance of deviance: The neighborhood context of racial differences. *Law and Society Review, 32,* 777-804.

Sampson, R., & Laub, J. (1992). Crime and deviance in the life course. *Annual Review of Sociology, 18,* 63-84.

Sampson, R., & Laub, J. (1993). *Crime in the making: Pathways and turning points through life.* Cambridge, MA: Harvard University Press.

Sampson, R., & Lauritsen, J. (1990). Deviant lifestyles, proximity to crime, and the offender-victim link in personal violence. *Journal of Research in Crime and Delinquency, 27,* 110-139.

Sampson, R., & Wooldredge, J. (1987). Linking the micro- and macro-level dimensions of lifestyle-routine activity and opportunity models of predatory victimization. *Journal of Quantitative Criminology, 3,* 371-393.

Schreck, C. (1999). Criminal victimization and low self-control: An extension and test of a general theory of crime. *Justice Quarterly, 16,* 633-654.

Shaffer, J., & Ruback, R. (2002). *Violent victimization as a risk factor for violent offending among juveniles.* Washington, DC: Office of Juvenile Justice and Delinquency Prevention.

Singer, S. (1981). Homogeneous victim-offender populations: A review and some research implications. *Journal of Criminal Law and Criminology, 72,* 779-788.

Singer, S. (1986). Victims of serious violence and their criminal behavior: Subcultural theory and beyond. *Violence and Victims, 1,* 61-70.

Smith, D. (2004). *The links between victimization and offending: The Edinburgh study of youth transitions and crime, No. 5.* University of Edinburgh, Centre for Law and Society.

Sparks, R. (1982). *Research on victims of crime.* Washington, DC: U.S. Government Printing Office.

Sparks, R., Genn, H., & Dodd, D. (1977). *Surveying victims.* New York: Wiley.

Stewart, E., Schreck, C., & Simons, R. (2006). "I ain't gonna let no one disrespect me": Does the code of the street reduce or increase violent victimization among African American adolescents? *Journal of Research in Crime and Delinquency, 43,* 427-458.

Tonry, M. (2004). *Thinking about crime: Sense and sensibility in American penal culture.* Oxford: Oxford University Press.

Tseloni, A., & Pease, K. (2003). Repeat personal victimization: Boosts or flags? *British Journal of Criminology, 43,* 196-212.

Tseloni, A., & Pease, K. (2004). Repeat personal victimization: Random effects, event dependence, and unexplained heterogeneity. *British Journal of Criminology, 44,* 931-945.

von Hentig, H. (1948). *The criminal and his victim: Studies in the sociobiology of crime.* New York: Schocken Books.

Whitbeck, L., Hoyt, D., Yoder, K., Cauce, A., & Paradise, M. (2001). Deviant behavior and victimization among homeless and runaway adolescents. *Journal of Interpersonal Violence, 16*, 1175-1204.

Widom, C. (1989a). Does violence beget violence? A critical examination of the literature. *Psychological Bulletin, 106*, 3-28.

Widom, C. (1989b). The cycle of violence. *Science, 244*, 160-166.

Wikstrom, P., & R. Sampson (Eds.). (2006). *The explanation of crime: Context, mechanisms, and development.* Cambridge: Cambridge University Press.

Wittebrood, K., & Nieuwbeerta, P. (1999). Wages of sin? The link between offending, lifestyle and violent victimization. *European Journal on Criminal Policy and Research, 7*, 63-80.

Wittebrood, K., & Nieuwbeerta, P. (2000). Criminal victimization during one's life course: The effects of previous victimization and patterns of routine activities. *Journal of Research on Crime and Delinquency, 37*, 91-122.

Wolfgang, M. (1958). *Patterns in criminal homicide.* Philadelphia: University of Pennsylvania Press.

Wolfgang, M., & Ferracuti, F. (1967). *The subculture of violence.* London: Tavistock.

Wolfgang, M., Figlio, R., & Sellin, T. (1972). *Delinquency in a birth cohort.* Chicago: University of Chicago Press.

Wooldredge, J. (1994). Inmate crime and victimization in a southwestern correctional facility. *Journal of Criminal Justice, 22*, 367-381.

Ybarra, L., & Lohr, S. (2002). Estimates of repeat victimization using the National Crime Victimization Survey. *Journal of Quantitative Criminology, 18*, 1-21.

Development and Key Results from the First Two Waves of the Offending Crime and Justice Survey

by

David Matz
Formerly with the Research,
Development and Statistics Directorate
U.K. Home Office

Abstract: *The Offending Crime and Justice Survey (OCJS) is the first nationally representative, longitudinal, self-report offending survey of the general household population in England and Wales. Its main aim is to examine the extent of offending, antisocial behaviour and drug use. The 2003 wave covered people aged 10 to 65 and subsequent waves covered young people aged 10 to 25. Data was collected by Computer Assisted Personal Interviewing (CAPI) and, for more sensitive questions, audio-CASI (Computer Assisted Self-Interviewing). Key results have been obtained relating to the prevalence of offending (ever and in the last year), risk factors for offending, victimisation of young people, victim–offender relationships, antisocial behaviour, the volume and concentration of offences, co-offending and motivations.*

The Offending Crime and Justice Survey (OCJS) is the first nationally representative, longitudinal, self-report offending survey of the general household population in England and Wales.

Crime Prevention Studies, volume 22 (2007), pp. 77–98.

The Offending Crime and Justice Survey (OCJS) series for 2003-2006 was designed to meet a range of aims including the following:

- measuring the prevalence of offending and the number of offences committed by people in the general household population, including trends amongst young people and comparisons for different ethnic minority groups

- providing information on young persons' experience and perpetration of antisocial behaviours

- exploring links between offending and problem behaviours (drug use, alcohol use, antisocial behaviour) and with victimisation

- providing information about the proportion of offenders coming into contact with the criminal justice system

- exploring knowledge of, and attitudes toward, the criminal justice system

- investigating motivations for offending and the nature of individual offences

- providing longitudinal insight into young persons' behaviour to examine the pathways into and out of delinquency.

METHODS

Data were collected by Computer-Assisted Personal Interviewing (CAPI), and via Computer-Assisted Self-Interviewing (CASI). The OCJS was the first large-scale survey in Britain to utilise audio-CASI, whereby respondents were able to listen to questions and possible answers via headphones, thereby assisting respondents with literacy problems.

Data Collection Considerations and Results from Feasibility Studies

A range of methodological and design issues relate to the use of self-report offending surveys (see, e.g., Coleman & Moynihan, 1996), for example, defining what an offence is and what offences to cover.

Issues that were specific to OCJS included that it needed (a) question wording suitable for use with young children, as well as parental permissions; (b) the inclusion of particularly sensitive topics within a household environment, which implied the use of self-completion; and (c) dual requirements to monitor trends and to provide longitudinal information.

Detailed testing indicated that

- most respondents, whether adults or children, will answer sensitive questions about offending behaviour.

- most questions were well understood by adults;

- children's understanding of questions on victimisation and offending varied considerably;

- a reasonable response rate was achievable and could be improved on with a longer fieldwork period (see Lynn online report; BMRB online report (2005).

Sampling Design Overview - 2003 Wave

The survey employed random probability sampling using the Postcode Address File. An element of screening of addresses was involved for each of the three main parts of the sample. For the core sample, those addresses in which the residents were all aged 66 or over were not eligible to take part in the study. For the boost sample, respondents aged 10-25, addresses not containing any people in this age range were excluded. To minimise the cost of identifying such addresses, people contacted for the core sample were asked if neighbouring addresses contained anyone aged 10-25.

The core sample and the boost sample of young people were selected in two stages. The first stage was selection of postcode districts. They were divided into districts in police force areas (for which the sample required to be augmented to ensure a minimum achieved sample of around 100). Districts were then stratified by region and, within region, districts were ordered by population density and occupational profile. Once the districts had been selected, two postcode sectors were randomly selected. The sample was selected in a quarter of a postcode sector.

For the non-white boost sample, two sorts of areas were identified, based on 1991 census data: those with high incidence of ethnic minorities, and other areas. For the higher incidence areas, a random set of sectors was selected, and then 75 addresses were preselected in each, at which interviewers established eligibility, based on whether an address had at least one person aged 10-65 who self-identified as non-white. For other parts of the country, a separate random sample of postcode sectors was selected, within each of which 76 sets of 5 addresses (380 addresses in total) were selected and focussed enumeration used to determine if any of the 5 addresses contained someone who was non-white and eligible aged 10-65.

The sampling design used for the 2004 wave was broadly similar but covered 10- to 25-year-olds only, incorporated longitudinal follow up of the 2003 panel, and did not include an ethnic minorities boost.

Data Instrument Design and Methods (Including Use of Audio-CASI)

The questionnaire includes 15 different topic modules. Three different methods of computer-assisted interviews were used, depending on which module the respondent is answering:

- Computer-Assisted Personal Interviewing questions are administered by the interviewer, who reads the questions from a laptop and enters answers directly into the laptop.

- Computer Assisted Self-Interviewing, where respondents read the questions themselves on the laptop and enter their own answers, unaided by the interviewer.

- Audio-Computer Assisted Self-Interviewing (A-CASI), like the CASI but where the respondent can listen to the question through headphones. A-CASI allows respondents who have reading difficulties to answer questions without interviewer involvement.

CASI and A-CASI were used for the most sensitive modules. The modules in the 2003 and 2004 OCJS, in order, were as follows:

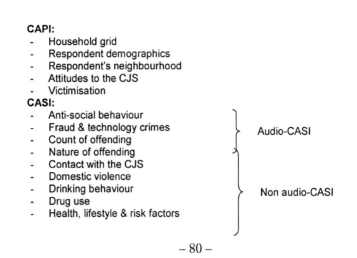

CAPI:
- Household grid
- Respondent demographics
- Respondent's neighbourhood
- Attitudes to the CJS
- Victimisation

CASI:
- Anti-social behaviour
- Fraud & technology crimes   ⎫
- Count of offending   ⎬ Audio-CASI
- Nature of offending   ⎭
- Contact with the CJS
- Domestic violence
- Drinking behaviour   ⎫
- Drug use   ⎬ Non audio-CASI
- Health, lifestyle & risk factors ⎭

The feasibility study recommended using audio-CASI to provide potential benefits to respondents who may otherwise find self-keying problematic. Using Audio-CASI, respondents do not need to read the questions and answers on screen (although they do need to recognise numbers on the key pad to enter their response).

Aside from helping respondents with literacy difficulties, early testing of the 2003 CJS identified other benefits of audio-CASI:

- Some younger respondents found this mode of interviewing more "fun" and engaging.

- Audio-CASI helped some respondents to concentrate more on the questions, minimising distraction from other people or noises (e.g., TV) in the room.

- As only the respondent could hear the questions being asked, the headphones helped emphasise to others who may have been in the room the importance of privacy.

The feasibility study conducted prior to the CJS 2003 suggested that where a choice between conventional CASI or audio-CASI was offered, virtually no one opted for the latter, possibly because respondents did not appreciate the potential benefits of this approach. Respondents reluctant to self-key tended to want the interviewer to ask the questions instead. However, minimising interviewer assistance for the CASI sections was desirable, to address concerns that respondents might not be totally honest if the interviewer knew their answers to sensitive questions and that respondents might be tempted to give more "socially desirable" responses. In the event, 7% of interviews in the 2003 wave were completed with the interviewer assisting with the self-completion questions (2%, 3%, 7%, and 12%, respectively for those aged 10-15, 16-25, 27-39 and 40-65).

Interviewer completion rates for the CASI section were higher for the ethnic minority boost sample (13%), those with literacy problems (21%), and those who had not used a computer before (27%). Amongst those requesting interviewer assistance, the most common reasons were (a) didn't like computer (61%), (b) problems reading/writing (12%), (c) couldn't be bothered (11%), (d) tending to children (8%), (e) language problems (7%), (f) ran out of time (7%), (g) other disability (7%), (h) eyesight problems (6%).

A decision was made to ask all respondents to complete certain sections in audio-CASI, rather than offering this as a choice. Interviewers were briefed to encourage respondents to use audio-CASI. If a respondent refused to put on the headphones, however, interviewers were briefed not to force the issue, and the respondent completed the CASI sections by conventional (non-audio) means. Respondents refusing to self-key (either with or without listening to the soundfiles) were allowed as a fallback option to have the interviewer ask the questions and record their answers.

One key drawback of audio-CASI is that it takes longer to complete, as respondents listen to questions read out more slowly than they can read questions on-screen. Therefore, audio-CASI was restricted to the key offending sections, that is, offending count, antisocial behaviour, and fraud and technology crime.

Tables 1 and 2 show the level of usage, and degree of perceived benefit of audio-CASI, by sample type, age and presence of reading/literacy difficulties. Table 1 shows that the non-white sample and children (aged 10-15) were slightly more likely than average to listen to all of the soundfiles: 16% of 10- to 15-year-olds did not listen to any of the soundfiles

Table 1: Percentage of Soundfiles Listened to by Subgroups

	Total	Core Sample	Non-white Sample	Aged 10-15	Aged 16-25	Aged 26+	Literacy Difficult-ies
Base: All respon-dents except those requesting interviewer completion	*11,149*	*9,511*	*1,638*	*2,180*	*2,875*	*6,089*	*533*
	%	%	%	%	%	%	%
All of questions listened to	49	48	54	54	40	51	58
Most questions	12	12	12	15	14	10	12
Just a few questions	14	14	13	12	17	13	11
None of the questions lis-tened to	22	23	19	16	25	23	15
Don't know/ refused	3	3	3	3	3	3	4

Source: 2003 Crime and Justice Survey (England and Wales): Technical Report.

Table 2: Usefulness of Audio-CASI According to Subgroups

	Total	Core Sample	NW Sample	Aged 10-15	Aged 16-25	Aged 26+	Literacy Difficult-ies
Base: All respon-dents except those requesting interviewer completion	11,149	9,511	1,638	2,180	2,875	6,089	533
	%	%	%	%	%	%	%
Very useful	29	27	36	41	22	28	50
Fairly useful	25	25	24	26	26	24	21
Not very useful	16	16	13	11	19	16	7
Not at all useful	18	19	14	12	19	20	11
Don't know/ refused	13	13	13	10	14	13	11

Source: 2003 Crime and Justice Survey (England and Wales): Technical Report.

compared with 24% of older respondents. Respondents with reading difficulties were also more likely than average to have used the audio feature (70% listened to most or all of the soundfiles compared with 61% in total).

Table 2 also clearly shows that children and respondents with reading difficulties were considerably more likely than average to have found the audio-feature useful. Forty-one per cent of 10- to 15-year-olds said this was "very useful" compared with around a quarter of other age groups; and half (50%) of respondents with reading difficulties said it was very useful, compared with 29% overall.

The positive association between level of use and perceived benefit of audio-CASI and presence of reading difficulty is very encouraging as it shows that audio-CASI has helped make the most important self-keying sections more accessible to those who might otherwise have struggled.

RELATION TO OTHER SURVEYS

OCJS is one of a wide range of different surveys of crime and justice in England and Wales, including the British Crime Survey (BCS), the Witness and Victim Experience Survey (WAVES), the Arrestee Survey, and local police user satisfaction surveys, as well as (to 2005) the Youth Justice Board's (YJB) annual Youth Survey. Some aspects of crime and antisocial behaviours have been covered by the British Household Panel Survey (BHPS), the Millennium Cohort Study, and the Longitudinal Study of Young People (LSYPE).

Additionally there are a number of location-based longitudinal studies: the Peterborough Adolescent Development Study, the Childhood Study (part of the Environmental Risk in the Origins of Disruptive Behaviours (E-risk) study), the Cambridge Study in Delinquent Development, the Sheffield Pathways out of Crime Study, the Avon Longitudinal Study of Parents and Children (ALSPAC), and the Edinburgh Study of Youth Transitions and Crime.

The key feature of the OCJS is that it is designed to investigate self-report offending, and associated factors for the general population, and that it covers multiple topics and multiple ages. OCJS includes victimisation primarily as a factor to be related to offending and provides unique victimisation data for 10- to 15-year-olds (not included in the BCS). Victimisation as covered by OCJS is much less detailed than in the BCS, using questions adjusted in light of the feasibility studies to be suitable for younger respondents. Additionally the context of the questions is different within the different surveys. Hence, the victimisation results for the two surveys are not directly comparable.

The BCS is a continuous, general household-victimisation survey covering around 50,000 adults aged 16 and above each year, and is the gold standard measure of victimisation for those offences it covers. (It excludes offences against children under 16 and against public or commercial bodies.) The survey first started in 1981. Since 2001 it has been running on a continuous basis with fieldwork conducted throughout the year. The interview is conducted face-to-face in respondents' homes. Its main aim is to provide a measure of criminal victimisation against adults living in private households in England and Wales, including incidents that are not recorded by the police.

For the crime types that it covers, the British Crime Survey is a better reflection of crime than police recorded crime because it includes crimes that are not reported to the police and those that go unrecorded once reported. The BCS count gives a better indication of trends in crime over time because it has measured crime in a consistent way since the survey first started and is not affected by administrative changes. Figure 1 shows the links between Home Office Crime and Justice Surveys.

Figure 1: How OCJS fits in: links between Home Office Crime and Justice Surveys.

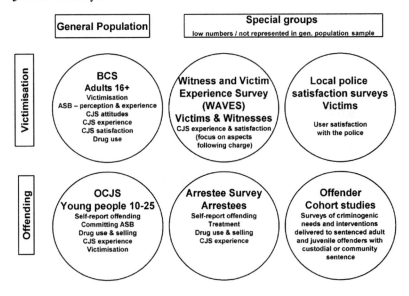

KEY RESULTS FROM THE 2003 AND 2004 WAVES

The results that follow provide a brief overview from a wide range of publications produced using OCJS data, available at http://www.home office.gov.uk/rds/offending_survey.html. Other results relate to the patterns of offending, age of onset/desistance, contact with the criminal justice system, the relationships between alcohol use and offending and between drug use and offending, antisocial behaviour, delinquent youth groups, and fraud and technology crime. Box 1 lists the seven offence categories and twenty core offences used in the OCJS.

Although a substantial proportion of 10- to 65-year-olds reported committing a core offence at least once in their lives (41%), offending in the last year was less common (10%). Young people, especially males, are most likely to be active (last year) offenders. Serious and frequent offending in the last year is less common still. Again it is concentrated among teenagers. Around a quarter of 14- to 17-year-old males were classified as serious or frequent offenders (13% for females of that age). (See Figures 2a and 2b and Table 3.)

The 2003 OCJS estimated that there were 3.8 million active offenders in England and Wales (see Table 4). A small minority of the most frequent

---

Box 1: The Seven Offence Categories and 20 Core Offences

PROPERTY OFFENCES

1. **Burglary**: domestic burglary*; commercial burglary*
2. **Vehicle related theft**: theft of vehicle,* attempted theft of a vehicle; theft from outside vehicle; theft from inside vehicle; attempted theft from a vehicle
3. **Other thefts**: from work; from school; shoplifting; theft from person,* other theft
4. **Criminal damage**: to a vehicle; to other property

VIOLENT OFFENCES

5. **Robbery:** of an individual,* of a business
6. **Assaults:** with injury,* without injury

DRUGS

7. **Selling drugs:** Class A drugs,* other drugs

Denotes a serious offence.

---

offenders were responsible for the vast majority of offences. Just 2% of the whole sample (26% of active offenders) accounted for 82% of all offences reported. Young people accounted for a disproportionate share of the volume of offences. (Of incidents measured, 35% were committed by 10- to 17-year-olds and 31% by 18- to 25-year-olds, who comprised 14% and 13% of the sample, respectively.) Table 5 shows the proportion of offences, offenders, and sample accounted for by sex and age.

The 2003 OCJS estimates a mean annual offending rate of 0.77 offences averaged across the sample (Budd, Sharp, & Mayhew, 2005). This equates to 770 offences per 1,000 10- to 65-year-olds in England and Wales, based on the 20 'core' offences. Many minor offences will be included and some incidents that will have taken place outside England and Wales. The estimate is also subject to a relatively wide margin of error, with a 95% confidence interval that (based on offences respondents reported) the "true" number of offences committed per 1,000 population lies between 560 and 980.

In the 2004 OCJS, a quarter (26%) of young people aged from 10 to 25 reported committing at least one of the 20 core offences in the last year; many had offended only occasionally or committed relatively trivial offences (Budd, Sharp, Weir, et al., 2005). Of all young people aged from 10 to 25, 8% reported committing an offence six or more times in the last year (classified as frequent offenders); 12% said they had committed

Figure 2a: Offending in the last year.

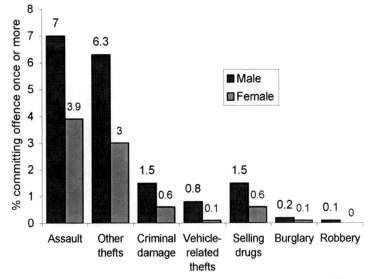

Source: Budd and Sharp (2005).

Figure 2b: Serious, frequent offending in the last year.

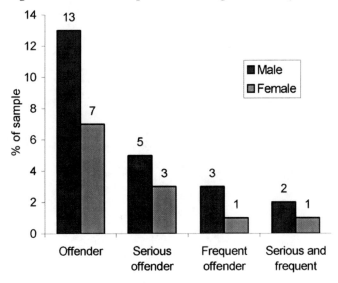

Source: Budd and Sharp (2005).

Table 3: Last-Year Prevalence of Offending (Committing Once or More)

Percentage Committing	Property Offence	All Violent Offences	More Serious Violence[1]	Drug Selling	Any Offence	Base n
Males	7	7	4	2	13	*4,676*
10 to 11	9	14	9	-	20	*313*
12 to 13	15	18	12	< 0.5	25	*375*
14 to 15	17	33	20	2	41	*328*
16 to 17	25	30	23	6	42	*318*
18 to 19	16	18	14	8	29	*276*
20 to 25	10	9	6	5	20	*602*
26 to 35	8	5	3	1	13	*595*
36 to 45	5	3	2	1	9	*672*
46 to 65	3	1	1	-	4	*1,197*
Males 10-17	16	24	16	2	32	*1,334*
Females	4	4	3	1	7	*5,050*
10 to 11	3	5	3	-	8	*271*
12 to 13	9	15	8	< 0.5	21	*338*
14 to 15	13	18	12	2	23	*299*
16 to 17	10	15	11	2	21	*327*
18 to 19	9	11	8	5	20	*204*
20 to 25	6	6	4	1	11	*723*
26 to 35	3	2	2	1	6	*742*
36 to 45	2	2	1	< 0.5	3	*700*
46 to 65	1	1	< 0.5	< 0.5	2	*1,446*
Females 10–17	9	13	8	1	18	*1,235*
All	5	5	3	1	10	*9,726*

[1]Excludes assault without injury.
Source: 2003 Crime and Justice Survey. Based on all respondents (Budd, Sharp, & Mayhew, 2005).

Table 4: Offenders in England and Wales (in millions)

Number Committing . . .	Best estimate	Lowest estimate	Highest estimate
Any offence in last 12 months	3.8	3.6	4.1
Violent offence in last 12 months	2.1	1.9	2.3
Property offence in last 12 months	2.1	1.9	2.3
Drug selling in last 12 months	0.4	0.3	0.5

Source: 2003 Crime and Justice Survey. Lowest and highest estimates based on 95% confidence Interval range (Budd, Sharp, & Mayhew, 2005).

Table 5: Proportion of Offences, Offenders, and Sample by Sex and Age

	Male			Female			Total
	10-17	18-25	26+	10-17	18-25	26+	
% of all offences in last year	22	26	24	13	5	10	100
% of last-year offenders	22	15	28	12	9	14	100
% of the sample	7	7	36	7	7	37	100

Source: 2003 Crime and Justice Survey (Budd, Sharp, & Mayhew, 2005).
Results are based on the 9,612 respondents who had information on number of offences committed.

at least one of the more serious offences. Almost eight in ten of the incidents reported to the survey were of a less serious nature. The most numerous offences were non-injury assaults (28% of all incidents measured); the selling of non–Class A substances (19%) and thefts from the workplace or from school (16%).

Nature of Offences - Incidents Data for Young People on Co-offending and Motivations

A range of data was collected on individual offending incidents, for example, where and when it happened, what happened, details of victim(s), type of force used, motivation, and subsequent contact with the criminal justice system.

The utility of asking offenders about their motivations has been subject to some debate (Farrington, 1993). It has been argued that people find it difficult, if not impossible, to understand their complex mental processes and will have little insight into their motives. Offenders may also use the opportunity to minimise their culpability. It is also likely that people are more aware of immediate situational motives than longer-term factors that contribute to their offending.

Motivations (for 10-25-year-olds in the 2004 OCJS wave)

About 9 in 10 violent offence incidents and 8 in 10 property offence incidents were committed on the spur of the moment. The reasons given for committing offences varied. For example, assaults were mainly driven by being annoyed or upset with someone (47%), self-defence (30%), or revenge (17%), while vehicle-related thefts often happened because the offender was bored or wanted a "buzz" (44%) or was bored/had nothing else to do (42%). "Other thefts," which were most likely to be planned, happened most commonly because the offender wanted what was stolen (34%).

Co-offending (as reported by 10- to 25-year-olds in the 2004 OCJS wave)

A fifth of violent offences (assaults and robbery) and 40% of property offences (vehicle related thefts, burglary, criminal damage, other thefts) involved one or more co-offender. Co-offenders most often featured in vehicle-related thefts and criminal damage incidents (Budd, Sharp, Weir, et al., 2005).

Risk Factors for Young Peoples' Offending

Previous research has shown that some groups of young people are more likely to offend than others. The 2003 OCJS, for example, identified various factors associated with both a heightened risk of offending and antisocial behaviour (Hayward & Sharp, 2005).

Analysis of the 2004 OCJS also identified a range of factors. Table 6 shows the factors associated with significantly higher levels of offending,

Table 6: Groups of Young People at Higher Risk of Offending in the Last 12 Months, by Age Group (2004 OCJS)

Percentage in each group who said they had committed a core offence in last year	10- to 15-year-olds	16- to 25-year-olds	All 10-to25-year-olds
Personal demographics			
Male	31	35	33
Perceptions of local area			
One to three disorder problems in area	29	-	-
Four or more disorder problems in area	-	36	36
Does not trust local police	42	33	36
Lifestyle and behaviour			
Been a victim of personal crime in last year	42	46	44
Committed anti-social behaviour in last year	54	54	54
Been drunk more than once a month in last year	76	41	44
Taken any drug in last year	72	49	52
Highly impulsive	NA	55	NA
Visits pub once a week or more	54	34	35
Visits club once a week or more	-	37	37
Economically inactive – student	-	31	-
More likely to agree that criminal acts are ok	50	50	50
Family and friends			
Gets/got on badly with parents	55	-	39
Friends and/or siblings in trouble with police in last year	42	43	42
Parents perceived to have poor parenting skills	47	NA	NA
Spends little or no free time with parents	36	NA	NA
Parents' attitudes favourable towards delinquent behaviours	52	NA	NA
School			
Has been suspended or expelled ever	47	39	41
School perceived to have poor teaching skills and discipline	44	NA	NA
All	**25**	**26**	**26**

Source: 2004 Crime and Justice Survey. Results are based on respondents aged from 10 to 25 (Budd, Sharp, Weir, et al., 2005).

compared with the national average. The results are presented separately for 10- to 15-year-olds and 16- to 25-year-olds because some of the risk characteristics were only relevant to one of the age groups. For example, more questions relating to school experiences and parental attitudes/behaviour were asked of 10- to 15-year-olds.

Of course, the factors identified are not necessarily causally related to offending: they simply indicate which types of young people are more likely to be classified as offenders in the survey. In some cases, the association may exist because they are both expressions of delinquency. For example, 10-to 15-year-olds who had taken drugs or been regularly drunk were particularly likely to have committed a core offence. This does not mean that drug and alcohol use directly cause offending, but may simply reflect an underlying tendency to delinquency. Other risk factors may arise from delinquency rather than being a cause of it, for example expulsion from school. Although alcohol and drug use were particularly related to offending among 10- to 15-year-olds, impulsivity and believing certain criminal acts to be acceptable were important factors among 16- to 25-year-olds. Interestingly, measures of household income, personal employment status, and an area's "social capital" were not significant factors.

Prevalence and Risk Factors for Young Persons' Victimisation

These findings are based on 2004 OCJS (Budd, Sharp, Weir, et al., 2005):

- Just under a third of 10- to 25-year-olds said they had been the victim of one or more personal crimes (assault or personal thefts) in the 12 months prior to interview (Table 7).

- Overall, younger respondents (aged 10 to 15) were more likely to have been victims of personal crime than those aged 16 to 25 (34% versus 29%). Looking at age in more detail, however, shows the level of personal victimisation to be relatively stable between the ages of 10 and 21 (ranging from 32% to 35%), before falling significantly among those aged 22 to 25 (23%) (Table 7).

- The most common victimisation for young people was assault with and without injury (12% each) and other personal thefts (11%) such as from a cloakroom.

- Males were significantly more likely to say they had been a victim of personal crime in the last year than females. This held for both children and young adults. Over a third (36%) of all males (aged 10 to 25) were victims of personal crime in the 12 months prior to interview, compared with a quarter of females (26%).

Research among adults has shown that some groups of people are more likely to be victims of crimes than others. The BCS, for example, has consistently shown the following groups of adults to be particularly at risk of violent crime: young people, particularly males; single people; the unemployed; those who frequently visit pubs or bars; those living in flats or maisonettes and privately renting; and those living in areas with a high level of physical disorder (Walker et al., 2006). The 2003 OCJS found that the following characteristics were associated with higher risk of personal crime victimisation among 10- to 15-year-olds: being male; negative school environment; negative parenting experiences; friends in trouble with police; drug use; committing criminal or antisocial behaviour; living in households in financial difficulty and living in more disorderly areas (Wood, 2005).

The 2004 OCJS also showed that the likelihood of victimisation amongst young people varies considerably according to a range of factors. Table 8 shows the factors that are associated with a higher risk of being a victim of personal crime (compared with the national average).

Victim-Offender Overlaps Amongst Young People

Offending is strongly associated with victimisation (Lauritsen & Laub, 2006). Just over a half (52%) of those who reported offending in the last year had also been a victim, compared with 23% of nonoffenders. Involvement in crime in the last year, either as a victim, offender, or both, by age groups, is shown in Table 9.

Just over half of 10- to 15-year-olds and 16- to 25-year-olds said they had not been a victim of personal crime or committed a core offence in the last year. The proportion of those who had been both an offender and a victim was 14% for children and 13% for young adults. The younger age group were significantly more likely than young adults to be victims only.

Victim-Offender Relationship for Offenders Aged 10-25

Offenders were asked how well they knew the victim(s) prior to the incident. From 2004 OCJS, offenders already knew victims in some way for most incidents (excluding those that were directed against a business or organisation) – in 10% of non-injury assaults and 20% of assaults with

Table 7: Young People Aged 10 to 25 Who Were Victims Once or More in the Last 12 months

Percentages	10 to 11	12 to 13	14 to 15	16 to 17	18 to 19	20 to 21	22 to 23	24 to 25	10 to 15	16 to 25	10 to 25
Any personal crime[1]	**34**	**35**	**33**	**32**	**32**	**34**	**24**	**22**	**34**	**29***	**31**
Any personal theft	**20**	**19**	**19**	**17**	**18**	**18**	**14**	**12**	**20**	**15***	**17**
Robbery	2	3	4	3	4	4	2	1	3	3	3
Theft from the person	5	7	9	8	8	6	7	4	7	7	7
Other theft of personal property	15	13	12	10	9	11	9	9	13	9*	11
Any assault	**24**	**24**	**20**	**21**	**20**	**20**	**13**	**13**	**23**	**17***	**19**
Assault (no injury)	19	17	13	13	13	11	6	7	16	10*	12
Assault (with injury)	13	14	11	13	11	14	8	8	13	11	12
Base n	*524*	*886*	*909*	*853*	*655*	*454*	*479*	*445*	*2,319*	*2,886*	*5,205*

Source: 2004 Crime and Justice Survey. Results are based on respondents aged from 10 to 25 (Budd, Sharp, Weir, et al., 2005).
[1]Includes theft from the person, robbery, other personal theft and assault.
*Significant differences at the 5% level against 10- to 15-year-old age group.

Table 8: Groups of Young People at Higher Risk of Personal Victimisation by Age Groups

Percentage of Victims (Personal Crime)	10- to 15-year- olds	16- to 25-year- olds	All 10- to 25-year- olds
Personal demographics			
Male	39	33	36
Lifestyle and behaviour			
Committed antisocial behaviour in last year	50	45	47
Committed a core offence in last year	55	50	52
Been drunk more than once a month in last year	*	38	38
Taken any drug in last year	43	42	42
Highly impulsive	NA	51	NA
Visits pub once a week or more	50	35	36
Visits club once a week or more	*	39	39
More likely to agree that criminal acts are ok	50	40	43
Family and friends			
Gets/got on badly with at least one parents	38	49	45
Friends and/or siblings in trouble with police in last year	43	43	43
Household getting by with income	40	*	*
Parents perceived to have poor parenting skills	49	NA	NA
Spends little or no free time with parents	39	NA	NA
School			
Has been suspended or expelled ever	52	41	44
School perceived to have poor teaching skills and discipline	48	NA	NA
Perceptions of local area			
Negative attitude towards local area (10 to 15)	43	NA	NA
Negative attitude towards local area (16 to 25)	NA	37	NA
One to three disorder problems in area	40	*	*
Four or more disorder problems in area	58	46	48
Does not trust local police	47	36	39
All	*34*	*29*	*31*

Source: 2004 Crime and Justice Survey. Results are based on respondents aged from 10 to 25 (Budd, Sharp, Weir, et al., 2005).
Asked of those aged 10 to 15.
*Not a risk factor for the particular group. NA indicates factor not measured for group. NA is used in the all column if the factor is not covered in both age groups. Definitions of risk factors are given at Budd, Sharp, Weir, et al. (2005), Appendix C.

Table 9: Profile of Young Peoples' Involvement in Crime

Percentages	10- to 15-year-olds	16- to 25-year-olds	All 10- to 25-year-olds
	%	%	%
Neither victim nor offender in last year	55	58	57
Victim only in last year	19	15	17
Offender only in last year	11	13	12
Victim and offender in last year	14	13	14
Total	100	100	100
Base *n*	*2,319*	*2,886*	*5,205*

Source: 2004 Crime and Justice Survey. Results are based on respondents aged from 10 to 25 (Budd, Sharp, Weir, et al., 2005).
Figures may not sum to 100 due to rounding.

injury the victim/all victims were strangers. In over half (59%) of assault incidents the offender knew the victim(s) well, with victims most commonly being a friend (42% of assault incidents).

Assaults committed by females, and by those aged 10-15, were more likely to involve victims known well. Females knew victims well in 81% of incidents compared to 49% for males. Likewise 68% of assaults committed by 10- to 15-year-olds and 52% of those by 16- to 25-year-olds were against victims known well (Budd, Sharp, Weir, et al., 2005).

CONCLUDING REMARKS ON OCJS DEVELOPMENT AND OPTIONS FOR THE FUTURE

Self-report offending surveys are not new in England and Wales. Nationally representative studies, however, are relatively recent, first occurring in the 1990s (the Youth Lifestyles Surveys), and longitudinal self-report studies of offending have also become more common in recent years. The OCJS has provided a wide range of evidence about offending and other problem behaviours, and associated risk factors, victimisation of young people, victim-offender relationships, drug use among vulnerable groups of young people, offending by different minority ethnic groups, and delinquent youth groups.

New questions have been added to the survey to address new policy issues, for example, to measure the extent of delinquent youth groups, building on definitional work by the Eurogangs network (Sharp et al., 2006).

Longitudinal analysis will allow comparison of offending careers, and of risk factors for onset, continued offending, and desistance. It will be important to consider the characteristics of attrition (those who drop out of the survey in later waves).

Other potential methodological work that may be possible, includes the following:

- investigating the reasons for nonresponse

- follow-up studies of particular types of offenders

- comparing results and data collection instruments with other youth cohort studies or with general studies such as the Millennium Cohort Study, or the Longitudinal Study of Young People in England (LSYPE)

  Current plans for the survey are under review.

✦

Address correspondence to: Alison Walker, 5th floor, Peel Building, 2 Marsham Street, London SW1P 4DF; e-mail: alison.walker@home office.gsi.gov.uk

Acknowledgements: The efforts of everyone involved in the development and analysis of the OCJS are appreciated by the author. Special thanks are due to Paul Wiles, Jon Simmons, Alison Walker, Tracey Budd, Clare Sharp, Debbie Wilson, and other RDS colleagues. We are also grateful to all the research teams and interviewers at the National Centre for Social Research and BMRB Social Research, and particularly to the members of the public who kindly agreed to take part in this survey.

REFERENCES

BMRB Social Research. *Crime and Justice Survey: General population feasibility study.* Home Office online report 04/05. Available at http://www.homeoffice.gov.uk/ rds/offending_survey.html

Budd, T., & Sharp, C. (2005). *Offending in England and Wales: First results from the 2003 Crime and Justice Survey*. London: Home Office Findings No. 244.

Budd, T., Sharp, C., & Mayhew, P. (2005). *Offending in England and Wales: First results from the 2003 Crime and Justice Survey*. London: Home Office Research Study No. 275.

Budd, T., Sharp, C., Weir, G., Wilson, D., & Owen, N. (2005). *Young people and crime: Findings from the 2004 Offending, Crime and Justice Survey*. London: Home Office Statistical Bulletin 20/05.

Coleman, C., & Moynihan, J. (1996). *Understanding crime data: Haunted by the dark figure*. Buckingham, England: Open University Press.

Farrington, D. (1993). Motivations for conduct disorder and delinquency. *Development and Psychopathology, 5*, 225-241.

Farrington, D. (2003). What has been learned from self-reports about criminal careers and the causes of offending? Home Office Online Report. Available at http://www.homeoffice.gov.uk/rds/offending_survey.html

Hamlyn, B., Maxwell, C., Hales, J., & Tait, C. (2004). *2003 Crime and Justice Survey (England and Wales):Technical report*. London: National Centre for Social Research/BMRB Social Research.

Hayward, R., & Sharp, C. (2004). *Young people and anti-social behaviour: Findings from the 2003 Crime and Justice Survey*. London: Home Office Findings No. 245.

Lauritsen, J. L., & Laub, J. H. (2007), Understanding the link between victimization and offending: New reflections on an old idea. In M. Hough & M. Maxfield (Eds.), *Surveying crime in the 21st century, Vol. 22 of Crime Prevention Studies*. Monsey, NY: Criminal Justice Press.

Lynn, P. Methodological issues in the development of a survey to measure the prevalence of offending. London: Home Office. Available at http://www.homeoffice.gov.uk/rds/offending_survey.html

Office of National Statistics. (2005). *Crime and Justice Survey: Communal establishments feasibility study*. London: Home Office Online Report 05/05. Available at http://www.homeoffice.gov.uk/rds/offending_survey.html

Sharp, C., Aldridge, J., & Medina, J. (2006). *Delinquent youth groups and offending behaviour: findings from the 2004 Offending, Crime and Justice Survey*. London: Home Office Online Report 14/06. Available at http://www.homeoffice.gov.uk/rds/offending_survey.html

Walker, A., Kershaw, K., & Nicholas, S. (July 2006) *Crime in England and Wales 2005/06*. London: Home Office Statistical Bulletin 12/06.

Wood, M. (2005). *The victimisation of young people: Findings from the Crime and Justice Survey 2003*. London: Home Office Findings 246.

The Distribution of Household Property Crime Victimisation: Insights from the British Crime Survey

by

Tim Hope
Centre for Criminological Research
Keele University

Abstract: *The British Crime Survey is at once an instrument for observing crime-related phenomena, a source for the discovery of insights about crime, and a means of communication between government and citizens. These uses embed the BCS within a complex system of knowledge and action, as likely to generate error as value. This paper seeks to review some discoveries made from BCS data about the social distribution of crime victimisation risk and "community safety." A particular focus is placed upon the role of key insights derived from the BCS, including the epidemiological components of crime rates; the concentration of property crime victimisation amongst neighbourhoods; the distribution of private security activities amongst the population; and the role of social contextual attributes of neighbourhoods in influencing individual crime victimisation risk. An attempt is made to extract insights that might help to suggest hypotheses about some of the reasons behind the trend in household property crime observed from BCS data over the past 25 years.*

A recent Home Office *Review of Crime Statistics* asserted that there is now a general agreement that the "overarching purpose for collecting information on crime should be to reduce the impact of crime on society" (Home Office, 2000, p. 9). Yet the *Review* was much less clear as to *how* crime statistics – in this case, the British Crime Survey (BCS) – might achieve this end. One primary way is for the BCS to serve as an *observatory* to collect facts and indicators about crime, including trends over time, so that government and the general public alike can take appropriate actions within their purview that would, it is to be hoped, lead to reductions in these problems. Yet facts never speak for themselves and need to be interpreted within a framework of meaning, whether provided by politics, common sense, or scientific theory. Because applying different frameworks of meaning can both confirm and refute previously held conjectures about the interpretation of data, the BCS has also been an instrument of *discovery*. Not only has it provided observations but it also has been used to discover new ways of conceptualising crime and disorder issues. Most obviously, this includes the discovery of crime victimisation that has not been reported to the police, but also other concepts, including "fear of crime" (see Ditton & Farrall, in this volume), "repeat victimisation" (see Farrell & Pease, in this volume) and "crime flux" (discussed further on). Yet, like any social survey, the BCS is vulnerable to selectivity and bias. Nor is discovery simply a matter of observation (Popper, 2002). So it is also important to satisfy ourselves that observations from the BCS mean what we think they mean, if we are to accept the validity of the discoveries made from them.

Furthermore, the BCS (in its analysed and published forms) is also a means of *communication*. Simplifying, the government uses it to collect information from the general public about their problems, in order to formulate policy and to report on its own performance in implementing such policies. The public may look to the BCS for information about problems in their society and community (helped by interpreters such as academics and the media) and also to find out about the performance of their government in addressing these problems (Matrix & Hope, 2006). Yet, paradoxically, because governmental social survey instruments like the BCS mix observation – discovery and communication together, with each activity containing its own forms of error and bias – there are also risks involved in using them as guidance for action. Scientific instruments and discoveries, including those associated with the BCS, not only cannot be divorced from the various frameworks of meaning in which they are embedded but, by virtue of their public use, also affect governmental policy and people's everyday activities. In turn, this affects the phenomena that the BCS seeks to measure. As Ulrich Beck (1992) has warned, the deployment of scientific instruments and frameworks as a guide for solving social problems also risks magnifying misunderstanding and misattribution in explanation, with potentially serious consequences both for policy making and for social life. Though it might have been hoped that the institution of the BCS would give an objective view for policy, these prevailing conditions of *reflexivity* that characterise contemporary *risk society* (Beck, 1992) mean that complexity and complication have also emerged to obfuscate, as much as to clarify, policy and practice.

In the light of such reflexivity, this chapter seeks, first, to review some discoveries made from BCS data about the *social distribution* of crime victimisation risk and community safety; and second, to apply those insights to help interpret the trend in household property crime observed by the BCS over the past 25 years. The "discoveries" have stemmed chiefly from academic "secondary analysis" of the BCS,[1] though they have had some influence on policy making, if not so much on the popular imagination. In particular, these include discoveries about: the repeat victimisation of individuals; the concentration of property crime victimisation amongst neighbourhoods; the distribution of private security activities amongst the population; and the role of social contextual attributes of neighbourhoods in influencing individual crime victimisation risk. This chapter does not constitute a comprehensive review of these topics (see Tseloni et al., 2002; Hope, 2005). Rather, an attempt is made to extract insights that might help to suggest hypotheses about trends in household property crime observed from BCS data, which is seen as the consequence of a reflexive interplay between real-world phenomena and the various constructions placed upon them.

CLUSTERING IN THE BCS

The BCS has a complex, multistratified sampling design, which requires statistical weighting to "readjust" it to representativeness, once interview data has been collected (Mayhew, 2000). As described in most of its technical reports, the Primary Sampling Unit (PSU) of the BCS (however it has been defined) is a *nested cluster sample* of respondents living in close, spatial proximity to each other. Common geo-coded spatial referencing has always allowed two kinds of operation: first, it has been possible to aggregate individual responses according to the strata and clusters present within the BCS sampling structure – for instance, to form *pseudo-neighbourhoods* based on such clusters; and second, it has been possible to use common geo-referencing systems[2] in order to attach exogenous data – most usually from the U.K. Census[3] – to characterise contexts or environments, again most usually pseudo-neighbourhoods. For these facilities, the BCS has been much admired (Bursik & Grasmick, 1993) and used in widely referenced academic research (e.g., Sampson & Groves, 1989). They can also provide some clues as to how crime victimisation is distributed amongst the population and how that might be related to trends over time.

Crime Flux

In a seminal article, Trickett and colleagues (1992; see also Trickett, Ellingworth, et al., 1995) introduced a novel way of conceptualising crime victimisation rates by taking advantage of the BCS sample design. Figure 1, calculated from BCS data (see Hope, 2001a, for details), illustrates the distribution of two household-property crime victimisation rates:[4]

1. the *incidence* rate – that is, the *per capita* number of household crime victimisation incidents within samples from each PSU. In Figure 1,

Figure 1: Incidence and prevalence of property crime.

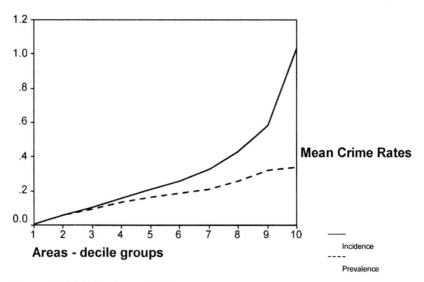

Source: British Crime Survey, 1992.

– 102 –

these PSUs are ranked according to deciles (from low to high) and the average crime incidence rate computed for each decile.

2. the *prevalence* rate – that is, the proportion of the PSU samples that experienced one or more victimisation incidents, again computed as decile means.

From these two rates, a third can be computed:

3. the *concentration rate* – that is, the number of crime victimisation incidents per victim.

These rates are related arithmetically (Trickett et al., 1992):

If the number of victims = V, the size of the population = P and the count of the number of victimisation incidents = C, then:

$$\text{Prevalence} = V/P;$$
$$\text{Concentration} = C/V; \text{ and}$$
$$\text{Incidence} = (V/P) \times (C/V).$$

The distribution of household-property crime victimisation incidence rates in Figure 1 has also been modelled statistically from microlevel household and area-contextual data (Osborn & Tseloni, 1998): specifically, in conditions of low risk (low incidence) "crime appears to be random, but in high-crime [conditions] there are fewer victims and higher concentration [rates] than anticipated with a random crime assumption" (Osborn & Tseloni, 1998, p. 326). This constitutes powerful support for the hypothesis that the distribution observed in Figure 1 represents the distribution of crime victimisation across the population (Trickett et al., 1992). Consequently, it was hypothesised that a substantive, nonrandom relationship might underlie the arithmetic relationship observed between the three crime rates – a combinational process termed *crime flux* (Barr & Pease, 1992).

This conceptual apparatus promised both to provide a basis for evaluating hypotheses about empirical change in crime victimisation (Hope, 1995) and for providing new insight into the distribution of crime victimisation between constituent communities within the general population (Farrell et al., 1996). The shape of the distribution (in Figure 1) appears to suggest that if resources could be concentrated on high crime areas, this would lead to greater reductions, relative to effort, in the national crime rate (Pease, 1993). Further, because the crime concentration rate appears to exert a disproportionate influence on the crime (incidence) rate, especially in the highest crime areas, then efforts to affect concentration in these areas might achieve an even greater efficiency gain in reducing the national average. Similarly, because it seems that in most areas there are fewer victims than would be expected if crime victimisation was randomly distributed amongst their populations (Trickett et al., 1992), then concentrating effort on those fewer number of victims upon whom victimisation appears to be concentrated – so-called repeat victims – would produce yet more efficiency gain for prevention effort (Farrell & Pease, 1993). Extrapolating the cross-sectional distribution to a dynamic form suggests that changes in concentration rates may exert an influence on the level of the crime incidence rate. Consequently, microlevel targeting of crime prevention on repeat victimisation prevalence would bring about macrolevel change in crime concentration rates (Laycock, 2001; Pease, 1993). This hypothesis has been advanced in policy making not only through individual prevention projects (Farrell, 2005) but, since around 1995, by also inserting the goal of reducing repeat victimisation into national police performance management in England and Wales (Laycock, 2001).

Nevertheless, although the BCS shows that crime rates rose to a peak in the mid 1990s, and have fallen subsequently, Figure 2 suggests that changes in national crime victimisation incidence rates – such as the volume crime of domestic burglary – may have been driven chiefly by changes in prevalence rates. During the period, the rate of crime concentration has remained relatively stable, apparently exerting a negligible influence on the trend in the crime incidence rate. Figure 2 not only raises doubts about crime flux (and its derivative, repeat victimisation) as a useful discovery for guiding crime prevention policy, but also suggests a paradox with regard to the concept. On the one hand, variation in crime flux combinations appears to occur at neighbourhood level (Hope, 1995; Trickett, Ellingworth, et al., 1995), though admittedly these do not seem to occur in the expected combination (that is, a reduction in incidence accompanied by a substantial reduction in concentration; see Hope, 2002). On the other hand, in BCS data (at least until 1992), both aggregate concentration rates and individual-level repeat victimisation frequencies would seem to have had a relatively constant relationship with prevalence as components of the crime victimisation incidence rate (Ellingworth et al., 1995; Farrell, 1995; Farrell & Pease, 1993).

The two components of the crime incidence rate may be measuring different phenomena: Although prevalence may measure the *rate of exposure*

Figure 2: Burglary in England and Wales, 1981-2006: Incidence, prevalence, and concentration.

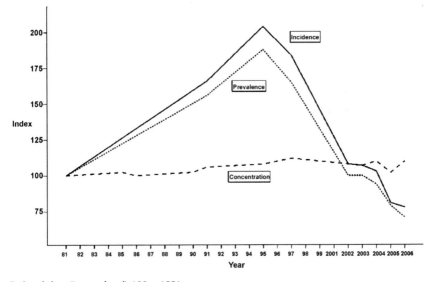

Indexed data (interpolated) 100 = 1981.
Source: British Crime Survey (HOSB 12/06, Tables 2.02, 2.03)

to crime victimisation amongst the general population, concentration may measure the *frequency rate* of crime victimisation to those so exposed – that is to say, there may be a "double-hurdle" process linking the two rates. Yet this does not warrant that concentration is *sufficiently* related to prevalence, other than by virtue of the necessary condition inherent in the microlevel double-hurdle process – that is, the impossibility of being a repeat victim without first having been a victim. For instance, Osborn and colleagues (1996) could find no additional factors that distinguished repeat victims from victims generally. Also, in a set of "trials" culled from victim survey data collected before and after various area-based British crime prevention experiments, changes in prevalence had a negligible correlation with changes in concentration and a higher correlation with changes in incidence (Hope, 2002).

As a characterisation of the crime rate, the concept of crime flux remains something of an enigma. First, the arithmetic definition of the concentration rate (C/V) comprises both the total number of victims (the denominator V) as well as the number of victimisations (the numerator C). So, it follows that change in the rate of repeat victimisation (as measured by the concentration rate) can be influenced both by changes in the prevalence of victims as well as by victimisation frequency. Second, the prevalence of repeat victims is relatively rare, never amounting to more than 20% of burglary victims since 1981 (Walker et al., 2006, Table 2c). So, for the incidence rate to be determined by the concentration rate, a decline in the concentration rate would have to be very substantial to overtake the effect of a reduction in the prevalence rate, because the latter may be simultaneously reducing the number of victims who would be exposed to further victimisation. As Figure 3 suggests, changes in the prevalence of burglary victims (which, according to Figure 2 has had the greater impact on the burglary incidence rate) would seem to have been driven far more by change in the prevalence of one-off (single incident) victims than by change in the prevalence of repeat (multiple incident) victims. Indeed,

Figure 3: Burglary in England and Wales, 1981-2006: Prevalence rates.

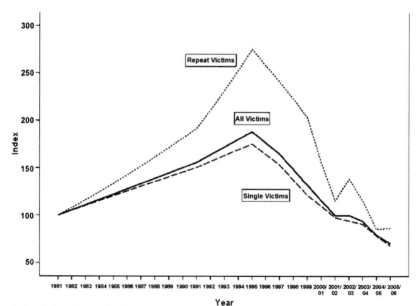

Indexed data (interpolated) 100 = 1981.
Source: British Crime Survey (HOSB 12/06, Tables 2c, 2.03)

only where there has been a very substantial change in the prevalence of repeat victims has there been any noticeable impact on the overall prevalence of victims, and these have been negligible. In sum, the role of repeat victimisation in driving crime rates via the concentration rate remains questionable. Notwithstanding the reality of repeat victimisation, or the apparent policy effort to reduce it, the BCS nevertheless has registered a substantial decline in burglary that seems to have occurred predominantly through changes in prevalence, particularly in the rate of one-off victimisation.

Victimisation and Community Context

The frequency distribution underlying Figure 1 implies that the top quintile (20%) of neighbourhoods alone contributes a half of the nations' household property crime incidents and over a third of the victims (Hope, 1997, Table 9.2). If the goals of policy are to reduce crime and ameliorate the inequity of its distribution, it would be advantageous to identify policy variables that predicted where high crime neighbourhoods were located and which, if manipulated, would bring about such policy goals. The implicit theory underlying Figure 1 is that knowledge of area crime rates alone might be sufficient for targeting action: Because high crime rate areas are produced by high crime concentration rates and concentration rates indicate the presence of repeat victimisation, then targeting action to forestall individual repeat victimisation based on information about prior victimisation would automatically lead to a reduction in inequality in the area-level distribution, because repeat victims are concentrated in high crime areas (e.g., Pease, 1993, 1998). In this hypothetical model, the between-household distribution of victimisation is a sufficient basis for policy, dispensing with the need to identify any additional, independent policy variables, either to target action or reduce crime. Nevertheless, because the burglary incidence rate appears to have fallen concomitantly with a reduction in the prevalence of single-incident victimisation (Figures 2 and 3), not only would it appear that the policy of reducing repeat victimisation is redundant, but also that knowledge of crime rates alone is insufficient as a predictor of the distribution of crime.

Multivariate statistical models of microlevel BCS data (i.e., for individuals and households), with varying specifications, have found *pseudo-neighbourhood socio-economic and demographic contextual variables* to have had a consistently significant effect on property crime victimisation in addition to household-level characteristics (Tseloni, 2006; Tseloni et al., 2002; Hope, Bryan, et al., 2001; Osborn et al., 1996; Ellingworth et al., 1997; Trickett, Osborn, et al., 1995)[5]. Amongst the variables identified as predicting the likelihood of becoming a burglary victim (i.e., prevalence) was an index of the level of deprivation in the victims' local area; this had a significant effect in addition to microlevel data that included prior victimisation (Ellingworth et al., 1997).[6] Figure 4 compares two distributions of household-property crime incidence rates across areas (ranked in deciles): first, by the Area Crime Rate (identical to Figure 1); and second, by the Area Deprivation Index variable (taken directly from the data used in Ellingworth et al., 1997).[7] The similarity in form of these two distributions suggests prima facie that there could be a similar kind of *concentration effect* on crime victimisation also occurring across neighbourhoods when characterised by their level of socioeconomic deprivation, and that a variable such as the Area Deprivation Index might serve as a means of targeting preventive action just as efficiently as the crime rate itself.[8]

Figure 4: Distribution of mean property crime victimisation rates by (1) area crime rate and (2) area deprivation level.

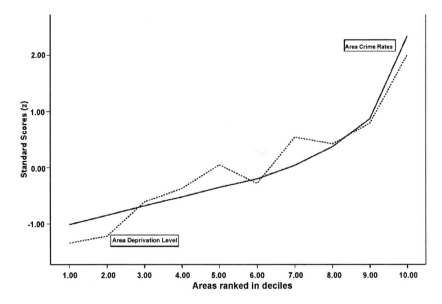

Data source: 1992 BCS/1991 UK Census. For definition of Area Deprivation Index see Hope (2001).

The distribution presented in Figure 1 implies an endogenous explanation – in effect, that crime is its own cause, and that it can be altered by directly targeted, crime-specific actions such as situational crime prevention and problem-oriented policing. In contrast, the distribution presented in Figure 4 suggest exogenous, socioeconomic predictors of area-level crime rates, pointing policy more towards social and economic actions to reduce crime. The similarity of the distributions – especially the concentration effect mirrored in the distribution of the Area Deprivation Index – is at least suggestive of the existence of a process similar to that identified by Sampson and Wilson (1995): *social dislocation within communities resulting from cultural isolation and social disorganisation engendered by social exclusion and concentrated poverty* (Sampson & Groves, 1989). Here, then, crime victimisation concentration may be a property of the social environmental context of particular kinds of neighbourhood, that is, neighbourhoods caught in a ratchet of social exclusion and internal cultural dislocation (see also Hope, 2001b, 1996, 1997; Pitts & Hope, 1997).[9]

The Role of Individual and Area Variables

Despite the importance played by area-level variables, models estimated at pseudo-neighbourhood alone have proven less robust in predicting either incidence or prevalence rates (Kershaw & Tseloni, 2005; Osbornet al., 1992), suggesting that individual-level variables nevertheless continue to play an important role in explaining the distribution of crime victimisation. Put another way, within-area variation in victimisation likelihood remains important, despite the explanatory value of between-area variation. This begs the question of the relative importance of macro- versus microlevel variables in predicting where to target preventive action. Simply, if area risk factors were more important, the area effect would thus exert a contextual influence on household-level victimisation, and serve as a justification for comprehensive community programmes to reduce crime. In contrast, if microlevel risk factors proved more important, the individual effect would comprise a composite influence on the area-level crime rate, and justify prevention programmes targeted on vulnerable households. The value of either strategy, and of choosing between them, would then depend upon the power, robustness, and clarity of the respective effects of macro- versus microlevel variables. Yet the empirical evidence from the BCS is ambiguous: On the one hand, Trickett, Osborn, and Ellingworth (1995, Table 1) estimated that area-contextual variables contribute more than 60% of the explanation of the likelihood of household victimisation; on the other hand, Tseloni has concluded that "area effects on household crimes are considerably weaker and fewer than effects of household characteristics" (2006, p. 220).[10] Part of the solution to this explanatory problem lies in the complexity of the interaction of households with the residential environments in which they are located.

Analysis of 1992 BCS data, presented in Table 1, illustrates some of these interactions (Hope, 2002). The effect of different risk factors appears to vary according to the Area Deprivation Index described earlier (see note 6). In general, in the most affluent areas, poorer households have lower than average risks, while households whose lifestyles may expose them to greater risk – because their homes may be unoccupied while they are out

Table 1: Risk Factors for Household Property Crime Victimisation by Level of Area Deprivation

	Level of Deprivation of Area (Quintiles)				
	low---high				
	Q1	Q2	Q3	Q4	Q5
Risk Factor					
Renter	0	0	+	+	+
Not in work	-	0	0	0	0
Young children	+	0	+	+	+
Lone Parent	0	0	+	0	+
Young Adult	+	0	+	+	0
No Car	-	0	0	0	0
Middle Aged	+	+	0	0	+
2+ Cars	+	+	0	0	0
Detached house	0	-	-	+	0
Property crimes Per 100 households	17	26	31	38	49

Key: + = a positive risk, - = a negative risk, 0 = no significant risk.
All differences in means significant at $p.<.055$ (Mann-Whitney U-Test)
Source: Hope (2001a).

at work, or they have more desirable property to steal because they are affluent (for instance, they own more cars, live in detached houses) – do appear to have higher risks than the average for their area, even though their neighbourhoods have low average property-crime risks. In contrast, in the most deprived neighbourhoods, it is still predominately the most socially vulnerable sections of the community that appear to have a heightened risk – including renters, and lone parent households (though the greater risk to the middle-aged probably indicates an unoccupied dwelling risk for the working population of poor areas). Thus, despite differential vulnerabilities between households, actual household risk seems to vary according to the level of risk inherent in the residential environment.

Variation in Risk Within Communities

Using 1982 BCS data, Trickett and colleagues (1992) estimated expected prevalence from prevalence rates observed over the deciles of the distributions of both personal and household property crime victimisation. Their analysis implied that significantly fewer people are victimised than would be anticipated if the chance of crime victimisation was distributed randomly amongst the population. As illustrated in Figure 5, observed prevalence rates differed significantly from that expected, over all decile groups, though dramatically so in higher rate areas.[11] Yet, although the disparity has been interpreted as evidence of excessive exposure of a minority of people (repeat victims), it can also be seen just as easily as indicating a nonrandom prevalence of immunity (i.e., nonvictimisation) amongst other residents. Thus, what is different about high-crime areas (and many other areas, see Figure 4) is not only nonrandom repeat victimisation but also nonrandom immunity. It is possible that the social environment of any high crime community may be composed at any one time of a segmented order comprising both the extremely vulnerable and the highly immune. The resulting neighbourhood pattern of crime flux may then reflect the outcome of conflicting forces of exposure and immunity, a process documented by Hope and Foster (1991) during a crime reduction "experiment" that resulted in specific, observable patterns of crime flux (Hope, 1995).

REFLEXIVE SECURITIZATION

Governmental policies of crime reduction often assume a top-down approach, reducing private citizens to passive, isolated individuals, while civil

Figure 5: Observed and expected prevalence: Household property crime victimisation.

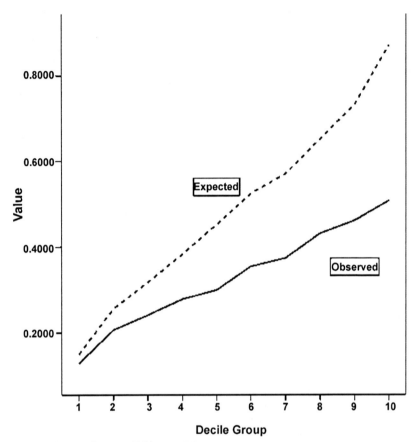

From Trickett et al. (1992, Table 1, p. 86).

society and its institutions remain a wasteland devoid of intention, morality, and purpose (Hope & Karstedt, 2003). Not surprisingly, the increasing use of the BCS as a source for governmental performance measurement (Matrix & Hope, 2006) tends to reinforce government's own self-image that it has (or ought to have) the dominant influence over society's crime (Garland, 2001). Arguably, because of this, governments find it difficult to come up with narratives to explain the changes in crime rates observed in their own national surveys: they are often reluctant to take responsibility when crime goes up; and at a loss to explain why it goes down. Part of their difficulty rests in failing to acknowledge sufficiently the active role played by private citizens and civil institutions within society (Hope & Karstedt, 2003).

As an alternative to governmental action, a key realm in which to look for explanations of crime rate change is that of private security. Both van Dijk (1994) and Philipson and Posner (1996) propose essentially similar models, which see crime rates, at any one time, as expressions of the aggregate outcome of a multitude of individual transactions between populations of offenders and victims. Because both populations interact and react to each others' actions, the general form of a crime rate trend is likely to follow that of a cycle of boom and bust: first, as with conventional criminological explanations, crime rates may rise primarily due to the actions of offenders – opportunities for crime may increase, or costs of committing crimes diminish, or rewards from conformity may seem less attractive, and so forth – leading to the increasing victimisation of citizens. Second, citizens respond by taking private security actions to avoid or protect themselves from crime risk, for example, by not visiting city centres in their cars, target hardening their homes, joining-in with their neighbours in mutual surveillance, or moving to a safer neighbourhood. Such actions reduce the social and spatial proximity and accessibility of potential victims to potential offenders, thus limiting the opportunities for the latter to commit crime against the former. As a result, crime rates will reduce subsequently. The crime victimisation rate is thus shaped, on the one hand, by elasticity in the respective preferences for crime (on the part of offenders) and for security (on the part of victims), and, on the other hand, by the supply of crime-facilitating goods and services to offenders, and of security-producing goods and services to citizens. Such reflexive security is provided by third parties of various kinds, including but not exclusively limited to the agencies of criminal justice (Hope, 2006).[12]

Private Security Consumption

The BCS does provide some insights into the role of reflexive securitisation on crime trends by providing data periodically on individual and household private-security consumption. In the first place, home security protection and membership of neighbourhood watch (NW) schemes now appear as significant predictors of a lower likelihood of burglary and household theft (Tseloni, 2006; Walkeret al., 2006), and this is a marked difference from models estimated on earlier sweeps of the BCS (cf. Ellingworth et al., 1997; Trickett, Osborn, et al., 1995). The BCS also records considerable increases in home security consumption since the early 1990s (Simmons & Dodd, 2003). Hope and Lab (2001) identified five distinct domains of crime prevention activity in 1994 BCS data, two relating to personal behaviour regarding the risk of street-crime, whereas three related to household and dwelling security. In each case, respondents' propensity to adopt a domain of private security behaviour reflected a combination of their experience or perception of crime victimisation risk and the resources available to them to facilitate the activity. For each of the household security domains,[13] respondents similarly were more likely to: think they had a high likelihood of burglary; be burglary victims; live in high crime areas; and live in detached dwellings.[14] Consistent with American research, a greater take-up of security was found amongst the more affluent: having higher incomes, educational levels and more types of goods liable to theft; and being home owners, older and more likely to be married (Hope & Lab, 2001). Thus, though it would seem that the experience or threat of crime has encouraged a greater level of private security consumption, it would seem likely to have benefited most the better-off and more established members of society (Hope, 2001a, 2001b).

Whereas neighbourhood watches might have been regarded once as a direct crime prevention measure, nowadays it tends to be regarded as having an indirect effect as a delivery mechanism for disseminating crime prevention information and promoting a "security consciousness" (Laycock & Tilley, 1995). From a set of models of BCS data, Hope and Trickett (2004) estimated that households' participation in NW may be prompted by two ostensibly countervailing factors: on the one hand, a sense of risk and worry about crime; on the other hand, a sense of neighbourly reciprocity. Generally, high fear goes along with high risk and diminished community satisfaction and reciprocity but households' actual participation in NW (as distinct from its availability) depends upon both perceived risk *and* actual resources being present. These resources are as much social as they are economic. Interpreting these data, it is amongst the better-off sections and communities that these tendencies come together (Hope, 2000). Thus, a key variable that differentiated the neighbourhood watch domain from the other household protection activities was whether the participant was also involved in other community social groups (Hope & Lab, 2001; see also Skogan, 1988).

The externality benefits produced by private security action in the exclusive suburb or urban enclave thus become a *club good*, retained for the benefit of the membership (Hope, 2000). The pooling of these benefits within a network of social capital is also likely to intensify their effects. Social capital leads to greater efficiency in the security accumulation process: social sanctions become less necessary the more exclusive the club because membership exclusivity ensures that the externalities of individual private security efforts will be retained within the club for the benefit of club-members only and will likewise not suffer from the threat of congestion and dilution of the club's security goods from external parties wanting a share of the benefit. Economic resources affect entry to exclusive club goods and serve to ration security production, while the social capital resources accruing from club membership operate to intensify the investment. As such, private security consumption becomes enriched and, arguably, more effective as a deterrent: security externalities are preserved, while negative, criminogenic externalities are excluded.

The theory of reflexive securitisation would seem a plausible way of linking crime victimisation with private security trends observed in the BCS and other national crime surveys.[15] Reflexive, joint consumption of private security goods and the consequent intensification of private security benefits, may affect midrange communities the most: very low crime communities have an excess of community over risk, and thus an excess of immunity; their investment in private security may be primarily symbolic. In contrast, high crime neighbourhoods have an excess of victimisation (Figure 1), which negatively affects trust and social capital formation (Skogan, 1988). Only perhaps where countervailing forces of immunity and victimisation are in constructive tension are security club goods likely to be generated (Hope, 1988).

CONCLUSION: THE FUTURE OF AREA-REFERENCED BCS RESEARCH

The sociodemographic structure of England and Wales has changed significantly since the BCS started. There have been major changes in the spatial distribution of income and wealth, particularly as it is expressed via the housing market. Patterns of housing tenure and of home ownership differ radically from the position 25 years ago Because the housing market has in the past had such a significant impact on the social ecology of crime in Britain (Bottoms & Wiles, 2002; Foster & Hope, 1993), it would be surprising if these changes were not also reflected in BCS data.

During the 1980s, it seemed possible to pick up the effect of these changes on the distribution of crime victimisation observed in the BCS –

for instance a shift in the distribution of crime victimisation from southern to northern regions, commensurate with a redistribution of the economy in the opposite direction (Trickett, Ellingworth, et al., 1995).[16] It was also possible to pinpoint from BCS data the concentration of crime victimisation in economically deprived public housing areas (Hope & Hough, 1988). Studies of public housing interventions at the end of the 1980s also registered the criminogenic consequences of the "residualisation" of public housing, and of the growing spatial concentration of poverty in England and Wales (Foster & Hope, 1993), including their impact on the distribution of victimisation (Hope, 1995). Consequently, if the distribution of crime victimisation mirrors that of socioeconomic deprivation (Figure 4), then it is also likely that both have concentrated in fewer areas (Trickett, Ellingworth, et al., 1995).

Notwithstanding studies by Kershaw and Tseloni (2005) and Tseloni (2006), BCS data sets with pseudo–area identifiers and contextual area data have not been made available to the academic community, which has meant that much of the analysis reported here cannot be replicated, as yet, on BCS data for the later 1990s and beyond, nor has it been possible to compare more recent patterns and distributions with those developed here for the early 1990s. One issue that arises is that it has not been possible either to evaluate the impact of the major sample redesign of the BCS that took place in 2000, particularly whether it would still be possible to detect the area-level inequality in crime that proved so informative in the past. At present, there remains some doubt. Until 1998, the BCS oversampled inner city areas on the grounds that this strategy would increase the amount of crime victimisation incidents available for analysis – an assumption substantiated by Figure 4. Commencing in 2000, the sample selection criteria for primary stratification changed: the procedure for oversampling inner city areas was abandoned in favour of creating representative samples for each of the Police Force Areas (PFAs).[17] Following from this decision, the BCS oversamples areas in the more rural PFAs (to ensure a reasonable sample size) and proportionately samples more suburban areas from metropolitan PFAs. Commensurately, inner city areas are no longer oversampled.[18]

The analyses reported here highlight the importance of area in shedding light on the crime victimisation experiences of residents of both high crime (inner urban, poor) and low crime (suburban, affluent) areas, respectively. Yet the reliability and validity of these kinds of analysis are amongst those most vulnerable to changes in sample designs that have incorporated a clustered selection method (Lynn & Elliott, 2000, section 4.2.1). For general population estimation purposes, compensatory weighting schema have been applied to individual responses such that the sample redesign probably has had a negligible effect for general population estimation purposes (such as calculating crime victimisation rates). However, as Trickett and colleagues (Trickett, Ellingworth, et al., 1995) point out with regard to the previous weighting schema, "while the inner city weight corrects for the over-representation of inner city residents . . . it does not compensate for the over-selection of inner city constituencies themselves" (p. 348). And in this respect, the analyses reported here (especially in Figures 1, 4, and 5) were carried out on an unweighted selection of pseudo-areas that, not surprisingly, reflected the overrepresentation inner city areas (Figure 4). Additionally, the BCS now samples over a much broader range of addresses within the primary sampling unit than in the past. So, prima facie, there may now be a greater likelihood of underselecting those small numbers of inner city respondents (including clusters of repeat victims) within their own neighbourhoods, who between them produce high frequency counts of crime victimisation.

Not least of the difficulties is that the ensuing period has seen two significant social changes that have coincided with the redesign of the BCS. First, though the BCS affords an analysis of the social ecology of crime in contemporary Britain, it is also inevitably a reflection of the pace and rapidity of change occurring in that ecology. Second, this has coincided with the increasing political importance of the BCS as a tool for the performance management and accountability of the criminal justice system, particularly the performance of the police service, and of the Home Office itself, in the governmental project of crime reduction (Hope, 2004). Both may be constituents of a greater movement of late modernity in British society (see Young, 1999), which no doubt accounts at some higher level for their coincidence, finding its expression, prosaically, in the redesign of the BCS (Matrix & Hope, 2006). Yet it remains to be seen whether one of the unintended consequence of these global changes will be to make the task of the BCS that much harder in its role as an accurate instrument for measuring the distribution of crime victimisation in British society. Because the analysis of the BCS has been such a rich source of knowledge about the variety of crime victimisation experiences in contemporary society, it would be a great shame if, unreflexively, its methodology fell victim itself to the social and political changes that are shaping our crime victimisation experience.

✦

Address correspondence to: Professor Tim Hope, Centre for Criminological Research, Research Institute for Law, Politics and Justice, Keele University, Staffordshire, ST5 5BG. E-mail: t.j.hope@crim.keele.ac.uk

Acknowledgements: I owe a deep debt of gratitude to Alan Trickett over the years: friend and statistical wizard; founder of, and collaborator within, the Manchester Quantitative Criminology Group – a genuine scientific college, irrespective of institutions and governments. Although the interpretations in this chapter are entirely my own responsibility, they could never have materialised without Alan, or without the Bacon Bombers, Full English (no beans), Harry Rags, and Bitter Shandies!

NOTES

1. A large though not exclusive part of this work was initiated by a series of research grants from the Nuffield and Leverhulme Foundations, the Loss Prevention Council and the Economic and Social Research Council during the 1990s to researchers at the University of Manchester, who loosely denoted themselves as the Quantitative Criminology Group (QCG).

2. That is, the facilities in the U.K. that can link address-referenced/geocoded data together via the common Ordinance Survey Grid Referencing (OSGR) system: including postal geography (postcodes)and administrative boundaries via a standardised national system that links postal (postcodes), U.K. Census and electoral/administrative geographies together.

3. This has been either in the form of individual census variables, as in the work of the QCG (note 1), or a proprietary geodemographic classifications such as ACORN or MOSAIC.

4. Household property crime includes burglary, theft from dwelling, and criminal damage to property associated with the dwelling, its contents, or grounds.

5. Similar effects have been found in statistical models of violence in U.S. NCVS data (Lauritsen, 2001).

6. The area deprivation index is a standardised, additive scale constructed from 1991 U.K. Census data, consisting of the proportions of households with overcrowding, three or more children, social

housing association accommodation, and the proportion of adult males who are unemployed. Preliminary analysis had found these variables to possess a high degree of collinearity (Ellingworth et al., 1997).

7. NB. It is not necessarily the case that precisely the same areas fall into similar deciles on each, independent distribution, though clearly there has to be a high positive correlation between the two distributions (Ellingworth et al., 1997). An analysis using the Area Deprivation Index is also reported in Hope (2001a).

8. In this sense, the Area Deprivation Index serves as an "instrumental variable" for predicting the distribution of the Area Crime Rate.

9. Though as Veysey and Messner (1999) point out as a result of their reanalysis of Sampson and Groves' (1989) data, criminological processes other than, or in addition to, their specification of social disorganisation theory may also operate to link socioeconomic disadvantage to crime rates at the neighbourhood level.

10. Although Trickett, Osborn, and Ellingworth (1995) performed a direct test, Tseloni (2006) performs an indirect (Wald) test of this hypothesis which, even so, still found a significant independent effect for area characteristics.

11. This finding was replicated using data from the 1988 BCS (Trickett, Osborn, & Ellingworth, 1995).

12. For example, in the case of domestic burglary the loss-reduction interests of household insurers or the marketing capacities of private security providers may be as much, if not more, influential in shaping the probability of victim-offender transactions as the role of public police (Hope, 2006).

13. These were Neighbourhood Watch (consisting of activities that relied upon assurance from risk, including membership of a watch group, property-marking, informal neighbourly watching and household insurance); technological security (consisting of surveillance measures such as alarms and timer lights); and fortress security (consisting of physical resistance measures including locks, bolts, and bars) (Hope & Lab, 2001).

14. A type of property identified in BCS data as at greater risk of burglary (Hope, 1984, 1999).

15. Declining rates of burglary seem now to be the norm across the western advanced economies, and have been in long-term decline in the United States since the mid 1970s, accompanied in many cases by increasing private security consumption (van Dijk, 2006).

16. Generalising, during the 1980s, Southern regions especially the South East, experienced economic and population growth, particularly associated with the growth of the service economy; although the predominantly industrial and manufacturing regions of Northern England and South Wales saw deindustrialisation, economic stagnation, unemployment, and social deterioration.

17. The decision was essentially political – to create a data set more useful for the introduction of the police performance management regime (Matrix & Hope, 2006) – and taken without reference to its methodological implications. As Lynn and Elliott (2000,4.3.2) remark: "[W]e understand that [oversampling of inner cities] is unlikely to be reinstated in the future. We do not therefore consider the oversampling of inner cities in this review."

18. For instance, the eligible population of the rural PFA of Dyffed-Powys (at one extreme) is currently oversampled by a factor of 2.26:1, while that of the metropolitan PFA of Greater Manchester (at the other) is undersampled by a factor of 0.69:1. Within the PFA, sampling points are no longer stratified, and respondents are no longer clustered at such a microlevel as they were (Bolling, 2006). Given the greater number of outer-urban relative to inner-urban districts within Greater Manchester (and the latter's complete absence from Dyfed-Powys) it would seem prima facie that the probability of selection of respondents living in inner-urban areas has reduced since the sample redesign. And this change may interact both with the generally higher nonresponse rates of population subgroups that tend to cluster in inner-city areas and with changes to the weighting schema applied since 2000.

REFERENCES

Barr, R., & Pease, K. (1992). A place for every crime and every crime in its place: An alternative perspective on crime displacement. In D. J. Evans, N. R. Fyfe, & D. J. Herbert (Eds.), *Crime, policing and place: Essays in environmental criminology*. London: Routledge.

Beck, U. (1992). *Risk society*. London: Sage.

Bolling, K. (2006). Introduction to the British Crime Survey. ESDS Government. Available at www.ccsr.ac.uk/esds/events/2006-12-05/slides/bolling.ppt. Accessed 14 December 2006.

Bottoms, A. E., & Wiles, P. (2002). Environmental criminology. In M. Maguire, R. Morgan, & R. Reiner (Eds.), *The Oxford handbook of criminology* (3rd ed.). Oxford: Oxford University Press.

Bursik, R. J., & Grasmick, H. G. (1993). *Neighborhoods and crime*. New York: Lexington Books.

Ellingworth, D., Farrell, G., & Pease, K. (1995). A victim is a victim is a victim? Chronic victimisation in four sweeps of the British Crime Survey. *British Journal of Criminology, 35*, 360-365.

Ellingworth, D., Hope, T., Osborn, D. R., Trickett, A., & Pease, K. (1997). Prior victimisation and crime risk. *International Journal of Risk, Security and Crime Prevention, 2*, 201-214.

Ewald, U. (2000). Criminal victimization and social adaptation in modernity: Fear of crime and risk perception in the new Germany. In T. Hope & R. Sparks (Eds.), *Crime, risk and insecurity*. London: Routledge.

Farrell, G. (2005). Progress and prospects in the prevention of repeat victimisation. In N. Tilley (Ed.), *Handbook of crime prevention and community safety*. Cullompton, Devon: Willan.

Farrell, G. (1995). Preventing repeat victimisation. In M. Tonry & D. P. Farrington (Eds.), *Building a safer society. Crime and justice, a review of research*, Vol. 19. Chicago: University of Chicago Press.

Farrell, G., & Pease, K. (1993). *Once bitten, twice bitten: Repeat victimisation and its implications for crime prevention*. Crime Prevention Unit Paper 46. London: Home Office.

Farrell, G., Ellingworth, D., & Pease, K. (1996). High crime rates, repeat victimisation and routine activities. In T. Bennett (Ed.), *Preventing crime and disorder: Targeting strategies and responsibilities*. Cambridge Cropwood Series. University of Cambridge, Institute of Criminology.

Farrell, G., Clark, K., Ellingworth, D., & Pease, K. (2005). Of targets and supertargets: A routine activity theory of high crime rates. *Internet Journal of Criminology*. Available at http://www.internetjournalofcriminology.com/ijcarticles.html (accessed 11/16/06).

Foster, J., & Hope, T. (1993). *Housing, community and crime: The impact of the Priority Estates project*. Home Office Research Study No. 131. London: Her Majesty's Stationery Office.

Garland, D. (2001). *The culture of control*. Oxford University Press.

H. M. Treasury. (2004). *SR 2004: Public service agreements*. Ch. 6: Home Office. 12 July 2004. Available at www.hm-treasury.gov.uk/spending_review/spend_sr04_psaindex.cfm

Home Office. (2000). *Review of crime statistics: A discussion document*. London: Home Office.

Home Office. (2004). *National policing plan 2005-2008*. London: Home Office. Available at www.policefeform.gov.uk

Hope, T. (1984). Building design and burglary. In R. V. Clarke & T. Hope (Eds.), *Coping with burglary: Research perspectives on policy*. Boston: Kluwer-Nijhoff.

Hope, T. (1988). Support for neighbourhood watch: A British crime survey analysis. In T. Hope & M. Shaw (Eds.), *Communities and crime reduction*. London: Her Majesty's Stationery Office.

Hope, T. (1995). The flux of victimisation. *British Journal of Criminology, 35*, 327-342.

Hope, T. (1996). Communities, crime and inequality in England and Wales. In T. H. Bennett (Ed.), *Preventing crime and disorder: Targeting strategies and responsibilities*. (Proceedings of the 22nd Cropwood Roundtable Conference). Cambridge, England: Institute of Criminology.

Hope, T. (1997). Inequality and the future of community crime prevention. In S. P. Lab (Ed.), *Crime prevention at a crossroads* . American Academy of Criminal Justice Sciences Monograph Series. Cincinnati, OH: Anderson.

Hope, T. (1999). Privatopia on trial? Property guardianship in the suburbs. In K. Painter & N. Tilley (Eds.), *Surveillance of public space: CCTV, street lighting and crime prevention*. New York: Criminal Justice Press.

Hope, T. (2000). Inequality and the clubbing of private security. In T. Hope & R. Sparks (Eds.), *Crime, risk and insecurity*. London: Routledge.

Hope, T. (2001a). Crime victimisation and inequality in risk society. In R. Matthews & J. Pitts (Eds.), *Crime prevention, disorder and community safety*. London: Routledge.

Hope, T. (2001b). Community crime prevention in Britain: A strategic overview. *Criminology and Criminal Justice, 1*, 421-440.

Hope, T. (2002). The road taken: Evaluation, replication and crime reduction. In G. Hughes, E. McLaughlin, & J. Muncie (Eds.), *Crime prevention and community safety*. London: Sage.

Hope, T. (2004). Pretend it works: Evidence and governance in the evaluation of the Reducing Burglary Initiative. *Criminal Justice, 4*, 287-308.

Hope, T. (2005). What do crime statistics tell us?. In C. Hale, K. Hayward, A. Wahidin, & E. Wincup (Eds.), *Criminology*. Oxford: Oxford University Press.

Hope, T. (2006). Mass consumption, mass predation – Private versus public action?: The case of domestic burglary in England and Wales. In R. Levy et al. (Eds.), *Crime et insécurité* . Paris: l'Harmattan.

Hope, T., & Foster, J. (1991). Conflicting forces: Changing the dynamics of crime and community on a "problem" estate. *British Journal of Criminology, 32*, 488-504.

Hope, T., & Hough, M. (1988). Area, crime and incivility: A profile from the British Crime Survey. In T. Hope & M. Shaw (Eds.), *Communities and crime reduction*. London: Her Majesty's Stationery Office.

Hope, T., & Karstedt, S. (2003). Towards a new social crime prevention. In H. Kury & J. Obergfell-Fuchs (Eds.), *Crime prevention: New approaches*. Mainz, Germany: Weisse Ring Verlag-GmbH.

Hope, T., & Lab, S. P. (2001). Variation in crime prevention participation: Evidence from the British crime survey. *Crime Prevention and Community Safety, 3*, 7-21.

Hope, T., & Trickett, A. (2004). *Angst Essen Seele Auf*... but it keeps away the burglars! Private security, neighbourhood watch and the social reaction to crime. *Kölner Zeitschrift für Soziologie und Sozialpsychologie, 43*, 441-468.

Hope, T., Bryan, J., Osborn, D., & Trickett, A. (2001). The phenomena of multiple victimisation: The relationship between personal and property crime risk. *British Journal of Criminology, 41*, 595-617.

Kershaw, C., & Tseloni, A. (2005). Predicting crime rates, fear and disorder based on area information: Evidence from the 2000 British Crime Survey. *International Review of Victimology, 12*, 293-312.

Lauritsen, J. (2001). The social ecology of violent victimization: individual and contextual effects in NCVS. *Journal of Quantitative Criminology, 17*, 3-32.

Laycock, G. (2001). Hypothesis-based research: The repeat victimization story. *Criminology and Criminal Justice, 1*, 59-82.

Laycock, G., & Tilley, N. (1995). *Policing and neighbourhood watch: Strategic issues.* Crime Detection and Prevention Series Paper No 60. London: Home Office.

Lynn, P., & Elliott, D. (2000). *The British Crime Survey: A review of methodology.* London: National Centre for Social Research.

Matrix Research and Consultancy, & Hope, T. (2006, September). Review of crime statistics: Report to the statistics commission. *Crime statistics: User perspectives.* Statistics Commission Report No. 30, Part 2. London: Statistics Commission. Available at www.statscom.org.uk

Mayhew, P. (2000). Researching the state of crime: Local, national and international victim surveys. In R. D. King & E. Wincup (Eds.), *Doing research on crime and justice.* Oxford: Oxford University Press.

Olson, M. (1971). *The logic of collective action: Public goods and the theory of groups.* Cambridge, MA: Harvard University Press.

Osborn, D. R., Ellingworth, D., Hope, T., & Trickett, A. (1996) Are multiply victimized households different? *Journal of Quantitative Criminology, 12*, 223-245.

Osborn, D. R., Trickett, A., & Elder, R. (1992). Area characteristics and regional variates as determinants of area property crime levels. *Journal of Quantitative Criminology, 8*, 265-285.

Osborn, D. R., & Tseloni, A. (1998). The distribution of household property crimes. *Journal of Quantitative Criminology, 14*, 307-330.

Pease, K. (1998). *Repeat victimisation: Taking stock.* Crime Detection and Prevention Series Paper 90. London: Home Office.

Pease, K. (1993). Individual and community influences on victimisation and their implications for crime prevention. In D. P. Farrington, R. J. Sampson, & P-O. H. Wikstrom (Eds.), *Integrating individual and ecological aspects of crime.* BRÇ-Report 1. Stockholm: National Council for Crime Prevention.

Philipson, T. J., & Posner, R. A. (1996). The economic epidemiology of crime. *Journal of Law and Economics, 39*, 405-433.

Pitts, J., & Hope, T. (1997). The local politics of inclusion: The state and community safety. *Social Policy and Administration, 31*, 37-58.

Popper, K. (2002). *The logic of scientific discovery.* London and New York: Routledge.

Sampson, R. J., & Groves, B. W. (1989). Community structure and crime: Testing social disorganisation theory. *American Journal of Sociology, 94*, 774-802.

Sampson, R. J., & Wilson, W. J. (1995). Toward a theory of race, crime and urban inequality. In J. Hagan & R. D. Peterson (Eds.), *Crime and inequality.* Stanford, CA: Stanford University Press.

Simmons, J., & Dodd, T. (Eds.). (2003). *Crime in England and Wales 2002/03.* Home Office Statistical Bulletin 07/2003. London: Home Office.

Skogan, W. G. (1988). Community organisations and crime. In M. Tonry & N. Morris (Eds.), *Crime and justice: A review of research*, Vol. 10. Chicago: University of Chicago Press.

Trickett, A., Ellingworth, D., Hope, T., & Pease, K. (1995). Crime victimisation in the eighties: Changes in area and regional inequality. *British Journal of Criminology, 35*, 343-359.

Trickett, A., Osborn, D. R., & Ellingworth, D. (1995). Property crime victimisation: The roles of individual and area influences. *International Review of Victimology*, *3*, 273-295.

Trickett, A., Osborn, D. R., Seymour, J., & Pease, K. (1992). What is different about high crime areas? *British Journal of Criminology*, *32*, 81-89.

Tseloni, A. (2006). Multi-level modelling of the number of property crimes: Household and area effects. *Journal of the Royal Statistical Society, Series A*, *169*, 205-233.

Tseloni, A., Osborn, D. R., Trickett, A., & Pease, K. (2002). Modelling property crime using the British crime survey: What have we learnt? *British Journal of Criminology*, *42*, 109-128.

van Dijk, J. J. M. (2006). Plenary Address. Conference of the European Society of Criminology, Tübingen, Germany, August 2006.

van Dijk, J. J. M. (1994). Understanding crime rates. On the interactions between the rational choices of victims and offenders. *British Journal of Criminology*, *34*, 626-639.

Veysey, B., & Messner, S. F. (1999). Further testing of social disorganisation theory: An elaboration of Sampson and Groves's "Community Structure and Crime." *Journal of Research on Crime and Delinquency*, *36*, 156-174.

Walker, A., Kershaw, C., &. Nicholas, S. (Eds.). (2006). *Crime in England and Wales 2005/06*. Home Office Statistical Bulletin 12/06, July 2006. London: Home Office.

Young, J. (1999). *The exclusive society*. London: Sage.

The International Crime Victims Survey and Complementary Measures of Corruption and Organised Crime

by

Jan van Dijk

International Victimology Institute
University of Tilburg

Abstract: *Although household victimization surveys such as the ICVS are a proven tool to put levels of victimization by common crime in a global perspective, they cannot be used readily to measure victimization by emerging or global crimes such as grand corruption and organised crime. The strategy of looking at the impact of crimes upon vulnerable groups may be promising in other areas as well. In this chapter, data on the perceptions of business executives of the extent of racketeering are combined with perceptional data on grand corruption and money laundering as well as with rates of unsolved murders. By integrating data on such varied markers of mafia-related activity, a composite index is constructed of organised crime. Country and regional scores on the index can be used for analyses of the macro causes of organized crime and its impact upon society. It is argued that criminology should seek to supplement the results of crime victim surveys with results of new, imaginative ways of measuring emerging forms of global crime.*

Crime Prevention Studies, volume 22 (2007), pp. 125–144.

THE INTERNATIONAL CRIME VICTIMS SURVEY

In 1987, a group of European criminologists involved in national crime surveys took the initiative to launch a fully standardized survey in order to further comparative criminological research. In 1989, the first International Crime Victims Survey (ICVS) was carried out in 13 countries, mainly from Western Europe and North America (van Dijk, Mayhew, & Killias, 1990). In collaboration with the United Nations Interregional Crime and Justice Research Institute, the ICVS was later conducted in a broad selection of countries from all world regions. Results were published in the United Nations Global Report on Crime (Newman, 1999) and in several other publications.

The fifth survey was carried out in 2005 in more than 30 countries. Surveys in 18 European countries were cofunded by the Directorate General for Research of the European Commission (under the acronym EU/ICS). Reports on the EU and on global results are forthcoming (van Dijk, Manchin, & Van Kesteren, 2007; van Dijk, 2007). Since 1989, surveys have been carried out at least once in around 30 industrialized countries and in 50 major cities in developing countries and countries in transition. More than 320,000 citizens have been interviewed to date in the course of the ICVS.

In this chapter, there will be a brief summary of the key findings of the last rounds of the ICVS, also touching upon some of the methodological concerns often raised concerning the ICVS. In the second part of the chapter, we will discuss the need to supplement results of conventional surveys on common crimes with measures of emerging types of crimes such as corruption and organized crime. For such supplementary data on crime, other methodologies than sample surveys among the general public must be harnessed. Some results of exploratory work on the development of such measures will be presented.

Levels and Correlates of Volume Crime

The ICVS interviews samples of households about their recent experiences with the most frequently occurring types of conventional crime (volume crime). National samples include at least 2,000 respondents who are generally interviewed with the CATI (Computer Assisted Telephone Interview) technique. In the countries where this method is not applicable because of insufficient distribution of telephones, face-to-face interviews are conducted in the main cities, generally with samples of 1,000-1,500 respondents.

The ICVS provides an overall measure of victimization in the previous year by any of the eleven "conventional" crimes included in the questionnaire. A first group of crimes deals with the vehicles owned by the respondent or respondent's household; a second group refers to breaking and entering (burglaries); and a third group of crimes refers to victimization experienced by the respondent personally, including robbery, pickpocketing, assault, and sexual offences.

To increase comparability of victimization rates across the world, analyses at the global level are based on the subset of data from respondents living in cities of more than 100,000 inhabitants. The results of the ICVS 2000 show that on average 28% of citizens living in urban areas of 100.000 inhabitants or more suffered at least one form of victimization over the twelve months preceding the interview. Victimization rates are highest for city dwellers in Latin America (46%) and Africa (35%). Victimization rates are moderately high in Oceania (Australia only) and Western and Central Europe. Victimization rates below the global average are found in North America, Eastern Europe, and Asia.

The countries with the highest prevalence rates for conventional crime are mainly from Latin America or sub-Saharan Africa, with the exception of Mongolia, Cambodia, and Estonia. A high prevalence rate was also found in Papua New Guinea.

Countries of Europe and North America are almost without exception situated in the middle category. Contrary to common perception, overall rates of volume crime – such as burglary, robbery, and assault/threats – are not higher in the United States than in most parts of Western Europe. In fact, U.S. rates are significantly lower than those, for example, of England and Wales (Van Kesteren, Mayhew, & Nieuwbeerta, 2000). The overall rate of Canada is somewhat below the mean of the European Union and that of the United States.

Countries with the lowest rates form a fairly mixed group with a strong representation of Eastern European and Asian countries, including affluent Asian countries (Japan, South Korea) and poorer ones (China, Philippines, Indonesia). Switzerland, although less so than in the first rounds of the ICVS, still emerges as one of the safest countries in Western Europe.

It is noteworthy that the variation in regional rates does not fully conform to the commonly held notion that levels of crime are driven by poverty. The low victimization rates in Asia (e.g., India, Indonesia, and Cambodia) are clearly at odds with this notion and so are the relatively high rates of countries such as Australia, England and Wales, and The Netherlands. The rate of the Eastern European countries such as Bulgaria below that of Central and Western Europe also belies easy generalizations about the relationships between poverty and crime. As discussed elsewhere, levels of property crime seem to some extent determined by the availability of suitable targets of theft (van Dijk, 1994). This factor can help to explain comparatively high levels of common crime in many of the most affluent countries.

Regional victimization rates per types of crime show huge variation. Robbery in Latin America was 8 times higher than in Western Europe, North America, and Australia.

The data in respect of robbery confirm the specific problems with urban violence of several main cities in Latin America and Africa, including South Africa (Shaw, van Dijk, & Rhomberg, 2003). Contributing factors seem to be extreme poverty and socioeconomic inequality, postconflict instability, and widespread gun-ownership (van Dijk, 2007).

The crime category of assault and threat is defined in the ICVS as personal attacks or threats by either a stranger or a relative or friend, without the purpose of stealing. Analyses have shown fairly strong links between alcohol consumption rates and levels of threats/assaults (van Dijk, 2007).

Assaults on women are more likely to be domestic in nature than are assaults on men. In a third of the cases of violence against women, the offender was known at least by name to the victim. In one of five cases, the crime was committed in the victim's own house. The level of violence against women is inversely related to the position of women in society, with most developing countries showing much higher rates (Alvazzi del Frate & Patrignani, 1995).

Trends of Volume Crime

The preliminary results of the ICVS 2005 allow a comparison of the 2004/2005 rates with rates recorded in previous rounds of the ICVS for 30 developed countries Available trend data confirm the continued downward trend in victimization by common crime across developed countries since 2000. This universal drop in volume crime also has been observed in national crime surveys in the U.S., Great Britain, and The Netherlands (van Dijk, Manchin, & Van Kesteren, 2007).

Nearly all developed countries, including the U.S., Australia, Canada, and 18 EU member states show a curved trend of volume crime since the mid 1980s, with all-time peaks situated between 1995 and 2000 and steep declines of up to 50% thereafter. The only difference between American and European crime trends is that the drop in crime in the U.S. started 5 years earlier than in Europe. These strikingly uniform curvilinear crime trends suggest that a similar set of factors has been pushing up crime till 1995-2000 and pulling it down afterwards across the Western world.

American crime trends have been ascribed to the crack epidemic, quadrupling of prison population, and fluctuations in police deployment (Blumstein & Walman, 2006; Levitt & Dubner, 2004). These factors, however, show huge variation across Western countries showing the same curvilinear trends. For example, most European countries have never experienced a crack epidemic of any sort and prison populations in countries such as Finland, France, and Poland have fluctuated rather than gone up since the early 1990s (European Sourcebook, 2006). None of the factors highlighted in American analyses can explain convincingly the universal curvilinear trends in volume crime.

The issue of what mainly has caused the crime drop will have to be revisited from an international perspective. A possible explanation for curvilinear crime trends is that crime across countries has been driven by the availability of criminal opportunities (Felson, 1997). Opportunities of crime are likely to have undergone a curvilinear trend over the past three decades. Opportunities expanded with the economy since the 1970s across the Western world and have subsequently shrunk due to improved self-protection of households and businesses in response to increased losses from crime (van Dijk, 1994). The ICVS provides some empirical support for this alternative interpretation by showing that the use of self-protection measures by households has increased consistently and universally across Western countries since 1986 (van Dijk, 2007). This alternative explanation accounts for the curvilinear crime trends but also for the advanced position of the U.S. where economic recovery after the Second World War came sooner than in European countries.

Methodological Concerns

The proposal for the first round of the ICVS was based on the argument that cost-saving modern techniques of data collection such as random digit dialling and CATI would justify periodic comparative surveys that could complement the well-established, nation-specific surveys of countries like the U.S., The Netherlands, Finland, Switzerland, the U.K., and Canada.

From the outset, the ICVS was designed with the objective to make broad comparisons across countries. This philosophy explains the use of relatively modest sample sizes (2,000 per country in developed countries). The two decades of experience of the ICVS has borne out that such sample sizes allow the identification of statistically significant differences across both countries and years. Larger samples are used in countries such as Poland and Argentina, where the ICVS is implemented to arrive at more precise estimates of national or regional levels of crime.

The results of the five rounds of the ICVS have empirically demonstrated that, notwithstanding trends noted above, the victimization rates of countries have remained remarkably stable over the years. The results also show that the trend of national rates mirror those of national crimes surveys using much larger samples.

Overviews of key methodological issues concerning the ICVS can be found in various reports (e.g., Mayhew & van Dijk, 1997; Van Kesteren, Mayhew, & Nieuwbeertaa, 2000). Most of the concerns relate to the quality of data collection methods and techniques employed and the extent of standardization achieved. According to Lynch (2006) nation-specific surveys produce higher-quality data on individual nations but ICVS provides, as intended, more comparable data across countries. Problems that have arisen with the extent of standardization flow mostly from the need to persuade all participating partners to follow jointly set guidelines. One of the recurrent challenges of the ICVS is the concentration of all fieldwork in the early months of the year, but due to the funding arrangements some variation has always been inevitable.[1]

A cause of concern about crime surveys is the under- or overrepresentation of subgroups in the sample. Considering the objective of the ICVS to obtain a rough profile of victimization by volume crime in comparative perspective, the sensitivity of sample surveys to sampling bias may be less than often is assumed. This can be illustrated with the theoretical example of a subgroup that makes up 5% of the population and experiences victimization rates that are *twice* as high as the average (e.g., 10% rather than 5%). If such subgroup would be completely absent in the sample, this omission would only marginally influence the national rate (namely, by +0.25).

In the latest sweep, response rates have declined compared to the second and subsequent sweeps, in line with general trends in population surveys. It is uncertain whether this fluctuation has affected victimization rates. In the fifth ICVS, respondents were recalled up to seven times.

Gallup/Europe has carried out experiments with the number of recalls showing that the number of recalls had no effect on the number of victimization incidents reported. Persons reached after many recalls did not show other response patterns on victimization or other crucial issues than those contacted sooner (van Dijk, Van Kesteren, & Manchin, 2007). This finding goes some way in allaying concerns that reduced response rates may have resulted in biased samples in terms of victimization experiences, for example, by oversampling those "eager to talk" about recent experiences.

In recent years, the increase of the proportion of mobile-only phone users in several countries has raised concerns about the representativeness of samples of landline phone numbers such as those used in the ICVS. Results of a special pilot study among mobile-only users conducted in Finland in the framework of the EU/ICS 2005 showed that mobile-only users differ significantly from the general population but not to the extent that victimization rates cannot be estimated reliably by reweighting data that are exclusively landline-based. In other words, the inclusion in the Finnish dataset of data collected among mobile-only users did not result in different victimization rates for Finland than those found before (van Dijk, Van Kesteren, & Manchin, 2007).

The conduct of international crime surveys will continue to face the ever changing methodological challenges facing survey research generally, including the increased use of mobiles. The biggest challenge for the ICVS seems the continued need to forge workable "coalitions of the willing" of partners agreeing to a minimum of standardization of their self-funded surveys. In this context, ongoing efforts to standardize crime surveys in the framework of the European Union may jeopardize the unique asset of the ICVS of providing globally comparable crime data.

Victimization as a Narrow Concept

In our view, the most fundamental limitation of the ICVS is that it focuses exclusively, as all conventional crime surveys do, on victims of traditional crimes that affect individuals and households. This limitation is becoming more and more problematic with the gradual shift of attention away from volume crime to emerging crime threats against the background of globalization. In recent years, the United Nations has adopted international treaties to address nonvolume crimes such as transnational organized crime (UNTOC, 2000) and corruption (UNCAC, 2004). These developments engender an urgent need of comparable statistics on new types of crime to establish benchmarks for internationally agreed-upon criminal policies against global crime.

Strenuous efforts are currently being made by involved international organizations such as the United Nations Office on Drugs and Crime (UNODC) and Europol to harmonize administrative data of police and courts on transnational organized crime and corruption. It seems doubtful that such data will ever be useful as indicators of the extent of these types of crime. In a global context, police-based information on organized crime and corruption – such as rates of arrest or convictions concerning such offences – is likely to be even more distorted by filtering processes than those on ordinary crime. In countries where organized crime is most prevalent, investigations into such crimes will be hampered by rampant corruption and political interference and fewer of such investigations will be initiated or successfully completed. Low rates of court cases on corruption or organised crime in a country may point to high rather than low prevalence of such types of crime. High numbers of arrests or convictions for corruption may similarly indicate a comparatively low prevalence of such crimes due to better policing (Lambsdorff, 2006). In the field of complex crimes, statistics of police-recorded or court-recorded crimes are a source of disinformation. The case of measuring levels of crime independently of the police is even stronger regarding organized crime and corruption than regarding volume crime.

Although victimization surveys are a proven tool to put levels of victimization by volume crime in a global perspective, they cannot be used readily to measure victimization by emerging or global crimes. Victimization surveys by definition collect information on crimes that directly victimize individual persons or households physically or economically. Many types of global crime – such as drug trafficking, subsidy or tax fraud, international corruption, money laundering, or environmental pollution – harm collective interests but few people will feel individually damaged by them.

A second major shortcoming of traditional victimization surveys is their use of samples from general populations. Even if individual respondents are able to report on experiences with emerging crimes, samples from general residential populations will be unable to pick up sufficient cases of such crimes. Few ordinary citizens ever will be confronted with cases of high-level corruption. The interviewing of household-based samples also means that no information is collected on the victimization experiences of nonresidents. Surveys among samples of residential women, for example, will fail to collect information on the victimization experiences of sexually exploited women who have been repatriated. Thus, new approaches must be found to collect information on the newly emerging global crime threats.

To arrive at estimates of the prevalence of global criminal victimizations, researchers are called upon to develop alternative methods of crime measurement. One approach is the systematic collection of information from public sources other than police records, such as reports of parliamentary rapporteurs, ombudsman, nongovernmental organizations, international organizations, and credible media. Groundbreaking efforts have been made by the RAND corporation with its database on terrorist incidents (http://www.mipt.org/terrorismdefined.html) and UNODC with its database on incidents and victims of trafficking in persons (UNODC, 2006). Using its database, UNODC has reported on countries most frequently cited as countries of origin, transit, or destination for human trafficking.

In cases in which little or no public source information is available, criminologists could look for the extent of social traces of crimes like corruption and organized crime. A promising research strategy would be to determine which special groups in society are most likely to be exposed to such crimes. This would mean measuring the extent of crime by looking at its impact on vulnerable parts of society, which mirrors the victimological strategy introduced by the crime victim surveys. The impact of emerging crimes on vulnerable groups will be measurable sometimes through survey research into the experiences and perceptions of groups such as business executives in the case of corruption. Such victim-centred information then can be combined with measures of the extent of other social traces of the criminal phenomena at issue. Examples of both types of social markers of complex crime will be presented next.

Corruption Indicators: Perceptions and Experiences

Corruption can be defined broadly as the abuse of public power for private gain. A distinction is often made between grand corruption and petty or street-level corruption. Grand corruption refers to corrupt practices that pervade the highest levels of government (local, regional, or national). Petty corruption involves the payment by individuals or companies of relatively small sums to gain preferential treatment from a public official in the conduct of their professional tasks (Langseth, 2006). One of the most common forms of corruption is bribery, the bestowing of (financial) benefits in order to influence unduly an action or decision.

The most commonly cited statistical indicator of nonconventional crimes is the Corruption Perceptions Index (CPI), designed and maintained by the Berlin-based Transparency International, generally known as TI (Transparency International, 2004). The CPI is a composite index of the perceived extent of both grand and petty corrupt practices in countries, drawing on more than a dozen different surveys. Recent versions of the CPI are based largely on results of surveys among business people and ratings made by country risks analysts (Lamsdorff, 2005, 2006). Although the CPI has had significant political impact, its methodology is increasingly criticized. One common criticism is that the sources used differ significantly across countries and years, thus compromising the comparability of the results (Galtung, 2006). Another criticism is that perceptions of business leaders and experts influence each other, and that high rankings could therefore be based on the mere echoing of unfounded, media-led beliefs. Perhaps the most salient criticism is that as an index measuring a broad range of perceptions of vaguely defined corruption problems, CPI does not accurately register changes in the actual extent of specific forms of corruptions in a country. In Bulgaria, for example, ICVS-type surveys among the public about victimization experiences with bribery have shown significant decreases in the level of street corruption. This drop in corruption was not reflected in CPI-type perceptions-based measures (Center for the Study of Democracy, 2006).

The International Crime Victims Survey (ICVS) includes a question on the respondent's actual experiences with street level corruption in the previous year. ("During the past year, has any government official such as a customs officer, police officer or inspector asked you or expected you to pay a bribe?") In older versions of the CPI, the ICVS country rates of victimization by corruption were incorporated (TI, 2004). The ICVS data on actual victimization by corruption seem one of the best available sources of reliable comparative information on petty corruption prevalence.

In 2004, TI contracted Gallup to conduct a public opinion survey (to be called the Global Corruption Barometer) in 64 countries among a total of 50,000 people to assess not just perceptions of corruption but also experiences (TI, 2004). The question used to measure actual victimization experiences reads as follows: "In the past 12 months, have you or anyone in your household paid a bribe in any form?" The question resembles the one used in the ICVS but, unfortunately, is not identical because it focuses on the actual payment rather than on solicitation ("have you paid?" rather than "were you asked or expected to pay?").

The analysis of the relationship between the prevalence rates of countries found in the ICVS 2000 and in the TI corruption barometer of 2004 revealed a high degree of agreement. The two measures of victimization by petty corruption were found to be strongly correlated ($r = 0.75$). On average, ICVS data are 9.9% higher than the Transparency International data, as was to be expected considering the wider scope of the question used in the ICVS.

In order to increase the coverage of the two studies and enhance the significance of the results, we have integrated the two datasets with an adjustment of the TI data to match ICVS data better (TI scores were multiplied by 109.9%). Through this operation we were able to calculate corruption victimization rates for 92 countries (van Dijk, 2007).

Countries with the highest scores are developing countries from across the world, with Eastern Europe, sub-Saharan Africa, and Latin America all containing several countries with the highest rates. Several Asian countries, such as India and Indonesia, also show comparatively high rates. Information on victimization by bribe-taking provides an important complement to the maps of ordinary crimes based on other ICVS results. One major difference is that several Asian countries with low rates of victimization by ordinary theft and violence show high levels of corruption. Corruption appears to be related more strongly to levels of development than ordinary crime.

Conventional wisdom says that corruption starts at the top and spreads downwards among lower-level officials. If this assumption is correct, the prevalence of street-level corruption could be used as a marker of grand or high-level corruption. In this special case, conventional crime surveys such as the ICVS among the general public can be used to collect useful information on complex crimes such as grand corruption that are seemingly victimless.

Diagnosing Organised Crime With the Use of Statistical Markers

An important source of information on specific types of transnational organized crime are victimization surveys among business executives about racketeering and extortion, one of the most important manifestations of organized crime in many countries (Alvazzi del Frate, 2004; Aromaa &

Lehti, 1996). Since 1997, the World Economic Forum has carried out surveys among CEOs of larger companies to identify obstacles to businesses in an increasing number of countries. From the onset, one of the questions in these executive opinion surveys asked about the prevalence in the country of "mafia-oriented racketeering, extortion (imposes or not serious costs on businesses)". The widespread perception among key persons that such activities are rampant in a country provides by itself no proof that this is actually the case, but it can be regarded as a statistical marker of organised crime.

The mean scores of mafia prevalence as perceived by business executives were found to be strongly correlated to the assessments of organized crime prevalence of an international risk-assessment group based in the U.K. called MIG ($r = .63$, $n = 102$, $p < 0.000$). In order to facilitate further statistical exploration, a composite index was constructed based on the averaged rankings of countries on the WEF surveys of 1997 to 2003 and these assessments. This so-called Organized Crime Perception Index (OCPI) refers to the level of different types of organized crime activities such as extortion and drugs and arms and human trafficking as perceived by potential victim groups and experts.

According to common definitions of organized crime in criminological literature and law enforcement practice (Levi, 2002), instrumental violence, corruption of public officials, and money laundering are regarded as universal secondary characteristics of organized crime. A fourth defining feature of mafia-infested countries is a bloated black economy. It is hard to imagine a high level of organized crime in a country without a significant amount of these systemic mafia-related phenomena.

Statistical indicators were selected for the prevalence of each of these four defining systemic characteristics of organized crime activity in countries: instrumental violence, high-level corruption, money laundering, and extent of the black economy (van Dijk, Shaw, & Buscaglia, 2002).

In an attempt to develop a proxy or stand-in measure of "mob-related violence," rates were calculated of the number of police-recorded homicides per country minus the number of convictions for homicide. Both types of data were drawn from the crime and criminal justice surveys of the United Nations. The resulting rates of "unsolved homicides" was used as proxy indicator of "mob-related homicide." The Organised Crime Perception Index, just mentioned, was found to be moderately strongly related to the indicator of mob-related violence ($r = .48$, $n = 51$, $p < 0.05$). Similarly, a proxy indicator of "high-level corruption" was derived from studies of the World Bank Institute and indicators of money laundering and the extent of the black economy were taken from the World Economic Forum reports (2003, 2004).

The moderately strong to very strong statistical relationships between the organized crime perception index and four other indicators of secondary manifestations of organized crime activity support the construction of a composite organized crime index combining the five interrelated indicators. An important strategic advantage of the composite index is the incorporation of at least one *objective* measure of organized crime activity: the rate of unsolved homicides according to official administrations. Scores on this composite index cannot be dismissed by governments as being based just on "perceptions." The scores are corroborated by the official "dead body counts" of their own police authorities as reported to the United Nations through the Crime Survey.

Table 1 depicts the regional distribution on the Composite Organized Crime Index (COCI), based on data from world regions. For diagnostic purposes, the picture presents both the ranked scores on the composite index and the rank orders for the five source indicators used. Higher scores and lower ranks indicate more corruption.

The regional scores and rank numbers of the composite index and those on its five constituting indicators show a high degree of consistency. Deviations from the overall pattern are relatively high rank numbers on informal sector and money laundering of the low-crime region of Central America. Among the high-crime regions, West and Central Africa shows relatively low rank number on homicides. This result could point to a shortcoming in the available statistics – for example, homicide statistics for Nigeria are missing – or to the different nature of organized crime in the region. Such blatant deviations at any rate suggest the need of focussed additional research.

Country Scores

The combination of data from different sources allows the calculation of scores for a large number of countries. To assess the organized crime situation of countries, both the scale values on the COCI and on the constituting indicators/markers should be taken into account. The rank numbers for different indicators are mostly in the same range as the COCI rank but significant deviations occur. Deviations of single indicators from the COCI rank can point to specific features of organized crime in the van Dijk

Table 1: Regional Mean Scores on Composite Organized Crime Index (COCI) and Data on Source Indicators: Perceived Organized Crime Prevalence, Grand Corruption, Money Laundering, Extent of Shadow Economy and the Rates of Unsolved Murders per 100,000 Population

	Average of the Composite Organized Crime Index	Organized Crime Perception (rank)	Informal Sector (rank)	Unsolved Homicides (rank)	High-Level Corruption (rank)	Money Laundering (rank)
Oceania	33	1	1	1	2	1
West and Central Europe	35	2	2	2	4	3
North America	44	4	4	4	6	4
East and South East Asia	45	5	3	7	3	6
Central America	50	4	13	3	8	13
Near and Middle East	50	7	6	11	1	2
World	*54*					
South Asia	54	14	8	8	7	11
North Africa	55	6	5	6		5
East Africa	55	12	9		11	9
Southern Africa	56	10	12	5	12	10
South America	58	11	14	10	13	12
Southeast Europe	58	15	10	12	9	14
West and Central Africa	60	13	11	15	5	8
East Europe	70	17	16	14	14	16
Central Asia and Transcaucasian	70	16		13	15	
Caribbean	70	9	15		16	15

Items and sources: Organized crime perception (World Economic Forum, 2003, 2004; Merchant International Group, 2004); Money laundering and informal sector (World Economic Forum, 2004); high-level corruption (Kaufmann et al., 2003); unsolved homicides (see UN Survey on Crime and Justice, 2002: www.UNODC.org).

country or, alternatively, to deficiencies in the data. At this stage of development, country scores should be interpreted with caution.

Within Europe, organized crime prevalence increases diagonally from the northwest to the southeast, with levels being low in England, Germany, and Scandinavia, higher in Spain and Italy, and by far the highest in Russia, Albania, Bulgaria, and Ukraine. In Asia, rates are the worst in parts of South Asia (Pakistan, Bangladesh). But China and India also are rated comparatively high on this composite index (higher than Italy). More research on the role of the organized-crime corruption in these two emerging superpowers countries seems warranted.

In Africa, Nigeria, Angola, and Mozambique stand out with the highest scores. Nigerian organized crime activity in both the country and the region has been well documented (Shaw et al., 2003; UNODC, 2006). A detailed account of how organized crime threatens to penetrate state and businesses in Southern Africa, notably in Mozambique, is given in Gastrow (2003). In Latin America, Haiti, Paraguay, Guatemala, Venezuela, and Colombia show the highest scores. High scores are also observed in Jamaica in the Caribbean.

The primary utility of the index lies in the possibility to carry out analyses of the macro-correlates of organized crime. Levels of organised crime are inversely correlated with measures of rule of law and of economic development (van Dijk, 2007).

Relationships Between Indicators of Types of Crime

Both for theoretical and for measurement purposes, it would seem crucially important to know more about the statistical relations between the level of victimization by volume crime and the extent of nonconventional crimes such as corruption and organised crime.

Figure 1 shows a scatterplot of country values on the ICVS 1992-2000 and the comprehensive organized crime index just discussed. The world map of organized crime emerging from this index differs fundamentally from that of conventional crimes. The perceived prevalence of organized crime and the overall ICVS rates of victimization by volume crime was found to be unrelated ($r = 0.001$, n.s.).

As shown in Figure 1, the level of volume crime in a country says very little about the level of organized crime. This result suggests that levels of volume crime and of organized crime are determined by different factors at the macrolevel (van Dijk & Nevala, 2002). As discussed, volume

Figure 1: Country scores on ICVS for overall victimization by volume crime (low to high) and on Comprehensive Organized Crime Index (low scores indicating high levels).

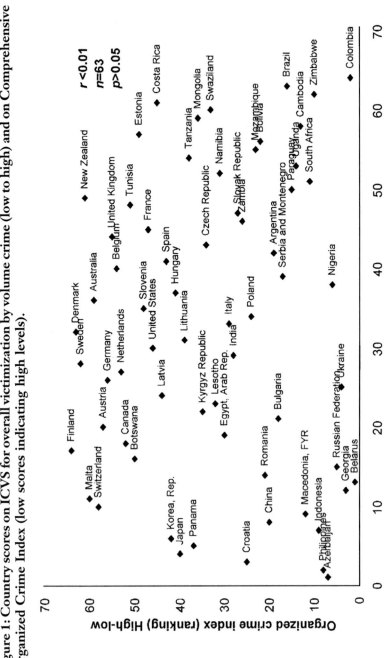

crime shows a clear downward trend in Western countries. There are no indications of similar declines in the level of organised crime or corruption (Lamsdorf, 2005). Complex crimes should be analysed separately from volume crime. This finding confirms the need of developing separate indicators of complex crimes that can complement the results of the ICVS.

CONCLUSION

Those convinced of the utility of collecting and analyzing comparative crime statistics for political and academic reasons find themselves in a quandary. Because of the intrinsic opposition of many national governments to air their dirty laundry in public, the production of international crime and justice statistics is historically underdeveloped. Few countries nowadays go as far as communist countries that regarded crimes statistics as state secrets, but most are still inclined to see international benchmarking of their crime situation as a threat to their sovereignty. Funding for the development of such statistics is difficult to obtain. As a result, the case for such statistics must be made on the basis of fragmentary, dated, and in some respects imperfect statistics. In this situation, many experts are inclined to stay on the scientifically safe side. If international crime statistics are discussed, it is to underline their intrinsic methodological weaknesses rather than to find ways to improve them and thereby enhance their potential to inform policy making at the macrolevel.

From a scientific perspective such a cautious approach might be commendable. But as Aebi, Killias, and Tavares (2003) as well as Kaufmann and colleagues (2003) have pointed out, it plays into the hands of those who – for particular political reasons – prefer such information not to be, or ever become, available. It means capitulating to political forces that would prefer comparative criminology to remain statistically challenged forever. In the current era of ongoing globalization, crime problems are increasingly transnational, with local crime problems spilling over to other countries and continents in many ways. The traditional position of governments that crime problems essentially are domestic affairs seems less and less tenable.

In our opinion, the time has come to break the politically imposed *omerta* of criminologists on comparative crime and justice statistics. A new generation of criminologists is well travelled and increasingly internationally oriented in its interests. It is to be hoped that they will revolt against the conspicuous absence of credible international statistics in their chosen field of study. The time has come to exploit fully the potential of survey research and growing availability of proxy indicators to arrive at indicators of both volume and complex crimes and to combine these with improved statistics on manpower and performance of law enforcement and justice. With the help of such a comprehensive set of international metrics on crime and justice, criminology will be able to break away from country-specific interpretations of (trends of) crime. Through such long-overdue internationalisation, it will increase the scope, validity, and policy impact of its products.

Finally, this chapter has demonstrated that traditional measures of volume crime from household-based samples tell a small part of the crime story. If transnational crime is breaking down national borders, corruption is undermining the integrity of government officials, and the victims of crime become harder to find, count, or even conceptualize, criminologists must become more creative in measurement.

✦

Address correspondence to: Jan.vanDijk@uvt.nl

NOTE

1. In the fifth round of the ICVS, fieldwork in some countries of the Continent took place much later than in the United Kingdom due to the delayed signing of contracts. In the report, an analysis is made of the possible impact of this variation with the conclusion that no major distortions seem to have taken place (van Dijk, Van Kesteren, & Manchin, 2006; Hideg & Manchin, 2006; see also www.Gallup-Europe.be/EUICS).

REFERENCES

Aebi, M. F., Killias, M., & Tavares, C. (2003). Comparing crime rates: Confronting the ICVS, the European sourcebook of crime and criminal justice statistics and Interpol statistics. In H. Kury (Ed.), *International comparison of crime and victimization: The ICVS, International Studies in Social Science*, special issue of the *International Journal of Comparative Criminology*, 2(1), 21–37.

Alvazzi del Frate, A. (2004). The international crime business survey: Findings from nine central eastern European cities. *European Journal on Criminal Policy and Research, 10,* 2–3, 137–161.

Alvazzi del Frate, A., & Patrignani, A. (1995). Women's victimisation in developing countries. *Issues & Report,* No. 5, UNICRI Series.

Aromaa, K., & Lehti, M. (1996). *Foreign companies and crime in Eastern Europe.* Helsinki, Finland: National Research Institute of Legal Policy, Publication no. 135.

Blumstein, A., & Wallman, J. (2006). *The crime drop in America.* New York: Cambridge University Press.

Buscaglia, E., & van Dijk, J. (2003). Controlling organized crime and corruption in the public sector. *Forum on crime and society,* Vol. 3, No. 1 and 2. United Nations Publication.

Center for the Study of Democracy. (2006). *On the eve of EU accession: Anticorruption reforms in Bulgaria.* Sofia, Bulgaria: CSD.

European Sourcebook of Crime and Criminal Justice Statistics – 2006. (2006). The Hague, Netherlands: Ministry of Justice, WODC.

Felson, M. (1997). *Crime and everyday life* (2nd ed.). Thousand Oaks, CA: Pine Forge Press/Sage.

Hideg, G., & Manchin, R. (2006). *Telescoping effect in EU ICS.* (Working paper). Gallup/EU.

Galtung, F. (2006). Measuring the immeasurable: Boundaries and functions of (macro) corruption indices. In A. Shacklock et al. (Eds.), *Measuring corruption.* Aldershot, England: Ashgate.

Gastrow, P. (ed.). (2003). *Penetrating state & business – Organized crime in Southern Africa,* Vol. 2. Tshwane (Pretoria), South Africa: Institute for Security Studies. Monograph #89 in the Monographs for the African Human Secuirty Initiative series.

Kaufmann, D., Kraay, A., & Mastruzzi, M. (2003). *Governance matters III: Governance indicators for 1996-2002.* (Policy Research Working Paper 3106. Washington, DC: World Bank. Available at http://www.worldbank.org/wbi/governance/pubs/govmatters3.html

Lambsdorff, J. (2005). Corruption perception index 2004. Transparency International. *Global corruption report 2005.* England: Yeomans Press.

Lambsdorff, J. (2006), Measuring corruption – The validity and precision of subjective indicators (CPI). In A. Shacklock et al. (Eds.), *Measuring corruption.* Aldershot, England: Ashgate.

Levi, M. (2002). The organization of serious crime. In M. Maguire, R. Morgan, & R. Reiner (Eds.), *Oxford handbook of criminology.* Oxford: Oxford University Press.

Levitt, S., & Dubner, J. (2004). *Freakonomics.* London: Penguin Books.

Lynch, J. P. (2006). Problems and promise of victimization surveys for cross-national research. *Crime and justice,* Vol. 34. Chicago: University of Chicago.

Mayhew, P., & van Dijk, J. J. M. (1997). *Criminal victimisation in eleven industrialised countries: Key findings from the 1996 International Crime Victims Survey.* The Hague, Netherlands: WODC, Ministry of Justice. Onderzoek en beleid, no. 162.

Merchant International Group Limited. (2004). *Grey area dynamics, organised crime figures 2004.* (Unpublished report to UNICRI).

Newman, G. (1999). *Global report on crime and justice*. United Nations Office for Drug Control and Crime Prevention, Centre for International Crime Prevention. New York: Oxford University Press.

Shaw, M., van Dijk, J., & Rhomberg, W. (2003). Determining global trends in crime and justice: An overview of results from the United Nations surveys of crime trends and operations of criminal justice systems. *Forum on Crime and Society*, *3*, No. 1 & 2.

Transparency International. (2003). *The coalition against corruption. Annual Report*. (www.transparency.org).

Transparency International. (2004). *Report on the global corruption barometer 2004*. (www.transparency.org).

United Nations Convention against Corruption (UNCAC). (2004). (untreaty.un. org).

United Nations Convention against Transnational Organized Crime (UNTOC). (2000). (untreaty.un.org).

United Nations Office on Drugs and Crime (UNODC). (2006). *Trafficking in persons; global patterns*. Vienna:

van Dijk, J. J. M. (1994). Understanding crime rates; on the interactions between the rational choices of victims and offenders. *British Journal on Criminology*, *34*(2), 105-121.

van Dijk, J. J. M. (2007). *World atlas of crime*. Thousand Oaks, CA: Sage.

van Dijk, J. J. M., Manchin, R., & Van Kesteren, J. (2006). *The burden of crime in the EU: Key findings of the EU/international crime victim survey 2005*. Brussels, Belgium, and Tilburg, The Netherlands: UNICRI/Gallup/Europe/Intervict.

van Dijk, J. J. M., Mayhew, P., & Killias, M. (1990). *Experiences of crime across the world*. Key findings from the 1989 international crime survey. Deventer, Netherlands: Kluwer Law and Taxation.

van Dijk, J. J. M., & Nevala, S. (2002). Intercorrelations of crime. In P. Nieuwbeerta (Ed.), *Crime victimization in international perspective*. The Hague, Netherlands: Boom Legal Publishers.

van Dijk, J. J. M., Shaw, M., & Buscaglia, E. (2002). The TOC convention and the need for comparative research: Some illustrations from the work of the UN Centre for International Crime Prevention. In H-J. Albrecht & C. Fijnaut (Eds.), *The containment of transnational organized crime. Comments on the UN convention of December 2000*. Freiburg, Germany: Max Planck Institut fur auslandisches und internationals Strafrecht.

Van Kesteren, J. N., Mayhew, P., & Nieuwbeerta, P. (2000). *Criminal victimisation in seventeen industrialized countries: Key findings from the 2000 international crime victims survey*. Onderzoek en beleid, No. 187. The Hague, Netherlands: Ministry of Justice, WODC.

World Economic Forum. (2003). *The global competitiveness report 2002-2003*. New York: Oxford University Press.

World Economic Forum. (2004). *The global competitiveness report 2003-2004*. New York: Oxford University Press.

The National Crime Victimization Survey at 34: Looking Back and Looking Ahead

by

Michael R. Rand
Bureau of Justice Statistics
U.S. Department of Justice

Abstract: *The National Crime Victimization Survey (NCVS) was initiated in 1972 because official sources of crime statistics in the United States were deemed inadequate to measure the extent and nature of the nation's crime problem as it existed at the time. Over the past three decades, the NCVS has become the nation's primary source of information on the frequency, characteristics, and consequences of criminal victimization. The survey has been instrumental in helping shape the national understanding of the nature and extent of crime.*

Today, violent crime rates have declined dramatically since the 1970s, but other offenses, such as identity theft, are becoming national concerns. Just as the nature of the "crime problem" has evolved and changed over time, the NCVS has changed as well. Over its 34 year history, changes have been implemented for a variety of reasons: to improve the survey's methodology; to obtain additional information about crimes, victims, and the consequences of being a victim of crime; and to reduce the cost of enumeration.

Crime Prevention Studies, volume 22 (2007), pp. 145–163.

The survey faces a number of challenges, including changing national priorities, rising costs of enumeration, increasing difficulties in obtaining interviews, and changes in technology. This chapter reviews the evolving nature of the survey and the challenges it faces, and discusses the new directions that the NCVS is likely to take over the next few years.

Today the National Crime Victimization Survey (NCVS) is widely accepted as a reliable source of information about the extent and nature of crime in the United States. In the first years following its 1972 birth as the National Crime Survey (NCS), this opinion was not widely held, nor was it always clear that the survey would survive to celebrate its 34th anniversary in July 2006.

In its earliest years, the survey was seen as expensive and unproven, and its findings were not widely cited. Support was mixed even within the Law Enforcement Assistance Administration (LEAA), the agency within the Department of Justice (DOJ) that sponsored the new survey. Elsewhere in DOJ, the survey was commonly viewed as an unwelcome competitor to the FBI's established Uniform Crime Reporting (UCR) program. For its first few years, survey estimates remained largely outside public consciousness, as initial estimates from the NCS were not released until 1975. The data itself, in the form of public-use data tapes, were accessible to only a few researchers prior to 1978 when NCS data were archived at the University of Michigan.

Throughout the 1980s, confidence in and use of survey findings and data by the press, researchers, and policy makers grew as did the understanding that the survey could provide information about the nature of violent and property crime in the U.S. not available from any other source. Survey estimates increasingly began appearing in news stories and in the popular press in articles related to crime and victimization. Much of our understanding of the nature of crime in the United States originally came from statistics from the NCS and NCVS, as evidenced by a Ripley's Believe It or Not cartoon circa 1986 about police reporting of crime (Figure 1). It can be argued that findings from the victimization survey were instrumental in helping fuel the growth in the 1980s and 1990s of programs devoted to assisting victims of crime and combating violence against women, rape, and sexual assault.

Even as the use of the survey was growing and its abilities to inform on the nature and extent of crime became increasingly recognized, financial support for the survey did not always keep pace with the cost of conducting

Figure 1: Believe it or not.

it. To keep the survey within available funding levels, on a number of occasions it has been necessary to implement cost-saving measures, including cuts in sample and reductions in quality control procedures.

Yet not all the changes made to the survey through the years have been negative. Questions have been added at various times to obtain new information about the nature and consequences of crime victimization. The survey underwent an extensive redesign (including a renaming to the National Crime Victimization Survey–NCVS) to improve its ability to screen for crimes and has been modified a number of times to improve question design and collect additional information about crimes and victims.

Through it all, the survey's core methodological attributes – including the two-part interview separating crime screening from attribute reporting, the 6-month reference period, the panel design, bounding to ensure accurate recall of offense dating, and interviewing all household members age 12 and older for themselves – have remained intact.

Over the past decade, however, the survey has experienced more cutbacks than growth, and in 2006, midway through the survey's fourth decade, the NCVS stands at a crossroad. Its reputation as a source of reliable information about the extent and nature of crime continues to be quite high, but its fiscal status remains precarious. In the past two years, the Bureau of Justice Statistics (BJS) has begun a process to evaluate survey procedures in order to reduce survey costs and place it on a more sound financial footing. In the coming year the evaluation will be broadened to examine every aspect and protocol of the survey in order to make whatever changes are required to avoid future budgetary crises and ensure that the survey can produce information about the kinds of crime that exist in today's world and also meet the challenges of tomorrow. It is likely that many of the survey's long-sustained core methodologies may not survive the anticipated survey redesign.

This chapter reviews some of the survey's history and methodology, discusses evaluations that are being undertaken currently, and explores some of the possible directions that the survey may take in the future.

The NCS - Origins

The National Crime Survey developed out of a perceived need for more comprehensive information about the extent and characteristics of crime in the United States. In 1965, in response to rising crime levels in our nation's cities, President Lyndon Johnson convened the President's Commission on Law Enforcement and the Administration of Justice to examine the root causes and characteristics of crime in the United States and recommend policies and programs to address what was seen to be a growing problem. The commission concluded that the extant source of crime data, the UCR program, was insufficient for the task of evaluating the extent and nature of crime. The UCR obtained information only on crimes reported to police and obtained little information on the costs of crime and characteristics of crimes and crime victims. Finding it "very difficult to make accurate measurements of crime trends by relying on official statistics," the commission undertook pilot studies to explore the viability of using sample surveys to obtain data on crime, including that not reported to police. Because "these initial experiments produced useful results that justify more intensive efforts to gather such information on a regular basis," the commission recommended that a national victimization survey be implemented (President's Commission on Law Enforcement and the Administration of Justice, 1967, p. 40).

The primary purpose of the new National Crime Survey, as implemented in 1972, was, "to measure the annual change in crime incidents for a limited set of major crimes and to characterize some of the socioeconomic aspects of both the reported events and their victims" (Kindermann, 1975).

The victimization survey program that was originally implemented in 1972 consisted of three surveys: a national household survey, a household survey of major cities, and a survey of businesses. The city surveys component of the program was designed to evaluate the impact of the federal crime fighting programs in major U.S. cities and were conducted in 12,000 households and 12,000 commercial establishments in each selected city. Eight "impact" cities receiving funding from the Department of Justice were surveyed in 1972 and 1975.[1] The nation's five largest cities were surveyed in 1973 and 1975.[2] One-time surveys were fielded in 13 additional cities during 1974.[3] The business survey was first fielded in 15,000 businesses in July of 1972 to collect data on robbery and burglary victimization of commercial establishments (LEAA, 1977).

Had it continued as originally implemented, the tripart program would have provided an ongoing comprehensive portrait of crime at both the national and local levels. However, the city surveys component was abandoned after 1975 due to its high cost, and the commercial survey was discontinued in September of 1977 because the sample was too small to produce usable estimates (Penick & Owens, 1976). The national household survey was therefore the only component to survive after 1976.

From its onset, the national household-victimization survey design incorporated trade-offs between accuracy and cost. To improve respondent recall of crime incidents, the survey incorporated a 6-month rather than a 12-month reference period (though not the 3-month reference period that was deemed to produce more accurate recall of events); in-person initial interviews; interviews of every household member for himself or herself; and the use of an initial bounding interview to anchor events more accurately in time. A rotating panel design was incorporated because it was a cost-effective way of increasing sample size.

The crimes measured by the NCS (and NCVS today) were selected to replicate, as closely as possible, those defined as UCR Part I offenses: rape, robbery, assault, theft, motor vehicle theft, and burglary. The offenses measured by the survey were not identical to those of the UCR. The NCS could not measure homicide, excluded crimes to businesses, and defined offenses somewhat differently than did the UCR. The survey also measured simple assault, an offense not included as a Part I UCR offense as well as aggravated assault, which is a Part I UCR offense.[4] As part of the survey's redesign, in 1992 the survey began measuring sexual assault other than rape, and also began collecting information about vandalism. In 2004, questions were added to measure identity-theft victimization.

NCS/NCVS History

Redesign

Within three years of the implementation of the NCS, LEAA contracted with the National Academy of Science (NAS) to evaluate the entire program. The resulting report, *Surveying Crime*, published in 1976, recommended a number of changes to the program.

- Eliminate the commercial survey and central cities samples.

- Revise the crime-screening questions to improve prompting respondents' memories.

- Add questions to allow examination of ecological factors and lifestyle activities associated with crime victimization.

- Add questions about crime preventive or protective measures taken by respondents (Penick & Owens, 1976).

Acting on these recommendations, LEAA commenced a long-term plan to redesign the survey. After an extensive research process, some revisions deemed not to affect rates were implemented in 1986. Revisions to the survey's screening questions, because they would impact the amount and nature of the offenses measured by the survey, were implemented in 1992. Revised crime-screening questions were designed to assist respondents better in remembering events they had experienced by adding specific cues and prompts, targeting some offenses such as violence by intimates and rape, and varying the frames of reference (e.g., acts, locales and relationship to offenders). The redesign also added sexual assault other than rape as an offense measured by the survey. The new screen questions were implemented in half the survey's sample for 18 months beginning in January 1992. The remaining half sample was enumerated using the old methodology, thereby enabling an evaluation of the impact of the new screening questions.[5]

The redesigned screening questions had a differential impact on each type of crime measured by the survey. For robbery, burglary, and motor vehicle theft, there was little or no difference between the estimates from the old and new methodologies. The rates of every other measured offense increased in the redesigned survey, and increases were greatest for difficult to measure offenses such as rape and domestic violence.

Because post-redesign estimates were obtained using a different screening process, they were considered to be not comparable to those of the earlier survey. The survey was renamed the National Crime Victimization Survey at about the time the redesign was implemented.

Post-redesign Period

The improvements made during the redesign have enabled the survey to become the benchmark for victimization estimates in the United States. The improved screening protocols and other methodological changes implemented in the redesign addressed a number of problems that had been identified in the NCS, and the questions added to the incident report expanded the information the survey could produce on the nature and consequences of crime victimization.

Since the redesign, BJS has avoided changing the crime-screening questions to prevent further breaks in series. At various times, questions have been added to the survey to comply with congressional mandates or obtain additional information about the characteristics of crimes and victims. For example, the 2001 Americans with Disabilities Awareness Act required that questions be added to the NCVS to obtain information on whether victims had a disability. In 1999 a battery of questions was added to determine whether offenses were hate crimes. Questions related to computer crime were added in 2001, and were replaced in 2004 by questions related to identity theft.

The post-redesign period also has seen increased use of telephone interviewing, especially computer assisted telephone interviewing (CATI). In July 2006, the survey converted from a paper and pencil instrument to a fully computerized instrument for both personal and telephone interviews.

NCVS as a Research Tool

Because the NCS was conceived primarily as a tool for measuring the extent and characteristics of crime victimization and crime trends, its use as a research tool developed well after the survey was established. Housed as it was (and remains) in the department's statistical agency, and not in its research arm (the National Institute of Justice), the survey's use as a research vehicle was never strongly advocated. Nevertheless, a set of survey objectives developed in 1983 to inform the survey redesign included the following objective: "To provide the research community with a database which constitutes the best available empirical information concerning crime victims and victimization" (Schlesinger, 1983).

Over the life of the survey, BJS has instituted a number of programs to encourage secondary research, first by making the data available at the National Archive of Criminal Justice Data (NACJD) at the University of Michigan, but also by holding seminars and workshops to assist researchers in working with the survey's large, complex data files. BJS has also developed some special data files, including longitudinal files that linked the data at the person level across all waves of the survey for a number of years.

BJS has also worked with the Census Bureau to allow researchers access to data files containing identifiers that are normally expunged from the public-use files under controlled conditions that maintain the confidentiality of the survey respondents. These files enable researchers to link the NCVS data with that from other sources, such as neighborhood-, city-, or state-level information.

Nevertheless, although BJS has gone to considerable effort to accommodate and encourage secondary research involving the NCVS, research remains a secondary, not a primary survey goal. There is no mechanism at present, nor has there ever been one, to allow research questions to drive survey content.

Budgetary Issues

From its earliest days, the NCS/NCVS has had an uneven funding history. Even as BJS was planning the survey redesign, funding shortfalls required reductions in a variety of survey protocols such as increased use of telephone interviewing. In 1992, while the redesigned survey was being introduced in half the survey's sample, further cost-saving measures were taken, including a 10% sample reduction.

Since the redesign, budget shortfalls have required additional cutbacks to survey protocols and reductions in sample. In 2005, lack of funds forced a year's delay in the introduction of a new sample in 2005 based on the 2000 decennial census. Overall, since 1985 the survey's sample has been reduced four times. The number of interviewed households in 2006 (38,600) is about three fifths the number interviewed during 1972, the NCS's first year (Figure 2). The number of interviewed persons in 2005 was about 42% of the number interviewed in 1972. The greater decrease in the number of interviewed persons is the result of declines in household sizes and increases in the personal non-interview rate.

As a result of the sample cuts and the declines in crime that the United States has experienced in the decade since 1994, the survey's ability to

Figure 2: Households and persons interviewed each 6 months.

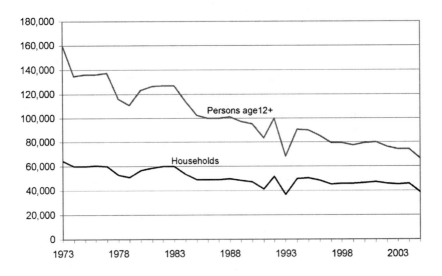

detect year-to-year changes in the crime rate has been severely diminished. To counter the declining precision, BJS began in 2003 to report short-term changes in crime using 2-year average annual victimization estimates. For example, Criminal Victimization 2005, released by BJS in September 2006 provided comparisons of average annual rates for 2004-2005 to those of 2002-2003.[6]

CURRENT SURVEY

Ironically, at a time when the NCVS has a diminished capacity to measure the nature and extent of the crime occurring in the U.S., its reputation in the public arena continues to be extremely positive and its utility continues to be recognized by public officials seeking to understand crime and crime trends.

Today the NCVS faces a number of challenges. The increasing cost of enumeration, rising non-interview rates, and changes in technology all create challenges for measuring a relatively rare phenomenon such as crime victimization.

Rising Survey Costs

The very methodologies that set the NCVS apart from victimization surveys conducted by other nations – a 6-month reference period, a panel design incorporating a bounding interview, and interviewing every household member age 12 and older – are the aspects of the survey that are most expensive to maintain. A 6-month reference period requires twice the number of interviews as a 12-month reference period to produce an annual estimate. Although the panel design is less expensive than a fully cross-sectional design, the bounding interview imposes a huge overhead. Moreover, the address-based sample has required a personal visit for the initial contact at each sample address.

Unfortunately, it is unclear whether BJS can continue to fund these methodological protocols indefinitely. Throughout the history of the survey, BJS has been able to respond to each fiscal crisis with a sample reduction or program change that reduced the cost of enumeration. Additional severe sample cuts have been avoided only because of funding received by other agencies within the Office of Justice Programs.[7] BJS cannot depend on outside sources to continue to make up the difference between appropriated funding and the cost of the survey. It is also clear that further sample cuts are not an option, as the precision of annual estimates has decreased substantially and many more cells in cross-tabulations have fallen below the threshold of statistical reliability.

The fiscal crisis has had an additional impact upon the NCVS program. Lack of funds has precluded methodological research, such as the effects of bounding or panel fatigue, or the impact of rising nonresponse rates. Therefore, at this critical stage in the survey's history, some basic structural information that could be useful in researching the program's future direction is not available.

Declining Participation Rates

NCVS response rates in 2006 were 91% of eligible households and 86% of eligible respondents in interviewed households. These response rates are among the highest of all household surveys conducted by the U.S. Census Bureau. Like other household surveys, the participation rates for the NCVS have declined for many years. The pre-redesign NCS household participation rate remained at or about 95% for 20 years before beginning to decline shortly after the redesign (Figure 3). From an unheard of rate

Figure 3: NCS/NCVS participation rates, 1973-2005.

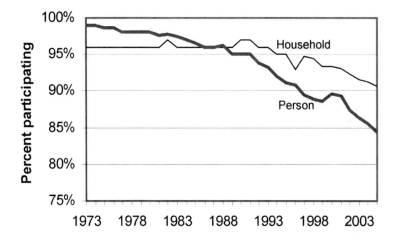

of 99% at the survey's inception, the person participation rate has declined across the survey's three decades, a decline most precipitous since the redesign. No studies have been conducted to explore the relationship between the redesign and declining participation rates, but this trend likely is largely the result of cultural changes, as other household surveys conducted by the Census Bureau have exhibited similar declines since 1990 (Bates & Stoner, 2004).

These increases in nonresponse are of concern for a number of reasons. The greatest nonresponse is among young minority males, who also exhibit the highest victimization rates. Though weighting adjustments account for nonresponse, there is concern, especially for some subpopulations, that the adjustments may be inadequate. Lack of funds has prevented conducting research to determine the impact of nonresponse on the estimates or the adequacy of the weighting adjustments.

Increasing nonresponse also drives up enumeration costs as interviewers must make more contacts with potential respondents to avoid even greater nonresponse. The impact of the increasing nonresponse is exacerbated by the declining sample sizes, and has contributed to the overall decline in the survey's ability to produce year-to-year change estimates or compare estimates for various demographic groups.

Changes in Technology

The technological advances that have occurred since the survey began in 1972 serve both as challenges to, and potential aids in, conducting household surveys. Continued telemarketing, despite telemarketing regulations passed in 2003, makes people reluctant to participate in telephone surveys. Caller ID and phone security systems create barriers for interviewers trying to reach prospective respondents. Abandonment of landlines for cell phone accounts presents another barrier, as the Census Bureau does not permit interviews with respondents using cell phones for reasons of confidentiality.

The technologies available to survey researchers in the 21st century are far greater than those available when the NCS began in 1972. Yet, until 2006, the majority of NCVS interviews were conducted using a paper questionnaire. Because of funding limitations, the NCVS was the last household survey conducted by the Census Bureau to be converted to a computer-assisted interviewing environment.

Even so, the questionnaire remains a computer version of a paper questionnaire, and therefore cannot yet take full advantage of the benefits of an automated instrument. One of the challenges the agency faces is working to streamline the instruments to take advantage of the computer-assisted interviewing technology.

BJS Responses to Current Challenges

It has become increasingly clear over the past few years that the survey as it is currently constituted cannot continue without substantial increases in the appropriations BJS receives. Past experience provides no reason to believe that these appropriations will increase to the levels necessary to sustain the survey.

In December 2005, BJS convened a panel of eight survey research experts who met for two days to explore strategies to reduce the survey's costs. The group discussed the necessity and importance of the NCVS, various methodological changes and their likely impact on survey estimates, and strategies for achieving cost savings. Varying degrees of consensus were achieved on different strategies, as well as a broad consensus that the "importance of the NCVS has not diminished over time," and that "the agency has done all it can to trim the costs of the survey without altering its basic design" (Lauritsen, 2006).

In examining various cost-reducing strategies, the panel explored possible methodological changes to the survey and assessed their potential impact. The panel rejected substituting victimization questions on another household survey for the NCVS because of the large effects on victimization estimates. Perhaps the panel's most important recommendation was to include the bounding interview data in the survey's estimates, and develop statistical adjustments to make the data comparable with previous years.

The panel deferred recommendations on a number of possible changes to the survey, including moving to a 12-month reference period and exploring whether a private survey firm could conduct the survey at lower cost. One interesting change the panel felt worth exploring would entail an additional eighth interview to the panel design that might offset an equivalent cut in sample size. This would achieve savings because subsequent telephone interviews are less expensive than initial interviews at a sample address, which must be in person. The panel concluded that some subjects could benefit from extensive study by the American Statistical Association or National Academy of Sciences.

Although implementing some or all of the panel's recommendation could reduce the cost of the NCVS, it was not clear whether such cuts would achieve real long-term reductions in the cost of the survey and avoid the possibility that the agency could find itself in a similar financial crisis within a few years. Therefore, rather than implement what could be just a short-term fix, BJS decided that it should research how the NCVS could be reconfigured to make it a more sustainable victimization survey.

Toward this end, BJS has requested that the Committee on National Statistics (CNSTAT) of the National Academy of Sciences conduct a broad scale evaluation of the entire NCVS. This evaluation, which will take about a year, is part of a larger 2-year project to evaluate the overall BJS program. BJS has given CNSTAT a mandate to examine every aspect of the survey, including what is being measured and how it is measured. The final report is due 1 year after the panel begins work in September 2006. Though it is not possible to predict what the evaluation may recommend, it is possible to provide some insight into the directions the American victimization survey is likely to move in the coming years.

A VISION OF THE NEXT GENERATION VICTIMIZATION SURVEY

The purpose of the NCS redesign implemented in 1992 was to create the ideal crime-victimization survey. The redesign consortium was specifically instructed not to consider costs in making recommendations for improved survey protocols. Ultimately, not every recommendation was implemented and many of those rejected were not implemented because of cost considerations. The objectives of the next survey redesign are much more limited: How do we build a survey program that is sustainable and can still achieve its major goals?

The survey's stated goals are important because "the objectives of a survey, and the relative emphasis on measurement or description versus analysis or explanation, will determine the questions to be asked of survey respondents" (Penick & Owens, 1976, p. 157). In fact, they determine more than just the questions, but can also dictate the nature and size of the samples used for the study.

The key question then is, What should the redesigned survey's objectives be? Should it be, as it has been in the past, primarily a counting system of reported and unreported crimes, crime trends, and the characteristics of victims? Or should it be more research focused, exploring such issues as vulnerability and risk, fear of crime, and the impact of crime on people and their communities?

The original goals of the NCS were fourfold:

- Measure the dark figure of unreported crime.
- Provide information on characteristics of crime victims and crime events.
- Estimate year-to-year change.
- Provide an independent calibration of police-based crime statistics at the national level.

I would argue that the survey's goals will shift towards more of a research orientation, but somewhat gradually. The survey cannot in the short term move dramatically towards becoming a research-oriented instrument. There is simply not enough time to reconfigure it. The fiscal crisis that has precipitated this survey's restructuring is too acute to allow either time or funds to conduct the basic methodological research that would be required to shift the survey's basic objectives dramatically.

Changes are likely to come in steps. The first will be to reduce current operational costs to keep the survey in the field, and to free up funds to conduct some methodological research and do the work necessary to redirect and retool the survey. Initial changes will likely include moving to a 12-month reference period and using the bounding interview for estimation. This will reduce the number of interviews required to produce annual estimates and save a substantial sum that can be redirected towards other changes.

In order to reduce the cost of the survey substantially and refocus the survey's objectives, it is probable that the NCVS will move in the direction that the British Crime Survey has taken, becoming a survey system rather than an omnibus survey. There will be a core survey that will be used to measure amounts and characteristics of crime and year-to-year changes. The survey will likely be primarily a telephone survey, because of the expense of conducting person-to-person interviews. The sample might be drawn from available lists of telephone numbers or might be conducted by random digit dialing. It will be cross-sectional, and the large scale panel design will be abandoned. Because of the high nonresponse, there might be oversampling of some population subgroups, such as Black or urban populations, and there might be targeted follow-up of noninterviews to reduce nonresponse among segments of the population that are hard to enumerate. If feasible and within cost constraints, there might be an address-based component to enumerate nontelephone households.

The core survey also will not cast as wide a net of offenses as does the current survey, but will focus on more serious offenses. The burdens and costs imposed by trying to measure minor offenses such as verbal threats and thefts of low-value items are simply too great, and prevent collection of information of greater potential value.

The survey will also incorporate modules to obtain information about the characteristics of victims and offenses. Because these don't change greatly over time, these modules will be either periodic or implemented within subsamples. This structure will enable creation of additional modules to measure attitudes and other non-crime measurement-related materials. Computer assisted interviewing will allow more complexity in designing the survey's questionnaires. Information collected earlier in the interview can be used to direct the flow of later sections of the instrument.

Additionally, the survey will also develop improved means to obtain information about offenses that are difficult to measure, such as intimate partner violence, rape, and sexual assault. These offenses have always proved problematic for the NCVS; the survey has historically been criticized for severely undercounting them. One possibility would be to replicate BJS methodology and utilize a small, dedicated sample using audio CASI, or similar technology, to increase response and protect respondent anonymity.

There are some methodological attributes of the current survey that I believe will not change in the reconfigured survey. The two-part interview

– first screening for offenses then obtaining detailed information in an incident report – has been a very successful approach, and will likely continue in the future victimization survey. I believe that the survey will continue to obtain information from each respondent within a household for himself or herself. Research has found that there is too much error associated with using one respondent per household. If the survey relies solely on a telephone frame, it may be possible to interview one person per household, but only about that individual person, not about other household members.

In the end, the survey will become a more flexible vehicle for exploring new issues related to crime and crime victimization. The old NCVS was built for stability and continuity. Changes have been difficult to implement. The paper-and-pencil environment inhibited the ability to target questions to appropriate respondents. The new survey will be constructed to facilitate revision and introduction of new modules to respond better to emerging issues.

This new survey will not be the "ideal" survey, as was conceived in the previous redesign. Cost considerations will drive most decisions related to the survey. Methodologies or components deemed too expensive will be abandoned. Almost certainly, the changes contemplated above will entail increases in measurement error and will definitely constitute a break in the series. At the same time, the changes will offer new opportunities, pushing the survey in directions it never has gone, and opening new areas to explore concerning the extent and nature of crime and its impact upon the public and our institutions.

CONCLUSION

Today's NCVS is longer and more comprehensive and uses a different crime-screening protocol than the original survey, but it remains a close relative of the NCS, a survey that was considered state-of-the-art at its inception 34 years ago. The stability in methodology has positive as well as negative ramifications. It enables analyses of trends and changes in characteristics over an extended period. One can have confidence that the changes (or lack thereof) one observes are not artifacts of changing methodologies. At the same time, that the survey is no longer considered state-of-the-art indicates that BJS has been unable to retool it to address changing societal conditions or to take advantage of improvements in survey methods and data collection.

The improvements introduced in the 1992 survey redesign set the stage for the NCVS to flourish as a tool for providing an understanding of the nature and extent of crime in the U.S. Even as the redesigned survey was being introduced, however, the survey began to experience the impact of tight funding. It is regrettable that there were not funds available even to fully assess the impact of the redesign or to study the impact of various aspects of the survey's methodology such as bounding or panel fatigue.

The evaluation that BJS is now undertaking follows a long period of fiscal hardship for the agency and the survey. A list of the program cutbacks taken during the past two decades is long, and cuts across virtually every component of the survey process. Last year the survey averted a fiscal crisis that would have engendered another large sample cut only because funds were provided by another agency. Clearly if this situation continued, the survey itself would have been in jeopardy.

For some time, the Bureau of Justice Statistics has characterized the NCVS as "the nation's primary source of information on criminal victimization," providing "the largest national forum for victims to describe the impact of crime and characteristics of violent offenders" (Patsy, 2002, p. 2). The evaluation now being undertaken is an opportunity to reestablish the survey on a firm fiscal footing so that it can continue to provide a forum for victims into the foreseeable future.

✦

Address correspondence to: michael.rand@usdoj.gov

This chapter was prepared for the conference to mark 25 Years of the British Crime Survey, London, England, October 16-17, 2006. The views expressed in this chapter are those of the author and do not necessarily represent those of the Bureau of Justice Statistics or the U.S. Department of Justice.

NOTES

1. Atlanta, Baltimore, Cleveland, Dallas, Denver, Newark, Portland, and St. Louis.
2. Chicago, Detroit, Los Angeles, New York, and Philadelphia.

3. Boston, Buffalo, Cincinnati, Houston, Miami, Milwaukee, Minneapolis, New Orleans, Oakland, Pittsburgh, San Diego, San Francisco, and Washington, DC.
4. For definitions of NCS/NCVS offenses see the Methodology section of Criminal Victimization in the United States-Statistical Tables on the Web at http://www.ojp.usdoj.gov/bjs/pub/pdf/cvus/cvus05mt.pdf
5. For information about the NCVS redesign see Kindermann, Lynch, and Cantor (1997) and Rand, Lynch, and Cantor (1997), available on the BJS Website at http://www.ojp.usdoj.gov/bjs/pub/pdf/erve.pdf and http://www.ojp.usdoj.gov/bjs/pub/pdf/cv73_95.pdf, respectively.
6. See Catalano (2006), available on the BJS Website at http://www.ojp.usdoj.gov/bjs/pub/cv05.pdf
7. The Office of Justice Programs comprises a number of bureaus and offices (of which BJS is one) with different missions related to providing leadership and assistance in preventing and combating crime in the United States. See www.ojp.usdoj.gov

REFERENCES

Bates, N., & Stoner, K. (2004). *Noninterview rates for selected major demographic household surveys 1990–2003* [internal memorandum]. Washington, DC: U.S. Census Bureau.

Baum, K. (2006). *Identity theft, 2004*. Washington, DC: Bureau of Justice Statistics Bulletin.

Catalano, S. (2006). *Criminal victimization 2005*. Washington, DC: Bureau of Justice Statistics Bulletin.

Dodge, R. W., & Turner, A. (1971). Methodological foundations for establishing a national survey of victimization. Reprinted in R. G. Lehnen & W. G. Skogan (Eds.). (1981). *The national crime survey: Working papers, vol. I: Current and historical perspectives*. (NCJ-75374). Washington, DC: U.S. Department of Justice.

Groves, R. M., Fowler, F. J., Jr., Couper, M. P., Lepkowski, J. M., Singer, E., & Tourangeau, R. (2004). *Survey methodology*. Hoboken, NJ: Wiley.

Hubble, D. (1996). *NCVS time-in-sample patterns, 1995 and 1988*. Unpublished analysis conducted for the Bureau of Justice Statistics.

Kindermann, C. (1975). Internal LEAA memorandum. In B. Penick & M. Owens (Eds.). (1976), *Surveying crime*. Washington, DC: National Academy Press.

Kindermann, C., Lynch, J., & Cantor, D. (1997). *Effects of the redesign on victimization estimates* [technical report]. Washington, DC: Bureau of Justice Statistics.

Klaus, P. (2002) *Crime and the nation's households, 2000*. Washington, DC: Bureau of Justice Statistics Bulletin.

Lauritsen, J. L. (2006). *Evaluation of NCVS methodology and costs: Report for the Bureau of Justice Statistics* [internal memorandum]. Washington, DC.

Law Enforcement Assistance Administration. (1977). *Report concerning the future of the national crime survey* [internal memorandum]. Washington, DC: Author.

Lepkowski, J., & Groves, R. (1986). A mean squared error model for dual frame, mixed mode survey design. *Journal of the American Statistical Association, 81,* 930-937.

McMullan, P. S., Jr., Collins, J. J., Gandossy, R., & Lenski, J. G. (1978). *Analysis of the utility and benefits of the National Crime Survey.* Research Triangle Park, NC: Research Triangle Institute.

Penick, B., & Owens, M. (1976). *Surveying crime.* Washington, DC: National Academy Press.

President's Commission on Law Enforcement and Administration of Justice, Task Force on Assessment. (1967). *Crime and its impact: An assessment* [task force report]. Washington, DC: U.S. Government Printing Office.

Rand, M., Lynch, J., & Cantor, D. (1997). *Criminal victimization, 1972–95* [special report]. Washington, DC: Bureau of Justice Statistics.

Rand, M., & Rennison, C. (2005). Bigger is not necessarily better: An analysis of violence against women estimates from the National Crime Victimization Survey and the National Violence Against Women Survey. *Journal of Quantitative Criminology, 21,* 267-291.

Rand, M., & Saltzman, L. (2003, Winter). The nature and extent of recurring intimate partner violence against women. *Journal of Comparative Family Studies, 4,* 137-149.

Schlesinger, S. (1983). *Objectives for NCS* [internal memorandum]. Washington, DC: Bureau of Justice Statistics.

Skogan, W. G. (1981). *Issues in the measurement of victimization* (NCJ-74682). Washington, DC: U.S. Department of Justice.

U.S. Department of Commerce. (1968). *Report on national needs for criminal justice statistics.* Washington, DC: U.S. Government Printing Office.

Woltman, H. F., & Bushery, J. M. (1977). *Update of the national crime survey panel bias study* [memorandum]. Washington, DC: U.S. Census Bureau.

Survey Assessments of Police Performance

by

Wesley G. Skogan
Institute for Policy Research
Northwestern University

Abstract: *This article considers the British Crime Survey (BCS) as a vehicle for monitoring police performance. The BCS has two complementary foci on the police: monitoring reports of general confidence in the police and tracking encounters between police and the public. These raise substantive and methodological issues, and have implications for survey design. Among these are response validity, or the issue of whether "confidence" questions actually reflect the quality of policing on the ground. We also need to ensure that the measurement process measures what it does with maximal accuracy. This paper reviews validity and reliability issues in the context of assessing general confidence and tracking public encounters with the police. It calls for a program of methodological research to document the error structure of the data and guide improvements and decisions about key features of the survey.*

"BUT THEY ARE JUST PERCEPTIONS"

One objection to the use of surveys to monitor public confidence in police performance in any official way is that "they are just perceptions." The obvious rejoinders that perceptions are important and that they are real in their consequences are certainly true, but those are different matters, and the complaint raises serious issues. At root, it is a response validity question, and the query that needs answering is, "Do survey assessments of the quality of policing measure what they claim to measure?" There are reasons to believe that a significant component of the general confidence in police that is measured by surveys is only tangentially related to the empirical reality of the moment, so the question cannot be put off. If policy makers are seeking survey data to answer the question "How are we doing?" it is not clear that they will always be getting a meaningful answer. After reviewing some of this evidence, I propose that a performance assessment survey is better off focusing on change measures rather than on level measures, a decision with survey design and cost implications.

Validity of Confidence Measures

The research literature provides ample challenges to assumptions about the validity of measures of the general confidence people have in the police. One challenge is issued by research on public encounters with the police (which constitutes an important component of what the police do on the street), and the impact of those experiences on general confidence measures (which are to provide an answer to the "How are we doing?" question). Another challenge comes from research comparing public opinion with independent measures of the quality of policing. Both point to shortfalls in the interpretability of general confidence measures.

Causal Order

An important question is whether experiences that people have recently had with police affect their confidence in the police strongly enough that general confidence measures can be used as an indicator of on-the-ground performance, and especially recent improvements in performance. Research suggests that this is not necessarily the direction in which the causality of attitudes toward the police runs. A study addressing the issue of causal direction found that the effect of recent experiences with the police (as recalled in a survey) on their general confidence was not very large. A counter effect – that of people's general views of the police on how they interpreted their recent experiences – was stronger (Brandl, Frank, et al., 1994). In the authors' view, people stereotype the police and selectively perceive even their own experiences. Although Brandl and colleagues do not make the link, since their 1994 article social psychologists have begun to stress a parallel hypothesis: that general, preexisting attitudes strongly affect how people interpret their experiences. They find that individuals read their experiences in the light of their prior expectations, perhaps more than specific recent experiences affect their expectations. In any slice of time, general attitudes affect people's evaluations of their experiences, rather than the reverse. If further research on the direction-of-causality issue (which is greatly needed) indicates that this is the case, it challenges the assumption that confidence measures are useful for answering the question "How are we doing?"

Asymmetry of Impact

There is also evidence that any impact of the public's direct experiences on their confidence in the police is asymmetrical. That is, police get little or no credit for delivering professional service, while bad experiences deeply influence views of their performance and even legitimacy. This brings into question whether positive experiences that people have recently had with police affect their confidence to such an extent that confidence measures can be used as an indicator of performance quality.

I examined the asymmetry issue in a recent article on public contacts with police (Skogan, 2006a). It is based on self-report survey data from Chicago assessing police-initiated and citizen-initiated contacts with police. Like the BCS, the survey screened for recent encounters and asked six follow-up questions about the nature of any contacts. Overall, about 20% of adults recalled being stopped by the Chicago police in a year, and half reported contacting them about some matter. A majority of these respondents recalled a favorable experience, even when they were stopped. The study addressed the relationship between the positive or negative character of those experiences and a six-question index of confidence in police performance and their effectiveness in addressing community problems. Statistically, the impact of having a bad experience was 4 to 14 times as great as that of having a positive experience. Worse, the coefficients associated with having a good experience – including being treated fairly and politely, and receiving service that was prompt and helpful – were not statistically different from zero. Bad police-initiated and bad citizen-initiated encounters both had large negative consequences, with the latter actually having a stronger effect. This does not mean that bad police work, as assessed from the public's side of encounters, was common; on the contrary, most respondents gave the police high marks even in police-initiated traffic and foot stops. However, all of this good police work counted for little, when it came to the public's expressions of confidence in the police.

So strong was the asymmetry in the Chicago data that in another section of the 2006 paper I replicated this finding using surveys of residents of seven other urban areas located in three different countries, including a BCS urban subsample for England and Wales. The pattern was everywhere the same, in places ranging from St. Petersburg in Florida to St. Petersburg in the Russian Federation. It is consistent with findings reported for the British Crime Survey, in which the most favorable attitudes are reported by those who have had *no* recent contact with police; those who had contacts of any kind are generally unfavorable (Allen, Edmonds, Patterson, & Smith, 2006). If good practice is not reflected straightforwardly in general confidence measures, this also challenges the assumption that confidence measures answer the question "How are we doing?"

Confounding Variables

Another reason for skepticism is my experience in rating the quality of community policing programs in Chicago's neighborhoods. There, confounding variables apparently overwhelmed any evidence of direct program effects on public opinion. This study concluded that public opinion did not reflect in any straightforward way the quality of policing that we had directly observed on the ground. This also questions the assumption that confidence measures answer the question "How are we doing?"

In the study, we conducted fieldwork in 12 police beats. The areas were chosen to reflect a broad range of race and class configurations. We interviewed police officers, attended beat meetings and surveyed those in attendance, rode along with officers on patrol, reviewed their formal plans identifying priority issues, and discussed the local situation with community informants. Our community policing quality ratings were developed along four major dimensions: the commitment and support of district management, beat team leadership, beat team activities, and the efforts of the district's specialized neighborhood relations unit to mobilize residents in support of community policing projects. Ratings were developed on 4 to 10 subdimensions for each of these, and a cluster analysis based on all of the ratings was used to construct a summary, four-category ranking of each beat. We labeled the twelve programs either "excellent," "reasonable," "struggling," or "failing." All of the details regarding the study are presented in Skogan, Hartnett et al., 1999.[1]

In parallel, we conducted a telephone survey of the study areas. A total of 1,290 households were surveyed, including at least 100 respondents in each of the 12 beats. Respondents were selected from telephone listings, and the response rate for the survey was 78%. Interviews were conducted in English and Spanish, a must in Chicago. Among the questions, respondents were asked to rate police working in their neighborhood in terms of their "responsiveness to community concerns," "dealing with the problems that really concern people in your neighborhood," and "working together with residents in your neighborhood to solve local problems." These questions targeted key goals of the city's community policing program. In each case, police were rated as "very good," "good," "fair," or "poor." Responses to these three questions were highly interrelated, and were combined together to produce an overall opinion index.

The survey results were unrelated to our laboriously arrived-at on-site observations and rankings, which are illustrated in Figure 1. On the

Figure 1: Observational and survey measures of policing quality.

Observational Policing Quality Index

horizontal axis, it arrays police units from "failing" to "excellent," based on the fieldwork. On the vertical axis, it arrays beats by the average rating score awarded by residents in our beat surveys. The names we gave the areas (all described in detail in Skogan et al. [1999]) are presented to mark where each beat fell. Figure 1 also presents a regression line, which indicates that there was no relationship between the two measures.

It is apparent in Figure 1 that opinion was not clearly linked to ratings of police on the ground. The best policing was being delivered in Two-Turf, a name we bestowed on this beat because half its residents were Mexican and half Puerto Rican (but all were poor). Police were also doing an excellent job in Bungalow Belt (a White, blue-collar area) and Norte (a stable, largely Puerto Rican neighborhood). Resident ratings of those three areas were all over the map, however, ranging from the lowest to the second-highest in the study. On the other hand, policing in Stir Fry stunk; it was our lowest-rated beat. The population there was evenly divided among Whites, African Americans, Asians, and Latinos. Policing was not much better in Pride, one of the most upscale Black communities in Chicago, and in Old Guard, which was also a middle-class African American enclave. Pride and Old Guard were the third- and fourth-rated policing operations in the eyes of the public, however. Fiesta, where police could care less about the community, was completely Mexican-American in character. Yet except for Fiesta, public ratings of the police working in these areas were relatively positive.

As this sociological tour suggests, what was really affecting opinion rankings were race and class. Property Values and Bungalow Belt were our only predominately White areas, and Old Guard and Pride were certainly the equal of Bungalow Belt when it came to their middle-class status. Their's were the four most highly rated policing units, based on public opinion. The lowest opinion ratings were from residents of three almost uniformly Latino (and mostly low-income) beats, and from poor African Americans living in Rebuilding.

Although a modest study, it may be the only one that holds popular views of the police up against an independent measure of the quality of service being delivered, in order to document the relationship between them. If our field ratings are taken as the gold standard against which to assess the convergent validity of the survey measure of policing quality, it was zero. Public opinion was measuring something, but it was not policing on the ground.

In a report published by the Home Office, I noted in the introduction that "[T]his report focuses on people who have had contact with the police because those people's experiences and opinions should give a better basis for assessing the police's efforts" (Skogan, 1994, pp. 1-2). However, direction-of-causality issues, strong asymmetry in the impact of the good and bad service delivered by police, the zero credit that the public gives to police actions even when they themselves describe them in positive fashion, and – on the evidence of the observational study – the lack of fit between independent measures of policing quality and public opinion say otherwise. They provide fuel to the view that survey-based confidence measures do not, without considerable massaging, adequately represent the reality of policing on the ground at the time. These findings are also bad news for police administrators intent on solidifying their support among voters, taxpayers, and the consumers of police services. The message of the asymmetry finding is, unfortunately, "You can't win, you can just cut your losses." No matter what you do, it only counts when it goes against you (Skogan, 2006a, p. 119).

None of these validity issues is unique to the police. There has been a tremendous amount of research on the relative merits of objective versus subjective measures of service quality by students of "urban service delivery," a subcategory in the field of public administration. They still have not figured it out. In 2003, Kelly issued a discouraging summary of the state of the art: "[D]ecades of research on citizen satisfaction have not yielded a decisive answer to the validity question – whether citizens' evaluations of service quality reflect objective changes in service quality" (Kelly, 2003, p. 857). Research cited in my 2006 (Skogan, 2006a) article indicates that asymmetry of effects is the rule rather than the exception when it comes to subjective measures of the quality of service delivered by government agencies. In the case of the police, we are interested in utilizing subjective measures of performance quality because survey indicators seemingly go directly to the heart of our concerns about policing: that it is fair and effective, and reinforces or rebuilds their legitimacy. Most of the quality measures that fall out of police information systems, on the other hand, concern inputs (money, people), activities (how fast they drive to crime scenes, in order to fill out reports), and intermediate outputs (cases solved), but they do not tell us much about important outcomes that we seek to achieve. This does not mean, however, that subjective measures can be accepted at face value.

Assessing Changes in Confidence in Police

One way out of the "they are just perceptions" box may be to shift focus from *levels* of confidence to *changes* in confidence over time. With an appropriate survey design, changes over time can be benchmarked against the level of early measures in the series. Earlier measures should incorporate (for example) stable race and class differences in area predispositions toward the police. This would highlight later changes in assessments of the nature and quality of policing. Focusing on changes in confidence reflects the logic of evaluations of innovations in policing, which typically gather "before" measures that provide benchmarks for assessing shifts in "after" measures, because the first-wave measures incorporate many potentially confounding factors. Note that this recommendation is not low cost. It raises the stakes considerably in terms of the frequency with which areas should be revisited. It also has implications for local-area sample sizes, because the design would need to have the capacity of reliably identifying change over time. The BCS is already producing some area estimates of confidence in police, including for 10 Government Office Regions (Allen et al., 2006) and for 42 subregions within them (Nicholas, Povey, Walker, & Kershaw, 2005). It might be possible to push further down the geographical ladder for confidence measures, but monitoring encounters with the police at the local level – an issue to be considered in the next section – will be more demanding.

A Chicago Example

The BCS is not conducted in the context of field experiments, however, and does not require a research design that aides in inferring causation. Instead, it could become an exercise in repeated measures at the area level. An example of how opinions can change in a context in which police are innovating rapidly can be found in the results of surveys monitoring public attitudes in Chicago. An evaluation of community policing monitored public opinion in a series of surveys conducted between 1993 and 2003 (Skogan, 2006b). Relying on one or two very general satisfaction questions would reveal little about the shortfalls and accomplishments of the police; rather, I worked out a set of questions that tapped the major goals of the department for this and related projects. The resulting 10 questions balanced coverage of the substantive domains of interest and scarce questionnaire space. Because single-item measures of attitudes are mostly dominated by error variance, I strove to have at least three questions addressing

Figure 2: Trends in confidence in Chicago police.

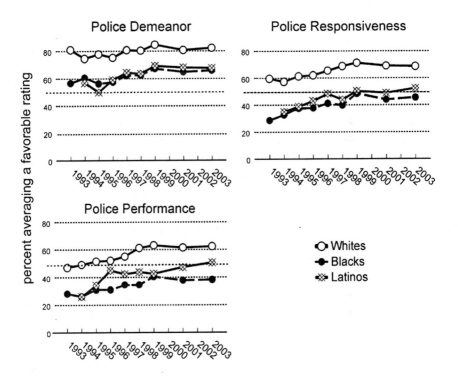

each domain. The resulting subscales were quite reliable in light of that still limited number.

As illustrated in Figure 2, during the evaluation period there were observable changes for the better in perceptions of several aspects of police service. Opinion improved steadily between 1993 and 1999, before leveling off at a new high in the after 2000. In addition, on every measure, positive changes in opinion were apparent among Whites, African Americans, and Latinos alike. At the same time, substantial gaps between the races were apparent in the first survey, and those gaps remained about the same despite the positive trends. The opinion gaps are equivalent to the race (and class) predispositions illustrated in Figure 1, except that they can be accounted for using repeated measures.

Chicagoans were asked to rate police using 10 questions representing three opinion dimensions. The first was *demeanor*, which was measured by responses to questions asking about the politeness, concern, helpfulness, and fairness of police in their area. Police *responsiveness* was measured by responses to questions about their responsiveness to community concerns, "dealing with problems that really concern people in your neighborhood," and "working together with residents in your neighborhood to solve local problems." Police *performance* of their traditional duties was tracked by questions about how good a job they were doing preventing crime, helping victims, and "keeping order on the streets and sidewalks." Figure 2 charts the percentage of respondents averaging a positive rating (the two best of four rating categories) on each index. Separate trend lines are presented for Whites, African Americans, and Latinos. The 1993 survey was conducted only in English, so the data point for Latinos is omitted in that year.

Before community policing began, almost two thirds of the respondents already averaged a positive score on the police demeanor index. As in our neighborhood studies, there were notable differences between the races in how they initially rated the police. In general, Whites perceived that police treated people well even in the early 1990s, and there was not much room for improvement. However, positive perceptions of police demeanor rose by about 10 percentage points among both Latino and African American respondents and ended on a high note. Perceptions of police responsiveness to community concerns improved steadily until 1999; overall, the responsiveness index rose by nearly 20 percentage points during the 1993-1999 period. Perceptions of responsiveness went up most between African Americans and Latinos, rising by almost 20 percentage points between 1993 and 1999. The views of Whites, which were more positive even before the program began, improved by about 10 percentage points. Finally, at the outset Chicagoans were mostly negative in their views of how well police performed their traditional tasks. Yet over time, the index measuring this aspect of police service improved significantly, rising from a low of 36% in 1994 to a high of 51% in 2003.

Note again that, for all of these changes, the gaps between the races closed not at all. The earliest surveys provided a baseline documenting interfacial differences in opinions of the police that persisted until the very end of the series. Yet having taken that into account, positive trends in the data were also apparent.

Sample Size and Statistical Power

Shortchanging on area-level sample sizes would be a mistake. Other things being equal, the smaller the sample size, the larger any changes in reports of policing quality would need to be in order to be statistically reliable. Small samples could raise the bar impossibly high for local police.[2] How big is big enough? A sample size sufficient for detecting a 10% shift in general confidence for an analytic area would be about 160 respondents in each wave.[3] A 10% shift in confidence over a multiyear time frame is a plausible one. For police responsiveness (see Figure 2), the average year-to-year shift in opinion in Chicago during the 1990s was about 5%. The 2003-2004 BCS sample targeted completing 600-700 sample interviews in each police force area (and 37,000 overall), which would have allowed making small-area estimates of general confidence for about four subareas within each police force area, as they were defined at that time. A subject for discussion is the administrative level of the police at which the findings of surveys would be of interest. The priorities from that discussion could be matched to these figures, to determine if the current survey could provide the desired coverage.

Of course, if analysts are interested in the views and experiences of subgroups, the sample requirements would be the same at that level. In Chicago the most important were Latinos who could not speak English and had to be interviewed in Spanish, and they constituted about 16% of the overall sample. Based on the same assumptions, to track a year-to-year change reliably in a group this size required overall samples of about 1,000 respondents in each wave. In any survey, subgroups that are targeted to be of analytic interest will have to be chosen judiciously. Two groups of great interest are people who have contacted the police or have been stopped by them; they are considered next.

"YOU CAN'T BE 'THE FRIEND OF THE PEOPLE' AND DO YOUR JOB"

What I hope my informant, the Chicago police officer who is quoted above, meant was that cool professionalism and an aloof manner, rather than the "customer-friendly" policing that was being discussed in the front of the room, was the appropriate demeanor for "real" police. His statement is a reminder that many officers do not aspire to be friendly and accessible, believing it puts them at risk on the street. However, the quality of service rendered when police and the public come in contact is one of the things that administrators can actually hope to control. Through their training and supervision practices, departments have some capacity to shape the relationship between residents and officers working the street. Whether police are polite or abrasive, concerned or aloof, and helpful or unresponsive to the obvious needs of the people they encounter depends importantly on actions taken by department leaders. This led a National Research Council review panel to recommend more attention to what was dubbed "process-oriented policing" (Skogan & Frydl, 2004), in addition to community- and problem-oriented policing. The trick is to identify the dimensions of behavior that are important, and where police should fall on them.

Screening and Recall Issues

Currently, the BCS hands respondents a card displaying 17 common reasons that respondents could have contacted the police in the past 12 months, to help them recall incidents. On the police-initiated side, the survey asks about vehicle and pedestrian stops in the same recall period. Follow-up questions are then asked about the most recent of each kind of contact that respondents recall having had. This procedure produces a reasonable random sample of all experiences, and presumably the most recent are most likely to be fresh in respondents' minds. However, as I note further on, the domain of police-initiated encounters is a larger one. There exists a broad range of police-initiated interactions that probably fall below the threshold of being a stop, and whether or not they are included makes a very large difference in the yield of the screener.

A key issue here is that we have no idea what the optimal length of the recall period is for accurately remembering encounters with the police. The current period is the 12 months preceding the interview, a date which is read to each respondent as part of the question. The length of the recall period is one of the most important design decisions for the victimization component of surveys, and a large number of field tests were conducted to determine how far back in the past crime victims could be relied upon to remember events. It turns out that the "time-dependent forgetting curve" is very steep, with victimizations occurring further than 3 months in the past going unrecalled with alarming frequency (for a review of these studies see Skogan, 1981). There is no reason to think that the various ways and reasons for which people encounter the police are any different from victimization with regard to time-dependent forgetting. The recall length decision is fraught with cost implications. A tighter recall window probably will yield a smaller number of more accurately recalled encounters. To ask the same questions as in the past (did they think they were treated fairly? were they satisfied with the experience?) would almost surely require larger samples due to the decreased yield (albeit greater accuracy) of each survey interview.

There is also no reason to think that the task of retrieving reports of encounters with police is immune from many of the other shortcomings of victimization measures. We know that victims underrecall events involving private or embarrassing circumstances, for example, when they were themselves culpable to some degree, when there was a relationship between the parties, when there was no insurance claim to be made, when alcohol was involved, and when the incident was not very serious. A long string of hypotheses about differential recall rates for different kinds of police-public encounters comes easily to mind. Research in North Carolina indicates that recall biases vary by race, with African Americans known to have been stopped reporting a smaller fraction of the criterion events, thus possibly underrepresenting the extent of racial disparity in police-initiated stops (Tomaskovic-Devey, Wright, Czaja, & Miller, 2006). Based on the "asymmetry" research described earlier, I fear that negatively rated encounters are much more readily recalled than positive rated ones, overrepresenting the extent to which they are not "the friend of the people."

The legitimacy of any official use of survey-based evaluative measures of police-public encounters could depend upon a program of research that identifies the error structure of the data, and ensures that the questionnaire design is optimal for maximizing the accuracy of the data. The most important tool for doing so would be reverse record checks. They would involve selecting samples of persons known to have encountered the police and then testing questionnaire drafts to determine the rate at which the criterion encounters are recalled in interviews. The encounter samples would be selected to represent dimensions along which we expect difficulties with recall – including the length of time in the past in which they occurred – across indicators of event seriousness, when respondents were themselves culpable, and other factors. Respondents would also be chosen to represent population groups presenting a range of challenges to response validity, for example, by immigration status and age.

Sample Size

Of course, a big impediment to producing reliable estimates of encounter characteristics for smaller geographical areas is sample size. As with victimization, features of encounters and those involved in them can only be ascertained among those recalling experiences at the screener stage. Special challenges are posed by important but less frequent forms of encounters, including pedestrian stops and those involving relatively small population groups. In the United States, nontraffic police-initiated encounters very heavily target young minority males, a group that usually proves particularly elusive in surveys. Another key factor would be what questions about encounters the survey intends to answer; just knowing the percentages involved in them is not very revealing. An example considered further on is the rate at which individuals who are stopped under various circumstances are searched.

In any event, incorporating encounters with police into the area-level agenda of the BCS would doubtless call for scrapping of the current supplement-based policing module in favor of questionnaire items that would be administered to all main and booster sample respondents. In parallel with local-area victimization estimates, only the more frequent kinds of encounters between the police and the public could be examined.

When it comes to monitoring encounters, all sample-size calculations will begin with estimates of the proportion of respondents who will have experiences with the police to report upon. Currently the BCS finds that about 20% of respondents nationwide recall initiating an encounter with the police, and about 22% recall being stopped. This will vary by area – a large victimization survey estimated that 38% of Londoners sought contact with the police in a year's time (during 1999-2000), and 12% were stopped (Fitzgerald, Hough, Joseph, & Qureshi, 2002). Some of this difference is doubtless due to methodology. When the London study added being "approached" by the police to the "stopped" count, the police-initiated contact rate rose from 12% to 24%, and I think the latter definition more closely approximates that of the BCS.

The next most important subset of respondents is those who recall being searched during a police-initiated encounter. Searches raise the ante in police-citizen encounters. In studies of satisfaction with police, being stopped has a much smaller effect than the increment of dissatisfaction added by a search. Compared to stops, searches are much more tightly defined and monitored by the Police and Criminal Evidence Act. The London survey put the search rate at 37% of pedestrian stops and 22% of vehicle stops, and notes that these rates seemed much higher than elsewhere in Britain. Any special focus on persons who are stopped in any BCS police monitor would impose an even greater burden on the sample.

Because of the importance of certain low-frequency public experiences that are heavily concentrated among harder-to-reach populations, it might also be worthwhile considering conducting supplemental interviews with samples of persons known to have encountered the police. This would involve stepping outside of the BCS sampling frame, into the world of jurisdiction-level "customer satisfaction" surveys. The long list of problems in conducting these surveys is outside of the scope of this chapter, but they too are legion.

Evaluative Content

Miller, Bland, and Quinton (2001) review British research on factors that influence how people evaluate encounters with police, and recommend a set of evaluative dimensions. Thirty years of research on the views of crime victims and others who have called the police, and on the subjects of police investigations, have documented the importance of satisfaction with police fairness, courtesy, understanding, and capability. Satisfaction is higher when officers take adequate time to inform members of the public of how they would handle a complaint and what could be expected to come of their case. Victims who later receive a follow-up contact from police are more favorably inclined as a result, regardless of the news they receive. Highly rated officers are those who were thought to have made a thorough examination of the scene, informed victims about their situation, offered advice, listened to the parties involved, and showed concern for their plight. Satisfaction is very consistently linked to perceived response time as well. Police-initiated stops are also better received when subjects are given a good reason for the stop, and when it is conducted in a manner that does not belittle subjects in front of bystanders. Satisfaction plummets when officers make unproductive and apparently uncalled for searches, a rationale for economy in police aggressiveness. The more of these details that can be included in monitoring surveys, the more closely police managers can make use of the data to identify areas of practice that may be engendering dissatisfaction with the quality of police service.

CONCLUSION

This chapter considered two objections that doubtless will arise if serious managerial and evaluative uses are made of opinion data regarding the police. The objection that "it's just attitudes" implies that survey-based ratings are so abstracted from policing on the ground that they provide an uncertain guide to the service that is actually being delivered. There is considerable truth to this charge, but measures of change over time are more defensible than one-time measures of levels of confidence in police. The chapter also stressed the importance of ensuring that survey methodologies are employed that produce optimally accurate recall of encounters with police, and that research be conducted to illuminate problems and improve upon our ability to accurately assess encounters that respondents may be inclined to underreport. Underlying all of these specific concerns is a larger one: that the legitimacy of including public opinion on the list of official statistical performance indicators will be enhanced by directly addressing them proactively, rather than waiting for their inevitable appearance in the political realm.

Address correspondence to: Wesley G. Skogan, Northwestern University, Institute for Policy Research, Evanston, IL 60208, U.S.A.; e-mail: skogan@northwestern.edu

NOTES

1. The book is unfortunately out of print, but an exact digital image is available at www.skogan.org
2. The "statistical conclusion validity" question in every study is whether the data are robust enough to detect an effect of reasonable size. Robustness involves both sample size and the reliability of the measures. Small samples and bad measures can lead to false conclusions.
3. As illustration. I used sample means and standard deviations for my Chicago police performance scale, forecast an expected change in the mean of 10%, set the significance level at .05 and the power of the test at .9. For this hypothetical change to be statistically reliable, samples of 158 respondents would be needed in each wave.

REFERENCES

Allen, J., Edmonds, S., Patterson, A., & Smith, D. (2006). *Policing and the criminal justice system – Public confidence and perceptions: Findings from the 2004/2005 British Crime Survey.* London: Home Office.

Brandl, S. G., Frank, J., Worden, R. W., & Bynum, T. S. (1994). Global and specific attitudes toward the police: Disentangling the relationship. *Justice Quarterly, 11,* 119-134.

Fitzgerald, M., Hough, M., Joseph, I., & Qureshi, T. (2002). *Policing for London.* Devon, England: Willan.

Kelly, J. M. (2003). Citizen satisfaction and administrative performance measures: Is there really a link? *Urban Affairs Review, 38,* 855-866.

Miller, J., Bland, N., & Quinton, P. (2001). A challenge for police-community relations: Rethinking stop and search in England and Wales. *European Journal on Criminal Policy and Research, 9,* 71-93.

Nicholas, S., Povey, D., Walker, A., & Kershaw, C. (2005, July). *Crime in England and Wales 2004/2005.* London: Home Office Statistical Bulletin 11/05.

Skogan, W. G. (1981). *Issues in the measurement of victimization.* Washington, DC: U.S. Government Printing Office.

Skogan, W. G. (1994). *Contacts between police and the public: A British Crime Survey report.* Home Office Research Series. London: Her Majesty's Stationery Office.

Skogan, W. G. (2006a). Asymmetry in the impact of encounters with police. *Police & Society, 6,* 99-126.

Skogan, W. G. (2006b). *Police and community in Chicago: A tale of three cities.* New York: Oxford University Press.

Skogan, W. G., & Frydl, K. (2004). *Fairness and effectiveness in policing: The evidence.* Washington, DC: National Academies Press.

Skogan, W. G., Hartnett, S. M., DuBois, J., Comey, J. T., Kaiser, M., & Lovig, J. H. (1999). *On the beat: Police and community problem solving.* Boulder, CO: Westview.

Tomaskovic-Devey, D., Wright, C. P., Czaja, R., & Miller, K. (2006). Self-reports of police speeding stops by race: Results from the North Carolina reverse record check survey. *Journal of Quantitative Criminology, 22,* 279-298.

Survey Assessments of Police Performance in the British Crime Survey

by

Jonathan Allen
Research Development and Statistics Directorate
U.K. Home Office

Abstract: *This chapter provides a short introduction to the use that is currently made of the British Crime Survey (BCS) in measuring performance, in particular that of police forces in England and Wales, within the wider context of using surveys as performance measurement tools. The key role the BCS plays in the Home Office's Policing Performance Assessment Framework (PPAF) is examined, and the level at which data from the survey can usefully be provided is detailed, with reference to some recent findings.*

MEASURING PERFORMANCE THROUGH SURVEYS

In recent years, the BCS has become a key tool in measuring government performance-related targets, increasingly so as successive governments have refined their approaches to the performance management of public services. The BCS's capabilities in performance management were substantially enhanced by methodological revisions to the BCS implemented in 2001. These saw the survey move to continuous interviewing, adopt calibration weighting, and effectively double its sample size, to about 40,000 interviews per year. This increase in sample size has allowed much more precise estimates, and perhaps more important, greater depth and detail. Most notably, the survey provides summary-level data at police force area level that underpins some of the police performance assessments. In implementing these changes, great care was exercised to ensure the consistency of resulting estimates at the national level and the representativeness of those now available at force level. (For recent key results of the BCS, see Nicholas et al., 2005; Walker et al., 2006.)

The BCS has then been increasingly mined to provide baseline data and target monitoring for several wide-ranging government priority indicators, from the level of crime to perception of drug use in localities. The specific measures the BCS has been called upon to monitor will be summarised below. However, before doing so, it is worth considering some of the strengths and limitations in measuring agencies' performance via sample surveys more generally, as these naturally also apply to the BCS.

There are two particular strengths in the use of surveys for performance management. The first is that they provide largely comprehensive estimates of the experience and attitudes of the target population, and can do so consistently over time. This is in contrast to statistics generated through contacts with the agency under evaluation, which are skewed towards those who actually use the service in question. Second, surveys can yield measures that are independent of the agency under evaluation, and seen to be such. These strengths have provided government with a very significant set of new tools for managing public services.

There are counterbalancing limitations, of course. First, a key consideration is the reliance that can be placed in the robustness of outcome data. The sample size needs to be sufficiently large to detect statistically significant changes over time, for example, or across area. With a sample size currently approaching 50,000 per annum, the survey is sensitive to changes over time at the national level, and can also yield quite precise estimates for the 10 regions in England and Wales. Estimates for the 42 police force areas covered by the survey, however, are less precise. The requirement is to have a minimum subsample size of 1,000 for each police force area. This means that only headline measures can be provided and tracked at the police force level. The implicit need to detect changes in performance measures makes this a key limitation to be acknowledged.

Another key consideration is the temporal delay incurred through data collection, analysis, and presentation. With large-scale complex surveys, this delay can be substantial and potentially translates into diminished salience of a policy issue. This is especially true if a year's worth of data is required to reliably detect change over time and to counter the effect of short-term variation in the data. This is particularly acute for issues that rapidly gain prominence in the public consciousness; identity theft is an example. The results from the BCS are updated quarterly for regular monitoring purposes; it is necessary, however, to report on a full year of interview data for victimisation measures in order to have sufficient sample to detect changes reliably over time. This means that any analysis of trends needs to compare, at a minimum, results from the most recent 12-months' interviews with those in the previous 12 months. Thus, surveys often are not placed best to provide timely data on which to base performance measurement, especially if updates are needed frequently and with a minimum of delay between data capture and presentation.

In order to provide force-level data from the BCS it is also necessary to ask the relevant question to the whole sample. There is of course the tension here, in the context of assessing local performance through a national survey, of ensuring such questions are of relevance at the local level. Further, there remains the difficulty of maintaining consistency in performance-monitoring questions whilst retaining flexibility to introduce questions on emerging areas of interest. A further consideration is the limited depth of response that can be ascertained, given the rigidity necessitated by the quantitative survey format. Further, performance measures based on such batteries of items are in turn potentially limited in their scope.

Finally, it is worth considering the presentational problems arising from the use of survey data to inform performance measurement. Complexity is inherent when dealing with a survey tool, such as the BCS, operating with fixed recall periods that result in victimisation periods that do not directly map to interview periods. This complexity is antithetical to simple and transparent presentation and interpretation, which is often the goal in this arena. It is also often necessary to educate users of survey data in these various issues, as well as in those of statistical interpretation to facilitate correct use of the resulting data. All of the mentioned caveats potentially limit the survey tool as an instrument for performance measurement, and should be borne in mind in any such endeavour.

With the benefit of hindsight, using the BCS as a tool for "performance managing" the police looks like an inevitable development. The value of the survey was always seen in its ability not simply to count crime and track crime trends but also to chart people's attitudes to crime and justice and their experience of the criminal justice system. The various suites of questions on the police and policing have always been of particular value – even if their analysis was originally conceived of as research rather than organisational monitoring. With the expansion of the survey from 2001, and its increasing capacity to fill the role of performance measuring and monitoring, a key area that it has been called upon to provide such is in relation to monitoring the performance of the police nationally and at individual police force level. (In fact, the rationale for the expansion was partially provided by the desire to produce force-level estimates.)

CURRENT HOME OFFICE PERFORMANCE MEASURES

Policing Performance Assessment Framework

Over the past few years, a framework for police performance has been developed by the Home Office's Police Standards Unit (now rebadged as the Police and Crime Standards Directorate) and Her Majesty's Inspectorate of Constabulary (HMIC), with support from the Association of Police Authorities (APA) and the Association of Chief Police Officers (ACPO), with the overall aim of improving police performance. The framework is termed the Policing Performance Assessment Framework (PPAF). The PPAF concept originated in 2002-2003, at the time of the first National Policing Plan (NPP). Until the development of PPAF, the police service had tended to fall behind other public services in developing transparent performance assessment procedures.

Police performance assessments are intended to measure, compare, and assess the performance of forces in England and Wales in a clear, accessible, fair, and efficient manner. The assessments are used then not only to provide the public with a summary of performance, but also in the strategic management of forces. Once national priorities were decided and set out in the NPP and objectives determined, the performance indicators themselves were established.

PPAF operates by making two assessments for each force in seven key performance areas, based on a combination of performance data (see SPIs discussion in next section) and professional judgment. It is in the former arena that the BCS plays an integral part, across a number of the seven key performance areas:

- reducing crime
- investigating crime

- promoting safety

- providing assistance

- citizen focus

- resource use

- local policing.

Assessments in PPAF are made covering a wide range of police activities. In actual fact, in 2005-2006, 29 performance indicators were assessed, and HMIC used professional standards and judgement to assess 23 key areas of policing; these combined 54 components were then aggregated to form the assessment in the seven key areas.

Two sorts of comparative assessment are made for each force. First, there is a process of direct comparison to its peers (its "family" of comparator forces[1]). For this peer comparison, four "delivery" grades are possible: excellent, good, fair, or poor (although for BCS data only three grades are used – poor, fair, good/excellent). Peer comparison is made because forces operate within different environments and contexts and it is therefore natural and expected that performance will consequently vary – hence, it would be misleading to compare every force to each other. The second assessment relates to each force's "direction of travel" in its performance over time. Three direction grades are possible – improved, stable, or deteriorated.[2]

Statutory Performance Indicators

Statutory Performance Indicator (SPI) is the term used to describe the quantitative data (including of course the BCS measures) that are used to generate and monitor key aspects of police performance, which are then used in the assessments. They are set each year following consultation with partners. Several SPIs across the seven key performance areas are measured using the BCS at force level. These relate both to victimisation risk and perceptual measures, including fear of crime, antisocial behaviour, drug use and dealing, and confidence in the local police.

The victimisation element looks separately at risk of personal and household crime, whereas fear of crime and antisocial behaviour are primarily composite measures. Fear of crime is represented by three separate measures. Antisocial behaviour uses one combined measure based on responses to seven individual questions. The final key performance area in

PPAF, local policing, is a new method of assessing local performance based on setting local targets. Until this is in effect, however, local policing assessments for 2004-2005 and 2005-2006 have been made using the BCS public confidence in the local police SPI indicator, and an HMIC assessment of neighbourhood policing and community engagement. For this public confidence in local policing measure, other questions in the BCS are utilised to help understand the response to this SPI based on identified components of confidence in the police.[3]

As well as in the PPAF annual publication, the SPI data from the BCS are regularly provided to the Police and Crime Standards Directorate (formerly Police Standards Unit), both for individual forces and their most similar families, for inclusion on the iQuanta Web tool. This is a closed, password-protected Internet system accessible by forces, which supports the performance management of policing by enabling such crime data to be compared readily. The data are reported on once per quarter, for a rolling year's worth of interview data (data is also routinely provided to the Joint Performance Information Tool (JPIT).

Public Service Agreements

The BCS is also used at the national level for the Home Office Public Service Agreement (PSA) targets. The Home Office has several PSAs (at the time of writing), and BCS statistics form the key components of PSA1 and PSA2 and also contributes to PSA 4. PSA1 aims to reduce crime by 15% overall and further in high-crime areas, as measured by BCS victimization. PSA2 – to reassure the public, reduce the fear of crime and antisocial behaviour, and build confidence in the criminal justice system – is measured by the relevant BCS SPI questions noted earlier, with additional input from BCS questions on victim and witness satisfaction. The linkage of the PSAs, the SPIs, and the National Policing Plan is set out in Table 1.

Contextual Findings

The provision of BCS data consistently across forces has significant advantages over the alternative of individual forces being tasked to provide such for performance management. This would doubtless result in a plethora of varying survey designs, meaning direct interforce comparison would be severely limited if they were possible at all. There would also be significant

Table 1: PSAs, SPIs, and NPP Priorities

PSAs 2005/06-2007/08	PSA MEASURES 2005/06-2007/08	STATUTORY PERFORMANCE INDICATORS 2006/07	KEY PRIORITIES 2006-2009
1. Reduce crime by 15% and further in high crime areas	a BCS: overall crime	4a BCS risk of personal crime (proxy) 4b BCS risk of household crime (proxy)	Reduce overall crime by 15% by 2007-08 and more in high-crime areas
	b Recorded crime BCS comparator	5b violent crime 5f acquisitive crime	
		5e life-threatening/gun crime 8c value of cash and confiscation orders	Tackle serious/organised crime through improved intelligence and information sharing between partners
2. Reassure the public, reduce the fear of crime and anti-social behaviour, and build confidence in the criminal justice system without compromising fairness	a BCS: worry about becoming a victim	10a BCS fear of crime	Provide every area in England and Wales with dedicated, visible, accessible, and responsive neighbourhood policing teams; and reduce public perception of anti-social behaviour
	b BCS: feeling that ASB is a big problem	10b BCS perceptions of anti-social behaviour	
	c BCS: thinking local police do a good job	2a BCS: thinking local police do a good job	
	d BCS: confidence in CJS effectiveness		

(continued)

Table 1: *(continued)*

PSAs 2005/06-2007/08	PSA MEASURES 2005/06-2007/08	STATUTORY PERFORMANCE INDICATORS 2006/07	KEY PRIORITIES 2006-2009
	e HOCS: CJS agencies treat people equally including disproportionality measures	3b victim satisfaction by ethnicity 3c searches leading to arrest by ethnicity 3d detection for violent crime by ethnicity	
	f BCS: victim and witness satisfaction	1a-1e satisfaction of victims (for burglary, violent crime, vehicle crime, and RTCs) 3a satisfaction of victims (for racist incidents)	
		11a police officer time spent on frontline duties 8a domestic violence offences leading to arrest	
3. Improve the delivery of justice by increasing number of crimes where offender is brought to justice to 1.25 million	a Number of offences brought to justice	6b percentage of offences brought to justice 7a percentage of sanction detections	Bring more offences to justice in line with the government's PSA

Table 1: *(continued)*

PSAs 2005/06-2007/08	PSA MEASURES 2005/06-2007/08	STATUTORY PERFORMANCE INDICATORS 2006/07	KEY PRIORITIES 2006-2009
4. Reduce the harm caused by illegal drugs . . .	a Drug Harm Index (DHI)	10c *Perceptions of local drug use/drug dealing*	
. . . including increasing the number of drug misusing offenders entering treatment through the CJS	b Drug misusing offenders entering treatment		
5. Reduce unfounded asylum claims as part of a wider strategy to tackle abuse of the immigration laws and promote controlled legal migration	a Unfounded asylum claims		
6. Increase voluntary and community engagement, especially amongst those at risk of social exclusion	a Voluntary activity by those at risk of exclusion		
	b Voluntary and community sector contribution to delivering public services		

(continued)

Table 1: *(continued)*

PSAs 2005/06-2007/08	PSA MEASURES 2005/06-2007/08	STATUTORY PERFORMANCE INDICATORS 2006/07	KEY PRIORITIES 2006-2009
7. Reduce race inequalities and build community cohesion		3e police recruits from minority ethnic groups	
	a Perceptions of racial discrimination	*component of 2a (enhanced BCS measure of confidence)*	
	b Perceptions of community cohesion	*component of 2a (enhanced BCS measure of confidence)*	
SPIs not linked directly to SR04 PSA measures		3g percentage of female officers	
		9a number of people killed/ seriously injured in RTCs	
		12a delivery of efficiency targets	
		13a police officer sickness	
		13b police staff sickness	

Reproduced from *Guidance on Statutory Performance Indicators for Policing 2006/07 ANNEXES (2006)*. BCS-related measures are italicised.

cost implications. Even when providing a minimum of 1000 interviews in each force area per annum, however, only headline victimisation data can be provided at this geographical level – risk of household and personal crime, or key volume crime rates. It is not possible to monitor change over time at force level in rarer individual crime types or in victim satisfaction with services. In fact, separate surveys of user satisfaction are conducted for each force and included as an element within PPAF. Given that the BCS was originally designed with national-level estimates in mind, in order to provide the equivalent detail of data at force level would be prohibitively expensive. Notwithstanding these problems (and issues of industry capacity), there remains demand for highly detailed measures at the force level.

Despite these limitations, the BCS has provided some provocative, valuable, and possibly counterintuitive findings relating to police performance at the national level in recent years, additional to the headline data provided within police performance and PSA monitoring. The BCS has consistently shown the police to be the most highly rated agency within the criminal justice system; in 2005-2006, 51% of the population believed the police were doing an excellent or good job nationally. In 2004-2005, victims were less likely than nonvictims to give high ratings to CJS agencies in general or the police in particular. The survey has indicated that attitudes towards the police are negatively related to personal experiences of the police, both locally and in general. The local police were more likely to be rated as doing an excellent or good job by people who had no contact with them over the previous year than by those who had been in contact with them over this period. Among people who were stopped on foot, ratings of the local police were particularly low (see Figure 1).

The survey has also shown the variation in levels of confidence in the police, both locally and nationally, by various sociodemographics. For example, in 2004-2005, White respondents had a lower level of confidence in their local police (48%) and the police in general (48%) than Asian (53% and 52%), Black (56% and 52%), and Chinese and other (60% and 56%, respectively) respondents.

At a national level, the survey has also provided consistent information on victim satisfaction (Figure 2), and aspects thereof. In 2004-2005, more than half of all adult victims reported that they were satisfied with the police response (58%), the same proportion as the previous year – leaving a substantial unsatisfied minority. Victims who had face-to-face contact with the police were more likely to be satisfied with the way the police handled the matter than those who did not. Victims also felt they had

Allen

Figure 1: Rating of the local police by type of contact, 2004/05 BCS.

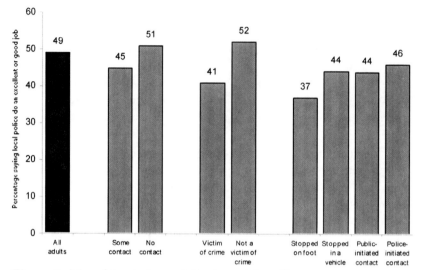

Figure 2: Trend in victim satisfaction with police response.

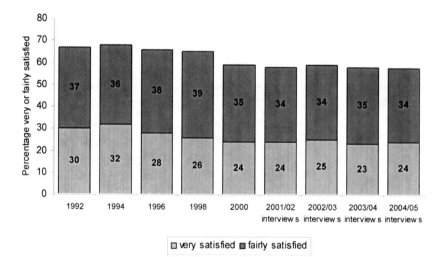

been kept well informed by the police in only 32% of all incidents the police came to know about. Of those respondents who had initiated some form of contact with the police, 65% were very or fairly satisfied with the way the police handled the matter, lower than those who had some form of police-initiated contact.

The survey has also provided some interesting data on stop and searches. Again for the latest period (2004-2005) the survey showed that 10% of adults reported having been stopped by the police while in a vehicle and 3% had been stopped while on foot in the 12 months prior to interview. Men were more likely to be stopped than women: 13% compared with 7% in a vehicle, and 4% compared with 1% on foot. Young men aged 16 to 24 were particularly likely to be stopped by the police; 28% were stopped in a vehicle and 20% were stopped on foot.

People from a mixed, Asian, or Black ethnic background were more likely than those in other ethnic groups to be stopped in a vehicle by the police (16%, 13%, and 15%, respectively). This compares with 9% of Whites and 6% of Chinese and other ethnic groups. The sample size for the proportions being stopped on foot, however, was too small to detect significant differences.

CONCLUSION

This chapter has given a synopsis of the use made of the British Crime Survey in assessing performance, and in particular its central role in the Policing Performance Assessment Framework. Some of the inherent limitations in measuring performance with survey data have been highlighted. Even the small selection of findings presented here, however, should be enough to give some indication of the capacity of the survey to yield valuable policing-related information.

The BCS long has been envisaged as a multipurpose vehicle. Whilst illuminating crime levels and trends was always a central aim, its modular structure allowed for coverage of experience of, and attitudes to, the criminal justice agencies. The coverage of policing issues in the 1980s and 1990s made a significant contribution to research knowledge about the police. In other words, the survey combined social indicator functions with research functions.

This remains the case as the survey moves into the 21st century, but the BCS has now acquired an important third function, which is to support central government's work in assessing and monitoring police performance. The survey has broadened in purpose from being a source of understanding and knowledge about crime and justice, to being part of the machinery of governmental control over the criminal justice system. How this function evolves and develops over the next decade remains to be seen. However, so long as there is a visible political commitment to ensure that public services are responsive to the public, it seems improbable that the salience of survey data in performance management will decline – whether in policing or in other areas of the public sector.

✦

© Crown copyright. Reproduced under the terms of click-use license C02W0005902.

Address correspondence to: Jonathan.allen@justice.gsi.gov.uk

NOTES

1. Decisions on which forces are allocated into which "family" are based on a range of demographic, regional, and socioeconomic factors.
2. As part of wider Home Office reform plans announced by the Home Secretary in July 2006, the Home Office made a commitment to introduce a new, simplified performance framework for crime, policing, and drugs. The new framework is being taken forward under the working title of Assessments of Policing and Community Safety (APACS).
3. These are termed Key Diagnostic Indicators (KDIs), and were developed following qualitative work, better to understand drivers of confidence.

REFERENCES AND ADDITIONAL SOURCES

Guidance on statutory performance indicators for policing 2006/07 ANNEXES. Available at: http://police.homeoffice.gov.uk/news-and-publications/publication/ performance-and-measurement/SPA_Guidance_Annexes_2006_v3.pdf

Nicholas, S., Povey, D., Walker, A., & Kershaw, C. *Crime in England and Wales, 2004/05.* Home Office Statistical Bulletin, 11/05. London: Home Office.

Walker, A., Kershaw, C., & Nicholas, S. (2006). *Crime in England and Wales, 2006.* Home Office Statistical Bulletin 12/06. London: Home Office.

Additional Sources

http://www.homeoffice.gov.uk/rds/pdfs06/rdsolr070 6.pdf
http://police.homeoffice.gov.uk/performance-and-measurement/performance-assessment/assessments-2005-2006/

http://www.opsi.gov.uk/si/si2004/20040644.htm

http://police.homeoffice.gov.uk/performance-and-measurement/assessment-methods/

http://police.homeoffice.gov.uk/performance-and-measurement/assess-policing-community-safety/

http://www.homeoffice.gov.uk/documents/ho-targets-autumn-report-06?view=Binary

Public Opinion and Criminal Justice: The British Crime Survey and Beyond

by

Mike Hough
Institute for Criminal Policy Research
King's College London

and

Julian V. Roberts
Centre for Criminology
University of Oxford

Abstract: *Measuring public attitudes to criminal justice has become an important goal of victimization surveys in Britain and around the world. In this chapter we trace the evolution and impact of attitudinal questions on the British Crime Survey (BCS). Although some questions on attitudes to crime and punishment were included in earlier sweeps of the BCS, an important step forward was taken in the 1996 administration when an entire component was dedicated to public knowledge of, and attitudes towards, sentencing and sentencers. This module resulted in a Home Office report and subsequent scholarly publications; it sensitized politicians to issues relating to confidence in justice; and it was one of the factors that led to the adoption of "confidence" performance measures by the Home Office. A number of other jurisdictions including Canada, Belgium, Barbados, Northern Ireland, South*

Africa, and New Zealand subsequently modified their crime or victim-
ization surveys to include modules exploring public attitudes. Most
recently the BCS has developed a range of questions on public confidence
in the criminal justice system and criminal justice professionals. These
developments are discussed, and we conclude by outlining a proposal
to improve our knowledge of public opinion in this vital area of
criminal justice.

The British Crime Survey (BCS) has emerged as the principal source of information about public attitudes to crime and punishment in England and Wales.[1] The research findings that have emerged since the mid 1990s have achieved a significant degree of international recognition, as can be seen in the proliferation of analogous surveys in other jurisdictions. Findings from the BCS also have made their mark on criminal policy, in particular by prompting a number of initiatives to bolster public confidence in justice. The BCS has also given rise to a stream of scholarly publications exploring public reaction to crime and criminal justice. For the first decade of the BCS, however, public opinion findings achieved the status of little more than criminological curiosities, and the coverage of the topic was essentially researcher-led, a result of the research interests of specific individuals.

This chapter traces the origin, evolution, and impact of attitudinal questions on the British Crime Survey that first appeared in the 1996 administration of the BCS. After discussing the emergence of these questions, we make some comparisons between findings emerging from the BCS and surveys in other jurisdictions. This is followed by a discussion of the role BCS findings played in the debate about crime and justice in Britain. The chapter concludes with a proposal to improve the state of knowledge with respect to this important issue in the field of criminal justice.

Questions about the punishment of offenders were placed on the first BCS in 1982, but they were posed only to crime victims. The specific question asked how victims wanted their offender to be punished. The results were described in brief and the authors concluded that despite problems in making comparisons with sentencing trends, victims' wishes were "broadly in line with present practice" (Hough & Mayhew, 1983, p. 28). These findings prompted the research team to devise a series of questions asked of both victims and nonvictims, exploring knowledge of and attitudes towards sentencing in the second BCS. For example, respondents were asked to select sentences for a range of offenders whose crimes were specified in minimal detail. The results, reported in Hough and Mayhew (1985) and Hough and Moxon (1985), again suggested that the widespread view held by criminal justice elites that the public was significantly more punitive than the courts had been rather overstated.

These BCS findings were consistent with surveys conducted at the same time in Canada, the only other jurisdiction in which public opinion regarding crime and justice had been systematically explored. In 1981, the Canadian federal government commissioned research to examine a wide range of interrelated issues, including public knowledge of crime statistics, knowledge and attitude towards sentencing, and parole (see Doob & Roberts, 1982, 1983). This poll was followed by a series of other surveys over the next 5 years (see Roberts, 1988).

The proliferation of empirical research in the early 1980s entered the scholarly literature when research findings from a number of countries, including Britain were assembled in a book, *Public Attitudes to Sentencing*, published almost 20 years ago (Walker & Hough, 1988). In his preface to that volume, Tony Bottoms observed that most criminologists until then had regarded the subject as "something of a side-issue" (Bottoms, 1988, p. xi). The reasons for this are fairly clear. At that time, there was a consensus amongst politicians, their officials, academics, and other opinion formers in Britain that it was necessary to manage – but not to respond to – public opinion about sentencing. If public opinion turned out to be more nuanced and less uniformly punitive than they had supposed, that was a bonus, but not a reason for any shift in policy direction.[2] In addition, policy makers appear to have assumed that the public were uniformly and strikingly more punitive than the courts.

The political climate in Western nations altered in the early 1990s in several important ways. As described by Giddens in particular (1990, 1991), late modern societies are characterized by a decline in public trust in expert opinion. This trend has been accompanied by an increase in the importance attached to public opinion as a guide to criminal policy development. In Britain, responsiveness to public views became a hallmark of the "new public management" approach to modernizing government that influenced both of the main political parties from the early 1990s onwards. New Labour's shadow Home Secretary at the time (Tony Blair) launched a highly effective challenge to the Conservatives' claim to be the party of law and order. According to their now-famous slogan, New Labour promised that if elected they would be "tough on crime, tough on the causes of crime." This challenge breached the cross-party consensus that imprisonment represented an ineffective response to crime. Finally, concerns were growing about declining public confidence in key institutions of justice. By the mid 1990s, public attitudes to justice began to emerge as a hot political topic and this generated increased interest in the findings from public opinion surveys.

Regrettably, the 1988 BCS dropped all questions about sentencing. Four years later, however, the 1992 BCS included a new module concerned with the sentencing of a set of offences with problematic or ambiguous status – date rape, domestic and acquaintance violence, and cannabis possession. The results were not published until 1998, and then only in an obscure nongovernment publication (Hough, 1998).[3] They revealed that the public was more equivocal than Michael Howard, the Conservative Home Secretary in the mid 1990s, about the proposition that "prison works." The public appeared skeptical about the value of imprisonment as a response to crime, with the exception perhaps of the most serious forms of violence. More interestingly, responses to this sweep of the BCS indicated that young people were much less tolerant than their elders of a range of violent and sexual crimes, with the reverse being the case for property crimes and drug offences. This finding was inconsistent with received wisdom about demographic trends in public punitiveness.

THE 1996 BRITISH CRIME SURVEY

In 1996, the Home Office commissioned the authors of this chapter to design and analyse a module on public knowledge of, and attitudes to, crime and punishment, and the new administration was more than ready to promote the findings. The results revealed considerable public cynicism about sentencers and sentencing, and widespread misperceptions about sentencing trends and the sentencing process.

The 1996 survey and subsequent sweeps of the BCS played a pivotal role in expanding our knowledge of public opinion and sentencing. This is clearly true for Britain but the BCS has also served as a model that spawned comparable surveys in other jurisdictions. Until the 1996 sweep, no systematic data were available regarding public knowledge of sentencing trends in Britain. Indeed, one has to reach back to 1961 to a brief article published in the *Criminal Law Review* to find some research addressing public knowledge of sentencing and the use of imprisonment in Britain (see Silvey, 1961). A number of "one-off" surveys contained questions measuring public *attitudes* to sentencing and criminal justice, but there was no way of gauging the true extent of public *knowledge* in this area of crime and justice. All this changed with the 1996 BCS, which contained a dedicated module exploring public knowledge regarding a number of interrelated issues, including knowledge of crime trends and sentencing patterns.[4]

The research reports describing the findings from this module (Hough & Roberts, 1998a, 1998b) resonated with the emerging political concerns about a sentencing system that was out of step with community views about legal punishment, and was consistent with the language of the "confidence agenda" – a shorthand that embraced both the need to be responsive to the electorate and the need to sustain institutional legitimacy.[5] It was certainly one of the factors contributing to the adoption of government performance indicators on confidence in justice. In 2000, the government's triennial spending review included a Public Service Agreement (PSA) performance target on "confidence in justice" for the first time, covering the period from 2001-2004: "To improve the level of public confidence in the CJS by 2004, including improving that of ethnic minority communities." The BCS has provided the data for assessing progress in achieving this and subsequent PSA targets on confidence.

At this point, we summarize some of the findings from the 1996 and subsequent surveys, placing them in some comparative international context (for further details of the 1996 module see Hough & Roberts, 1998a, 1998b, 1999). The questions designed for the 1996 BCS were intended to map both knowledge of crime and punishment and attitudes to crime and criminal justice.

Knowledge of Crime and Punishment Trends

One of the more important findings was that the British public has failed to notice the decline in crime rates that had begun in 1995. The 1996 module included a question – replicated on BCS surveys ever since – about trends in crime rates. Figure 1 shows the proportion of respondents in England and Wales that believed that crime rates had risen in the 7 years since 1996. Around two thirds of the population chose the "wrong" answer in each year. It is unsurprising that the downtrend went unnoticed in the mid 1990s, but much more remarkable 10 years later.

Whilst this is probably the best publicised and best known example of public misperceptions of crime, the 1996 BCS module identified and documented a number of other public misperceptions regarding crime and

Figure 1: Public perceptions of crime trends in England and Wales.

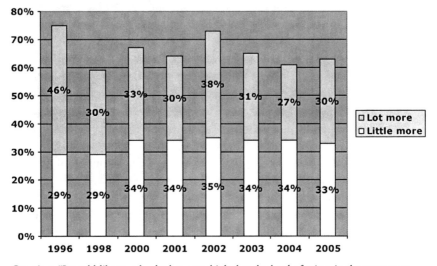

Question: "I would like to ask whether you think that the level of crime in the country as a whole has changed over the past two years. Would you say there is more crime, less crime or about the same amount (since two years ago)?"
Source: British Crime Survey.

justice. Most respondents underestimated the proportion of the population with criminal records; this is a sign that most people see crime as the activity of a small group of individuals in society. But the most significant for our purposes were those findings that demonstrated the extent to which people underestimated the severity of sentencing practices.

When asked to estimate the incarceration rates associated with a number of common offences, most respondents underestimated the proportion of offenders committed to custody. Later administrations of the BCS as well as other surveys measuring public opinion and youth court sentencing found essentially the same pattern of findings (see Mattison & Mirrlees Black, 2000; Roberts & Hough, 2005b). It became clear that misperceptions of sentencing and parole were linked to a more general perception that the entire criminal justice system was tilted in favour of offenders and against crime victims. This idea has recently been promoted by the government in Britain, and in particular by the current prime minister. Despite the intense media interest in sentencing and imprisonment in particular, public opinion has remained well insulated from the reality that sentencing has become progressively more severe the last decade, as can be seen from the rising and now record number of prisoners in England and Wales (see Hough, Jacobson, & Millie, 2003, for a discussion).

Attitudes to Sentencers and the Criminal Justice System

These findings with respect to public knowledge of the criminal process, and in particular those that relate to misperceptions of the use of custody help to explain the widespread view that courts are too lenient, and "out of touch with what the average person thinks." Sentencers – and in particular judges[6] – are poorly regarded by the British public. In 1996, four fifths of the population expressed the view that sentencers were too lenient. The same proportion thought that judges were out of touch, although public perceptions of magistrates were slightly less negative.[7]

Ironically, when asked to "sentence" offenders described in specific scenarios, the public responds with sentences that on average are less severe than current practice, even though they believe the opposite to be the case. The BCS asks respondents to choose an appropriate sentence for a 23-year-old burglar with two previous convictions for burglary. The vignette describes a daytime burglary of an empty house from which electrical goods were taken. The owner was an elderly man, and therefore a vulnerable individual. When the question was first posed on the 1996 survey, approximately half the sample (54%) chose imprisonment.[8] In 2002-2003 less than a third of the sample thought that the offender *would* get prison, while less than two thirds thought he *should* get prison. In reality, the burglar would now be at risk of a mandatory 3-year sentence, and currently sentences for this offence are harsher than they were a decade ago.[9]

Influence of the News Media and Politicians

A number of explanations may be offered to account for current trends in public attitudes to sentencing and sentencers. The two principal influences are undoubtedly the news media and the positions taken by politicians with respect to the punishment of offenders.

The tabloid media in Britain surely must be held responsible at least in part for the low levels of public knowledge of crime and justice. Coverage of crime and justice in some tabloids presents a greatly distorted view of crime trends and the criminal justice response to offenders. Home Office analyses of BCS data confirmed that tabloid readers were indeed less knowledgeable and more critical of criminal justice than were broadsheet readers. As noted, however, public opinion surveys conducted after the 1996 BCS revealed a similar pattern in very different jurisdictions. This suggests that basic news values or explanations invoking the ways that laypersons process attitudinally relevant information may account for the distorted public knowledge of information related to sentencing and parole. Tabloid journalism alone cannot be responsible for the gap that exists between the practice of the courts and public knowledge of sentencing trends.

Competing explanations exist for the levels of public concern about crime, and for the widespread sense that the governmental response is inadequate. One argument is that insecurities of this kind might reflect broader uncertainties of life in late-modernity; in other words, criminal justice serves as a lightning rod that attracts concerns about a social and natural environment that seems to becoming progressively more unpredictable. Another possibility is that people respond to the "signs of crime" that are to be found in social disorder and antisocial behaviour. That is, although the overall volume of crime has fallen over the last decade, people are more influenced by signs of low-level social disorder, of which there is no shortage in contemporary Britain. The prevalence of antisocial behaviour may therefore have a more important impact on perceptions of crime rates than the incidence of more serious but less visible crimes such as burglary.

Finally, people may simply be responding to the explicit or implicit messages about crime and social order that are conveyed by politicians and the news media. This is certainly the most parsimonious explanation. People may think that the criminal justice system is in disarray largely because this is the message they repeatedly receive from the media. Since 1992, elements of the media have been pursuing campaigns for tougher justice. For example, a concerted series of prominent articles in the *Sunday Times* and the *Sun* (11 and 12 June 2006, respectively) called for the removal of lenient judges. But politicians are also deeply implicated. Ever since 1992, when Tony Blair began to rival the Conservative party in terms of law-and-order policies, politicians on both sides have felt under pressure to out-tough each other. Opposition parties naturally question the competence of the government of the day, and challenge government crime policies. It is also to be expected that they will highlight unaddressed failures in the system.

New Labour has also consistently signalled to the public that the criminal justice system is in a mess. Senior Labour politicians have made public statements to the effect that judges' decisions are "bonkers" and "inexplicable or bizarre," that sentences are "unduly lenient," that probation is the "dagger at the heart of the criminal justice system," that we are "fighting 21st century problems with 19th century solutions," that the system "needs rebalancing in favour of the law-abiding majority," that the Home Office is "not fit for purpose" – to cite just a few. Prime Minister Blair's speech delivered at Bristol in June 2006 represents the clearest portrayal of the justice system in crisis (Blair, 2006). People might ignore such statements if they came only from opposition parties; after all, "they would say that, wouldn't they?" Coming from an administration that has been in power for 8 years, these views carry more weight.

RELATED RESEARCH IN BRITAIN AND OTHER COUNTRIES

When findings from the early administrations of the BCS were published, they were treated with caution. Nobody would want to construct or shape penal policy on the findings on public opinion from a single survey. The consistency of findings across countries and over time, however, is striking. Surveys in other jurisdictions have generated remarkably similar findings.

It will be remembered that from 1996 onward, the BCS has asked respondents whether crime has being rising or falling. Since then, this question has been posed in a number of other countries. Respondents in jurisdictions as diverse and far apart as Australia, New Zealand, Barbados, and Scotland generally hold the same view, namely, that crime rates are rising, regardless of the reality reflected in official crime statistics or crime victimization surveys (see Paulin, Searle et al., 2003; Nuttall, Eversley, et al., 2003; Justice 1 Committee, 2002; Weatherburn & Indermaur, 2004). For example, a sample of Australians was asked in 2004 about crime trends for six offences, most of which had been stable or falling. The majority of respondents held a different view, believing that crime rates for these offences had been rising over the period in question. Similarly in New Zealand, police statistics revealed a slight decline in the crime rate over the previous 2 years, but more than half of New Zealand respondents believed that there was "a lot more crime" than 2 years earlier. As Paulin and colleagues succinctly note, with respect to crime trends, "83% of our sample 'got it wrong'" (2003, p. 8). In Barbados, respondents were asked

Table 1: Public Estimates of the Percentage of Recorded Crime Involving Violence

Public Estimates	Canada (1988)	Britain (BCS) (1996)	Britain (BCS) (1998)	New Zealand (1999)	Barbados (2002)	Scotland (2002)
Accurate estimate	3	3	3	5	7	2
Small overestimate	15	19	19	29	24	15
Large overestimate	74	78	79	66	69	83

Sources: Roberts (1988); Hough and Roberts (1998a); Mattinson and Mirrlees-Black, (2000); Paulin et al. (2003); Nuttall et al. (2003); Justice 1 Committee (2002).

about crime trends over the previous 5 years. Examination of crime statistics suggested a slight rise over the 5-year-period, yet fully 69% of respondents expressed the view that there was "a lot more crime" (Nuttall et al., 2003). Similar misperceptions emerge from opinion surveys conducted in Canada (Roberts, 1994, 2001) and Northern Ireland (Amelin, Wills, Blair, & Donnelly, 2000).

There are international consistencies in responses to other questions. Table 1 summarizes responses to the following question drawn from the 1996 BCS survey: "Of every 100 crimes recorded by the police, roughly what number do you think involve violence or the threat of violence?" As can be seen, there is a remarkable degree of consistency in the pattern of responses across jurisdictions and over time.

Table 2 demonstrates similar cross-jurisdictional consistency, but this time with respect to attitudes to sentencing trends. One of the most frequently posed questions is whether sentences are too harsh, too lenient, or about right. As can be seen in Table 2, in all surveys conducted in the decade since the sentencing module on the 1996 BCS, a consistently high proportion of respondents have expressed the view that sentences are too lenient.

This replication of questions across jurisdictions serves several useful functions. First, it places the British Crime Survey trends in a comparative, international context. Interpretations of public confidence levels in criminal justice will change considerably when comparative data are available. For example, the ubiquitous perception of leniency is not restricted to the British public. Second, cross-jurisdictional analyses illuminate the origins of public misperceptions that must lie in some source common to disparate

Table 2: Perceptions of Judicial Leniency: 1996 BCS and Beyond[10]

Jurisdiction	Date of Survey	Percentage of Respondents Expressing the View That Courts Are Too Lenient
England and Wales (BCS)	1996	79
United States	1998	74
England and Wales (BCS)	1998	79
South Africa	1999	83
Northern Ireland	2000	76
Japan	2000	88
Scotland	2001	70
England and Wales (BCS)	2002/03	76
Barbados	2003	76
Netherlands	2004	84
Canada	2005	74

Sources: Hough and Roberts (1998a); Bureau of Justice Statistics (2007) Institute for Social Studies (1999); Amelin et al., (2000); Japanese Social Survey (2000); Mattinson and Mirrlees-Black (2000); Justice 1 Committee (2001); Nuttall et al. (2003); de Keijser et al., (2006); Roberts et al. (2007).

countries. Third, these comparisons show that some of these beliefs and attitudes are relatively invariant over time. Despite the fact that the prison population in England and Wales has risen at a vertiginous pace over the past decade, most people still think that sentencers are too lenient. If sentencers believe that imposing more or longer prison terms will placate a critical public, they are clearly mistaken. It is no surprise that public ratings of the judiciary have improved only marginally over the period in which sentencing became tougher.

REFINING THE MEASUREMENT OF PUBLIC ATTITUDES TO CRIME AND PUNISHMENT

The last decade has seen a rapid expansion of interest in attitudes to crime and punishment, but work in the field still stands in need both of conceptual refinement and of methodological development. There is also much scope – and a pressing need – to develop more cross-jurisdictional research.

Conceptual Refinement

Governments inevitably tend towards oversimplification in the presentation of their policies, and this is certainly true in the case of criminal justice. In Britain, for example, the government has used the label "confidence in justice" as a shorthand for referring to a collection of related initiatives about raising the level of public trust in the law, belief in the fairness of the law, and beliefs about the competence and effectiveness of criminal justice agencies. The fact that confidence in justice is self-evidently a good thing has tended to displace any serious critical examination of the different dimensions of confidence and of the possible rationales for seeking to improve confidence.

Research in the U.K. would benefit from greater engagement with the U.S. scholarship on procedural justice associated mainly with Tom Tyler and his colleagues (e.g., Tyler & Huo, 2002; Tyler, 2003). This work analyses – empirically and conceptually – the causes of compliance with the law, organized around the idea that procedural fairness can be as or more important than outcome fairness. The importance of this body of work lies in the linkage it makes between public attitudes towards institutions of justice and people's commitment to the rule of law. To use Etzioni's (1961) terminology, intelligent criminal justice systems should probably be aiming to secure *normative* compliance with the law – even if political rhetoric focuses on *coercive* compliance – and focusing on institutional legitimacy may be the surest route to normative compliance. British crime policy's "discovery" of confidence as an important issue has never been accompanied by any explicit justification for its importance. Does the government need to foster public confidence in justice because people are taxpayers, because they are voters, or because popular compliance with the law is what justice is all about? It is significant that the concept of fairness has now been introduced into the U.K. government's confidence-performance target – but as a factor constraining rather than supporting the pursuit of confidence.[11]

Assuming that the third answer is at least partly correct – that there are fundamentally important relationships between perceived justice and compliance with the law – a number of important questions need to be addressed. For example, in building institutional legitimacy, what is the relative importance of procedural fairness, outcome fairness, and system effectiveness? Is the quality of decision-making more important than the social and presentational skills of those who make the decision? Is it more important to foster trust in the system's fairness or in its effectiveness?

What characteristics do justice systems need to display – and to avoid – in order to command support? These questions are partly empirical ones, yet sensible answers can be found only if the empirical work is conducted within a conceptually coherent framework.

Methodological Innovation

Research has now established beyond doubt that the measurement of attitudes to punishment is a challenging process. As Stalans (2002) has discussed, different levels or layers of opinion can be tapped by different methodologies. It has been found that top-of-the-head reactions to quick prompts that deploy stereotypical images of the offender often tap into punitive views, which are often moderated when people are provided with more information and more time to think. Researchers clearly need to have thought through whether they are aiming to capture considered or unconsidered attitudes – and why.

A strategy that we have often deployed with some success is split-sample experiments, in which the same question is asked in different ways to different subsamples. (Computer-assisted interviewing makes such procedures easy to manage.) This enables one to get a clear idea of the lability of public opinion and of the sorts of factor that push and pull opinion in different directions. There are other research strategies for achieving the same end result – a better feel for the factors that shape opinion – such as incomplete factorial designs that rotate conditions in vignettes presented to respondents (cf. Applegate et al., 1996). The point we wish to emphasize is that the measurement of public attitudes to a phenomenon as emotionally charged as crime and punishment is inevitably difficult to get right. Crude methodologies will yield crude findings and little insight. Issues relating to the validity of survey-based measures of confidence are discussed elsewhere in this volume by Skogan. He makes the case in relation to measure of policing – though it is equally true in other areas of justice – that trends in measures of confidence tend to be more informative than point estimates relating to levels of confidence.

Cross-Jurisdictional Research

An important limitation on the field is the absence of a systematic cross-jurisdictional survey that explores public attitudes to punishment and related issues. The closest such instrument is the International Crime Victimization Survey (ICVS; see Mayhew & van Kesteren, 2002). Although it is conducted in a many jurisdictions the survey contains only a single, simple question on sentencing.[12] What is needed, surely, is a survey conducted periodically in several countries and that measures public punitiveness and related issues. At the present time, researchers wishing to explain variations in punitiveness across countries must rely on surveys conducted at different times, with varying sample sizes and methodologies, and that employ questions that are not completely comparable.

FUTURE DIRECTIONS: NEED FOR A PUBLIC OPINION CLEARING HOUSE AND WEBSITE

Our knowledge of public attitudes to criminal justice reflects the steady accretion of individual surveys. Apart from the BCS (and comparable annual or biannual surveys in other countries such as the GSS), however, there is an episodic nature to these polls. Many surveys are commissioned by news media outlets or special interest groups with an interest in a particular topic. A sudden burst of media coverage with respect to a specific issue often triggers an opinion poll. Little or no aggregation of findings takes place, with the consequence that the results from any particular poll are usually viewed in isolation. For example, if a survey finds that slightly over half of the polled public has a great deal of confidence in the police or that three quarters of respondents oppose parole, it takes considerable effort to place these findings in some historical context. These statistics represent a single data point in time, the true significance of which can be determined only by effecting comparisons with earlier surveys. Is public confidence in the police declining? Has public opposition to parole increased? The key to understanding the causes of public responses is having variation in outcomes over time. BCS findings may be accessed with relative ease, but the other, independently funded surveys are much harder for the average researcher to locate.

This is a regrettable state of affairs. Clearly an electronic repository of survey findings is needed which can be accessed and rapidly searched by researchers. The *Sourcebook of Criminal Justice Statistics* in the U.S. serves as a limited model in this regard (see www.albany.edu/sourcebook). One section of the *Sourcebook* is devoted to public attitudes to criminal justice, and for a number of issues findings are available over repeated administrations. Useful though it is, the U.S. *Sourcebook* is a very limited research tool; it contains only a small fraction of all surveys conducted and the range of issues explored is very restricted. The *European Sourcebook of Criminal Justice Statistics* (www.europeansourcebook.org/), now in its third edition, does not have a comparable section. The ESRC[13] question bank contains survey instruments from a number of social surveys including recent administrations of the British Crime Survey. However, it is a long way from being a useful research tool for researchers interested in public opinion and crime or criminal justice.

A comprehensive public opinion database is needed in Britain.[14] In addition to publicly funded surveys, the database should include findings from the archives of private polling firms. Most survey firms[15] release their polls into the public domain after a specified period, and it seems unlikely that these companies would object to the inclusion of their surveys in the database, with full citation of the polling firm and sponsor, if appropriate. Our proposal involves more than simply posting poll findings on a Website (although even this modest step would represent an advance). The organization maintaining the database would need to exercise some editorial scrutiny. This would include establishing clear criteria for inclusion in the database. These criteria might include the following:

- The exact wording of question

- The sample size

- The method of polling – with confidence limits

- Whether the survey was a stand-alone or omnibus survey

- Sponsor of survey and name of polling firm

- Contact details for the polling company.

If this information was unavailable, the survey should not be included. Once such a database was created, it would be possible for researchers, pollsters, policy makers, and other interested parties to have a more comprehensive and nuanced understanding of attitudes to a particular issue in criminal justice. It would be relatively easy to provide historical data in tabular and graphic form. Creation of a database and Website of this kind would be relatively inexpensive, and we urge the Home Office to give serious consideration to funding such a database for a trial period. The database could be established and maintained at one of the many centres or institutes of criminology throughout the country. The payoff in terms of deepening our understanding of public opinion would be significant.

Improving the Policy-making Process

In the previous section we were considering how the knowledge base on public attitudes to crime and justice can be consolidated and improved. Our starting point was that academic institutions need to think about the organizational infrastructure required to support academic work in the field. In parallel, however, survey measures of public opinion in general, including those relating to crime and justice, are increasingly being used as governmental tools for performance management. As noted earlier, the U.K. government's spending review in 2000 included Public Service Agreement targets on confidence in criminal justice. Subsequent spending reviews have refined these targets. At the time of writing, the current PSA target on confidence in justice, set in the 2004 Spending Review, PSA2 for 2005-2008, was as follows: "Reassure the public, reducing fear of crime and anti-social behaviour, and building confidence in the Criminal Justice System without compromising fairness."

This use of attitudinal data from sample surveys as part of the governmental systems of performance management is distinctively new. All the signs are that the trend is set to continue. In other chapters of this book, there are accounts of the ways in which survey data on policing and on anxiety about crime are being used to monitor police performance. Both in relation to these measures and to the PSA2 measure of confidence, survey questions are developed and deployed in a fairly pragmatic and ad hoc way. Although survey data are taking on a significant role in public sector governance, government departments have yet to recognise the full significance of this development. The difficulty, as we see it, is that although public attitudes to crime and justice have become a central topic for research and teaching, the subject of public opinion falls between the cracks with respect to institutional interest. Statistical agencies such as the U.S. Bureau of Justice Statistics, the Canadian Centre for Justice Statistics, and the Home Office appear to regard public opinion research as falling outside the domain of essential criminal justice statistics. The primary clients of these statistical agencies are found within the justice system itself, and none seems interested in a longer-term view of the state of public knowledge and opinion.

We would argue that establishing a rigorous and systematic database on public opinion is as important to the field of criminal justice as many of the issues on which data are routinely collected. In addition to containing findings from surveys, the sort of public clearing house that we are proposing could play an important role in helping government develop a more sophisticated understanding of the measurement of public attitudes to justice.

Certainly this could yield clear policy payoffs. All Western jurisdictions have experienced the phenomenon of "penal populism" – where ineffectual penal policies are promoted for electoral rather than penological reasons (see Roberts et al., 2003). These policies are usually described as reflecting the public's view. Advocates of policies such as mandatory sentencing, penal austerity, parole abolition, and the like often conduct one-shot polls in which public opinion is measured in a way that appears to generate support for the proposal under scrutiny.

At present, advocates of a more considered and evidence-based policy process seldom have the ability to place any claims about public opinion in context. If a database were available, claims about the views of the public regarding any issue could be evaluated in light of all available polls. Once a significant number of surveys had been conducted on an issue, it would also be possible to conduct the equivalent of metanalyses, in which a determination about public opinion can be made drawing upon the statistical power associated with a large number of independent samples of respondents. Finally, the ultimate goal would be to develop an international database that would permit researchers to make cross-jurisdictional comparisons. One of the limitations on the field at this time is fact that few cross-national studies exist, and there are limited opportunities for scholarship in this area to proliferate across borders.[16]

Improving Public Knowledge About Crime and Punishment

One final consequence of the 1996 and related British Crime Surveys should be noted. As noted, successive administrations of the BCS revealed low levels of public knowledge. The Home Office has responded to this pattern of findings by exploring ways of improving public knowledge of crime and criminal justice, with the hope that this will result in more positive attitudes towards the justice system. For example, Chapman, et al. (2002) report research that employed an experimental design to determine whether improving knowledge levels would change public attitudes. Salisbury (2004) reports findings from an experiment in which one quarter of respondents to the BCS survey were provided with a booklet about crime and sentencing. Comparison between the responses of this group and respondents who had not received the brochure suggested that provision of the information had a modest impact on improving levels of public confidence in criminal justice. In addition, since the publication of the 1996 BCS findings there has been an increase in the number of scholarly publications exploring ways to improve public knowledge, and subsequently attitudes to criminal justice system (e.g., Hough & Park, 2002; Mirrlees-Black, 2002).

Expectations have to be limited about what can be done to improve public knowledge in this field. Hutton (2005), for example, has argued that there are both practical problems in reaching significant proportions of the population and a growing resistance in the population to messages of any sort that emerge as expert knowledge from authorities. As Hutton himself argues, however, this should not be cause for total despair. The only sensible long-term strategy to improve public knowledge and understanding of justice is to ensure that modern communication techniques are used to provide better, and better targeted, information for the public about the work of the courts and other criminal justice agencies.

CONCLUSION

The field of criminal justice and public opinion has evolved considerably since publication of the first monograph to include systematic research on public attitudes towards sentencing. For certain issues – such as attitudes towards sentence severity – there is now a significant historical record on which to draw. The field will not progress beyond its current state, however, unless and until an attempt is made to consolidate the findings that have accumulated to this point. A decade ago our knowledge of public attitudes to criminal justice, and in particular sentencing, was very sketchy. Today we have a much clearer idea of the extent of public knowledge and the nature of public attitudes to sentencing and sentencers. We are also able to make some useful comparisons across jurisdictions, noting common trends and local variation. We know, for example, that the top-of-the-head reaction of people when asked about sentencing trends will appear punitive – whether the respondent lives in Barbados or Birmingham. In our view, the challenge to researchers is twofold: first, to consolidate the existing body of findings in a way that will make them more accessible and thus useful to policy makers; and second, to move beyond the descriptive nature of these findings and explore the nature of public opinion at a deeper level than has been the case to date.

Address correspondence to: Mike.Hough@kcl.ac.uk or to Julian.Roberts @crim.ox.ac.uk

NOTES

1. Findings from the Scottish Crime Survey can be found in Anderson and Leitch (1996).
2. One of the contradictions of the Thatcher administration was that despite the rhetoric of economic liberalism and social conservatism, the British government consistently pursued a penal policy designed to restrict the use of imprisonment. The reasons for this apparent paradox are to be found partly in the personalities of the two Home Secretaries of the time, William Whitelaw and Douglas Hurd, and partly in the fact that in the absence of any effective political challenge, penal parsimony made both political and fiscal sense.
3. This was largely but not solely because officials judged that the results had the potential for serious political embarrassment at a time when there was much political hostility to the whole enterprise of criminological policy research.
4. A copy of the questionnaire can be found in Appendix B of Hough and Roberts (1998a).
5. The Home Secretary of the day, Jack Straw, told the first author of this chapter that the study was one of the most important that he had seen since taking up office. Admittedly, he was new in the post, and one should in any case make allowances for political hyperbole – or, indeed, simple politeness.
6. England and Wales are unique among common-law countries in the respect that the vast majority of sentencing decisions are made by panels of lay magistrates. The most serious cases are sentenced by professional judges in the Crown court.
7. It is unclear why magistrates fare better than judges in public ratings of the two professions. One explanation is that the public are aware that magistrates are drawn from the community; people may have more faith in sentencing decisions made by laypersons. A more likely explanation is that the sentencing decisions of professional judges are more likely to involve serious offences and are more likely to attract the attention and criticism of the tabloid media.
8. This statistic derives from the respondents who received a "menu" of sentencing options prior to choosing which sanction to impose.

Support for imprisonment was higher when people were asked to impose sentence without having been provided with a list of sentencing options. This experimental manipulation demonstrated the importance of giving respondents the same range of options available to a sentencing court.

9. Unpublished analysis by Mike Hough.

10. Research in other jurisdictions using a somewhat different methodology generates the same pattern of findings. For example, respondents in Belgium were asked whether sentences for a series of offences were punished too severely, with sufficient severity, or not severely enough. Very high percentages of respondents chose "not severely enough"; see Parmentier, Vervaeke, Goethals, et al. (2005).

11. Local criminal justice areas are encouraged to build "confidence in the Criminal Justice System without compromising fairness."

12. The exact wording of the question is as follows: "People have different ideas about the sentences which should be given to offenders. Take for instance the case of a 21-year-old man who is found guilty of burglary/housebreaking for the second time. This time he has taken a colour television. Which of the following sentences do you consider the most appropriate for such a case: fine, prison, community service, suspended sentence, other sentence?"

13. Available at http://qb.soc.surrey.ac.uk/docs/surveys.htm

14. A comparable database to encompass opinion surveys in Europe would also be a useful project for the European Union to contemplate.

15. For example, a large number of surveys relating to crime and criminal justice can be found on the Website of the MORI company at www.MORI.com

16. Two rare examples of cross-jurisdictional initiatives are the conference on international trends in public opinion and the administration of justice held in Leuven in 2003 (see Parmentier, Vervaeke, Doutrelpont, & Kellens [2004] and the conference on public opinion and sentencing hosted by the Victoria Sentencing Advisory Council in Melbourne in July 2006.

REFERENCES

Amelin, K., Willis, M., Blair, C., & Donnelly, D. (2000). *Attitudes to crime, crime reduction and community safety in Northern Ireland.* Belfast, Ireland: The Stationery Office.

Anderson, S., & Leitch, S. (1996). *Main findings from the Scottish Crime Survey*. Edinburgh, Scotland: Scottish Office Central Research Unit.

Applegate, B., Cullen, F., Richards, P., Lanza-Kaduce, L., & Link, B. (1996). Determinants of public punitiveness toward drunk driving: A factorial survey approach. *Justice Quarterly, 13,* 57-79.

Blair, T. (2006). *Time for proper debate on law and order*. Speech delivered at Bristol, June 23, 2006. Available at www.number-10.gov.uk/

Bottoms, A. (1988). Foreword. In N. Walker & M. Hough (Eds.), *Public attitudes to sentencing. Surveys from five countries*. Cambridge Studies in Criminology. Farnborough, England: Gower.

Bureau of Justice Statistics. (2007) *Sourcebook of criminal justice statistics 2003* – Online. 31st edition. www.albany.edu/sourcebook

Chapman, B., Mirrlees-Black, C., & Brawn, C. (2002). *Improving public attitudes to the criminal justice system: The impact of information*. Home Office Research Study 245. London: Home Office, Research, Development and Statistics Directorate.

de Keijser, J., van Koppen, P., & Elffers, H. (2006, August). *Citizens in the judge's chair*. Presentation to the annual meeting of the European Society of Criminology, Tubingen, Germany.

Doob, A., & Roberts, J. V. (1982). *Crime: Some views of the Canadian public*. University of Toronto, Centre of Criminology.

Doob, A., & Roberts, J. V. (1983). *Sentencing: An analysis of the public's view*. Ottawa, Canada: Department of Justice.

Doob, A. N., & Roberts, J. V. (1988). Public punitiveness and public knowledge of the facts: Some Canadian surveys. In N. Walker & M. Hough (Eds.), *Public attitudes to sentencing*. Cambridge Studies in Criminology. Aldershot, England: Gower.

Etzioni, A. (1961) *A comparative analysis of complex organisations*. Glencoe, IL: Free Press.

Giddens, A. (1990). *The consequences of modernity*. Cambridge, UK: Polity Press.

Giddens, A. (1991). *Modernity and self-identity*. Cambridge, UK: Polity Press.

Hough, M. (1998). *Attitudes to punishment: Findings from the 1992 British Crime Survey*. Social Science Research Paper No 7. London: South Bank University.

Hough, M., Jacobson, J., & Millie, A. (2003). *The decision to imprison: Sentencing and the prison population*. London: Prison Reform Trust.

Hough, M., & Mayhew, P. (1983). *The British Crime Survey: First report*. Home Office Research Study No. 76. London: Her Majesty's Stationery Office.

Hough, M., & Mayhew, P. (1985). *Taking account of crime: Key findings from the 1984 British Crime Survey*. Home Office Research Study No. 85. London: Her Majesty's Stationery Office.

Hough, M., & Moxon, D. (1985). Dealing with offenders: Public opinion and the views of victims. *Howard Journal, 24,* 160-175.

Hough, M., & Park, A. (2002). How malleable are public attitudes to crime and punishment? In J. V. Roberts & M. Hough (Eds.), *Changing attitudes to punishment*. Cullompton, England: Willan.

Hough, M., & Roberts, J. V. (1998a). *Attitudes to punishment: Findings from the 1996 British Crime Survey.* Home Office Research Study No. 170. London: Home Office.

Hough, M., & Roberts, J. V. (1998b). *Attitudes to punishment.* Research Findings. Number 64. London: Home Office, Research, Development and Statistics.

Hough, M., & Roberts, J. V. (1999). Sentencing trends in Britain: Public knowledge and public opinion. *Punishment and Society, 1,* 11-26.

Hough, M., & Roberts, J. V. (2004). *Confidence in justice: An international review.* London: ICPR, King's College London. Available at www.kcl.ac.uk/icpr

Hutton, N. (2005). Beyond populist punitiveness? *Punishment and Society, 7,* 243-258.

Indermaur, D., & Hough, M. (2002). Strategies for changing public attitudes to punishment. In J. V. Roberts & M. Hough (Eds.), *Changing attitudes to punishment.* Cullompton, England: Willan.

Institute for Social Studies. (1999). *Attitudes to sentencing: Public opinion vs. legislation.* Nedbank ISS Crime Index, Vol. 3, No. 6.

Japanese Social Survey. (2000). Available at http://jgss.daishodai.ac.jp/english/eframe/englishtop.html

Justice 1 Committee. (2002). *Public attitudes towards sentencing and alternatives to imprisonment.* Available at www.scottish.parliament.uk

Mattinson, J., & Mirrlees-Black, C. (2000). *Attitudes to crime and criminal justice: Findings from the 1998 British Crime Survey.* Home Office Research Study 200. London: Home Office.

Mayhew, P., & van Kesteren, J. (2002). Cross-national attitudes to punishment. In J. V. Roberts & M. Hough (Eds.), *Changing attitudes to punishment.* Cullompton, England: Willan.

Mirrlees-Black, C. (2002). Improving public knowledge about crime and punishment. In J. V. Roberts & M. Hough (Eds.), *Changing attitudes to punishment.* Cullompton, England: Willan.

Nuttall, C., Eversley, D., Rudder, I., & Ramsay, J. (2003). *Views and beliefs about crime and criminal justice.* Bridgetown, Barbados: Attorney General, Barbados Statistical Department.

Parmentier, S., Vervaeke, G., Doutrelpont, R., & Kellens, G. (Eds.). (2004). *Public opinion and the administration of justice. Popular perceptions and their implications for policy-making in western countries.* Brussels, Belgium: Politeia.

Parmentier, S., Vervaeke, G., Goethals, J., et al. (2005). *Une radiographie de la justice. Les résultats du premier "baromètre de la justice" en Belgique: rapport final.* Gent: Academia Press.

Paulin, J., Searle, W., & Knaggs, T. (2003). *Attitudes to crime and punishment: A New Zealand study.* Wellington, New Zealand: Ministry of Justice.

Roberts, J. V. (1988). *Public opinion and sentencing: Surveys by the Canadian sentencing commission.* Research Reports of the Canadian Sentencing Commission. Ottawa, Canada: Department of Justice.

Roberts, J. V. (1992). Public opinion, crime and criminal justice. In M. Tonry (Ed.), *Crime and justice. A review of research* (Vol. 16). Chicago:University of Chicago Press.

Roberts, J. V. (1994). *Public knowledge of crime and criminal justice: An inventory of Canadian findings*. Ottawa, Canada: Department of Justice.

Roberts, J. V. (2001). *Fear of crime and attitudes to criminal justice in Canada: A review of recent trends*. Ottawa, Canada: Ministry of the Solicitor General.

Roberts, J. V., Crutcher, N., & Verbrugge, P. (2007). Public attitudes to sentencing in Canada: Some recent findings. *Canadian Journal of Criminology and Criminal Justice, 49*, 75-107.

Roberts, J. V., & Hough, M. (Eds.). (2002). *Changing attitudes to punishment: Public opinion, crime and justice*. Cullompton, England: Willan.

Roberts, J. V., & Hough, M. (2005a). Sentencing young offenders: Public opinion in England and Wales. *Criminal Justice, 5*, 211-232.

Roberts, J. V., & Hough, M. (2005b). *Understanding public attitudes to criminal justice*. Maidenhead, England: Open University Press.

Roberts, J. V., Stalans, L. S., Indermaur, D., & Hough, M. (2003). *Penal populism and public opinion. Findings from five countries*. New York: Oxford University Press.

Salisbury, H. (2004). *Public attitudes to the criminal justice system: The impact of providing information to British Crime Survey respondents*. Home Office Online Report 64/04. London: Home Office.

Silvey, J. (1961). The criminal law and public opinion. *Criminal Law Review*, pp. 349-358.

Stalans, L. (2002). Measuring attitudes to sentencing. In J. V. Roberts & M. Hough (Eds.), *Changing attitudes to punishment: Public opinion, crime and justice*. Cullompton, England: Willan.

Tyler, T. R., & Huo, Y. J. (2002). *Trust in the law: Encouraging public cooperation with the police and courts*. New York: Russell-Sage Foundation.

Tyler, T. R. (2003). Procedural justice, legitimacy, and the effective rule of law. In M. Tonry (Ed.), *Crime and justice – A review of research*, Vol. 30. University of Chicago Press.

Walker, N., & Hough, M. (Eds.). (1988). *Public attitudes to sentencing. Surveys from five countries*. Cambridge Studies in Criminology. Farnborough, England: Gower.

Weatherburn, D., & Indermaur, D. (2004). *Public perceptions of crime trends in New South Wales and Western Australia*. Crime and Justice Bulletin No. 80. Sydney, Australia: New South Wales Bureau of Crime Statistics and Research.

The British Crime Survey and the Fear of Crime

by

Jason Ditton

and

Stephen Farrall
School of Law
University of Sheffield

Abstract: *The BCS has been the lead provider of national fear of crime data in the U.K. since 1982. In that time, the subject has become a substantial area of concern for both research and public policy. The subject has never been adequately conceptualised, however, and measurement methods – once adequate – seem increasingly outmoded. The authors outline these deficiencies and suggest how more sophisticated questions might remedy the situation in the future. Alternatives to the repeat cross-sectional approach are suggested and benefits outlined. New subjects for future questioning are discussed, with some accepted (identity theft) and some rejected (terrorism).*

The fear of crime has been one of central topics in the history of the BCS (Mayhew, 1996). It has always been asked about in one form or another, and has been the focus of several key publications stemming from the BCS (for examples, see Maxfield, 1984; Hough, 1995). Certainly BCS input to our understanding of the fear of crime has been immense and we would be hard-pushed to review all of its contributions herein. Instead, therefore, we wish to focus on a number of areas. We shall start with an overview of what is meant by the term *fear of crime* and some of the problems associated with its measurement. We then turn to consider how questions about the fear of crime are currently asked, focussing on those questions used in the BCS. We shall critique these questions, before suggesting some possible improvements. Finally, we look towards possible future issues that the BCS may be used to explore.

WHAT THE LAST 25 YEARS HAS TAUGHT US ABOUT THE FEAR OF CRIME

First, "fear" is confused, and indeed, it is unclear that it even can be accurately measured. As Gibbs and Hanrahan (1993) put it, "we are not suggesting here that emotions cannot be measured. We believe, however, that such measurement is difficult when the emotion is fear, the object is crime, and the method is survey" (pp. 387-388). Further, fear is occasionally confused with worry and anxiety, which are considered by some as synonymous (Bilsky & Wetzels, 1997; Fattah, 1993). However, they are not. As Croake and Hinkle (1976) comment, "many studies that report fears may actually have investigated anxiety, and many reporting the results of anxiety studies may have been researching fears" (p. 197). Sarnoff and Zimbardo (1961) add that fear is aroused when somebody is confronted by an external object or event that is inherently dangerous. Fear is responded to with flight or fight. Anxiety is aroused by stimuli that are inherently innocuous.

Fear of prospectively becoming a crime victim is often confused with a general concern about societal levels of crime (Eve, 1985), with the latter diminishing in policy importance in favour of the former by governments and policy makers keen on transforming criticisms of their actions into the internal troubles of a fearful citizenry (Ditton & Farrall, 2000b, pp. i-xv; Furedi, 2005; Lee, 1999). Specific fear and general concern are separate topics. Brantingham, Brantingham, and Butcher (1986, pp. 140-141) put it this way:

> [C]oncern with crime and fear of victimisation are two separate but interrelated study areas . . . while frequently confused by politicians and popular writers, concern with crime and fear of victimisation are entirely different concepts: people who do not fear victimisation may be very concerned about crime as a social problem, while people who are more concerned about social problems other than crime may have powerful fears of victimisation. (pp. 140-141)

Further, as Ewald (2000) points out, expressed fear of crime is possibly just a proxy for general concerns about other things. It is unclear whether fear is to be seen as a mental state whose intensity we can quantify (Hough, 2004) or a mental event whose frequency we can monitor (Farrall, 2004a; 2000b; Farrall & Gadd, 2004; Gray, Jackson, & Farrall, 2006). The degree to which fear is state or trait is unclear (Gabriel & Greve, 2003), although independent measures of both seem to account for very little expressed crime fear (Chadee, Ditton, & Virgil, 2007). Surveys themselves have been believed to create the fear they apparently set out to measure (Rosenbaum, 1987), and when respondents are offered counterarguments to expressed levels of beliefs about crime, their levels of belief reduce considerably (Kerner, 1978). Split ballot tests of modes of inquiry (mail, telephone, or face-to-face) indicate significant variations in levels of expressed fear (Kury & Wurger, 1993; Kury, 1994; Jackson, Farrall, & Gadd, forthcoming).

Second, fear is by no means either the main or only emotional or other response to the prospect or reality of criminal victimisation. Some research has indicated that anger is far more dominant (Ditton, Bannister, Gilchrist, & Farrall, 1999; Ditton, Farrall, et al., 1999), confirmed by the 2000 BCS, which found 92% of those asked about burglary to be "very" "or fairly angry." Neither is crime the thing that most people worry about (Kanner, Coyne, Schaefer, & Lazarus, 1981; de Roiste, 1996), although this in part may be because offering response options in closed formats generates more apparent crime fear than when asked openly. In a split ballot experiment, wherein respondents were asked to name the "most important problem," 34.9% chose "crime" when offered in the closed version, but only 15.7% suggested it in the open version (Schuman & Presser, 1996, p. 85; see also Farrall et al., 1997b). When respondents in another crime survey were asked to name the five most important problems, only 9% named crime, and only 1% made it the most important problem (Clinard, 1978). Even when prompted to worry about crime, recent research has shown that people don't worry about it very much, or very often (Farrall & Gadd, 2004; Farrall, Jackson, & Gray, 2006).

Third, expressed levels of fear are highly unstable, or, rather, the nature of the questions asked generates data that "wobbles" significantly. Initially, this was discovered by accident. In the 1988 BCS, the question "Do the police do a good or bad job?" was asked twice. Of those who answered it twice, 35% gave a different answer the second time (22% more positive, and 13% less so. Mayhew (2000) explained this as follows: "There is little obvious explanation, except perhaps that having become more sensitised to crime issues as the questionnaire proceeded, respondents became more sympathetic to the demands on the police" (p. 111). This is a charitable explanation, to say the least. In a survey we ran in 1995, we asked people how much they worried about burglary on two separate occasions. The result? Thirteen percent who didn't worry about it the first time they were asked had become worried 20 minutes later. Further, 18% of those who worried about it initially had ceased to worry by the second time (Ditton, Farrall, Bannister, & Gilchrist, 2000; Ditton & Farrall, 2000a). Qualitative follow-up back checks on this project indicated that respondents did, indeed, vary their own fear state at different times of the day (Farrall, Bannister, Ditton, & Gilchrist, 1997a; Farrall & Ditton, 1999). Longitudinal research – unhappily a rarity in the fear of crime field – indicates that, at 12-month intervals, respondents can become more or less fearful (Ditton, Chadee, & Khan, 2003), often reversing this change after another year (Ditton, Khan, & Chadee, 2005). Finally, some small-scale research has suggested that there is a distinct seasonal affect to crime fear (Semmens, Dillane, & Ditton, 2002).

Fourth, a major problem with BCS fear questions is their direct nature, as this can generate socially desirable but wholly misleading responses. Recent research has demonstrated this to be the case. Using data from a lie scale we included in our 1995 survey, Sutton & Farrall (2005) have now shown that the one finding from all crime surveys (that women are more crime-fearful than are men) is a function of men wishing to appear brave, and of women wishing to appear timorous (see also Kury & Wurger, 1993; Gilchrist, Bannister, Ditton, & Farrall, 1998).

Fifth, with no temporal reference point, questions on the fear of crime as currently designed are inappropriate for before-after evaluation studies (Farrall, 2004a). Sixth, the use of descriptive codes ("very", "fairly" and so on) to help respondents select an answer may have the effect, whilst helping in the production of a normal distribution, of suggesting to journalists or politicians that these codes mean something beyond their convenience in assisting respondents during the survey (Hough, 2004; Jackson, 2006; Lee, 2001, 2007). In other words, the codes designed for ease of placing respondents on a continuum have been reified as part of a vibrant discourse about crime and anxieties about crime.

HOW IS KNOWLEDGE ABOUT THE FEAR OF CRIME GENERATED?

Knowledge about the fear of crime comes from one main source: respondents. There are no official or quasi-official sources of data in the same way that there are for police-recorded incidents, arrests, court appearances, or convictions. In part, this is the source of some difficulties, since respondents may use the questions to send a message to politicians or the local police that they are dissatisfied with their performance with regards to crime.

We have checked the 1982 BCS questionnaire with the 2006-2007 BCS questionnaire, and with one exception ("how safe do you feel walking alone in this area after dark?"), the fear of crime questions show remarkable variation. Taking one of the consistent questions, 1982 BCS respondents were asked:

"How safe do you feel walking alone in this area after dark? Would you say *[READ OUT]* very safe?"

(Note: If respondent never goes out alone at night, probe:)

"How safe *would* you feel? Fairly safe? A bit unsafe? Or, very unsafe"?

The 2006-2007 BCS respondents were asked the following:

"How safe do you feel walking alone in this area after dark? Would you say you feel *[READ OUT]*

1. very safe

2. fairly safe

3. a bit unsafe, or

4. very unsafe?"

Note: If respondent never goes out alone at night, PROBE: "How safe *would* you feel?"

Adopting a similar style, 2006-2007 BCS respondents were also asked how safe they would feel walking alone in this area during the day, and how safe they would feel when they are alone in their own home at night. A distinct downside in the design of this question is the inclusion of hypothetical responses. How can people who don't go out alone at night (a majority of most respondents; see Ditton, Farrall, Bannister, & Gilchrist, 1998) assess how safe they "would" feel? Indeed, even nonhypothetically worded questions are in one sense hypothetical. As Garofalo (1981) puts it, "it is unlikely that a respondent is experiencing actual fear during a survey interview" (p. 841). These questions, which don't mention crime, are sometimes called the "globals."

In contrast, questions more directly about crime, or more specifically about particular crimes are sometimes dubbed "specifics." The 1982 BCS asked respondents, "Do you ever worry about the possibility that you or anyone else who lives with you might be the victim of crime?" Those who said yes were asked, "Is this a big worry, a bit of a worry, or just an occasional doubt?" They were then asked whom in their household they worried about, and then, crucially, "What sorts of crime do you worry about most?" Their answers were recorded verbatim, but not probed. Later, each was asked, "When you are out, do you ever worry about the possibility that your pocket might be picked or your bag snatched?"; those with access to motor vehicles were asked, "Do you ever worry about the possibility somebody might steal your car or van or take something from it?"; and all were asked "When your home is empty, do you ever worry at all about the possibility somebody might break in?" These last three were followed by a yes/no filter and those who said yes were asked, "Is this a big worry, a bit of a worry, or just an occasional doubt?"

By 2006-2007, the specifics had evolved into a battery of crimes. Respondents are introduced to the topic with the following statement: "Most of us *worry* at some time or other about being the victim of a crime" and are then asked, "How worried are you about . . . having your home broken into and something stolen? being mugged and robbed? having your car stolen? having things stolen from your car? being raped? being physically attacked by strangers? being insulted or pestered by anybody, while in the street or any other public place? being subject to a physical attack because of your skin colour, ethnic origin or religion?" At the end of the list of specifics, they are asked, "And now thinking about all types of crime in general, how worried are you about being a victim of crime?"

For each, they are offered the following response set:

1. Very worried

2. Fairly worried

3. Not very worried

4. Not at all worried

5. (Not applicable)

They are then asked, "Of the following three types of crime, which, if any, are you MOST worried about happening?"

CODE ONE ONLY

1. Having your home broken into
2. Having your car stolen, or something stolen from it
3. Being physically or sexually attacked, or mugged
4. SPONTANEOUS ONLY: Not worried about any of these
5. SPONTANEOUS ONLY: Cannot choose one over another/equally worried about all three

The degree of inconsistency over time surprised us, not least because the resistance to question change by BCS managers has always been on the grounds that even poor questions should be retained to permit uncompromised comparisons over time. However, and looking on the positive side, this unexpected change over time presumably opens the door to the possibility that the BCS questions might be changed, with the aim being improvement, in the future.

SOME COMMON PROBLEMS WITH FEAR OF CRIME QUESTIONS

There is, of course, no such thing as the perfect survey question – a point that always ought to be borne in mind when discussing the relative merits and demerits of questions. There are a number of routinely encountered problems, however, relating to those questions that ask about the fear of crime (for reviews of these difficulties, see Ferraro & La Grange, 1987; Skogan, 1981b; Farrall et al., 1997a; Farrall, 2004a). There are three basic problems with the type of questions used in the BCS. First, far too many questions only yield nominal data, disdainfully dismissed by some as "qualitative" data (Kennedy, 1992). The limitation of nominal data is that it is impossible to test the association of it with other data except by assessing the probability that an association is by chance. With large samples, significant p values from chi-square testing often tend towards significance.[1] The strength and direction of any association is rarely calculated. An encouraging development would be to move nominal questions to ordinal ones, and ordinal ones to interval ones. One forceful methodological review suggests:

> We should now be beyond commonly used four-item Likert scales and headed toward better interval level measurement. The fact is

that multi-point, metric-ordinal rating scales yield lower measurement error and provide a closer approximation of true response positions. (Williams, McShane, & Akers, 2000, p. 7)

Second, attitudes are measured with single questions. Skogan (1981a) comments that "persuasive research evidence shows that one-item measures of attitudes have about a 50 per cent error variance" (p. 731) and suggests that a minimum of three are needed. In the same article, he also cautions against what he calls "vague quantifiers," such as "sometimes" and "most of the time," which are, of course, BCS staples.

Third, and most important, the BCS questionnaire commits the most basic sin of design, as it frequently asks the respondent to do the analysis. This takes various forms. Occasionally (2006-2007 BCS questions OutAlon2 and WeekDay), respondents are asked how often they do something "usually" or "on average." Even for simple questions, this expects respondents to generate what Jackson (2005, p. 299) calls a "difficult summary." The preferred professional form is to ask respondents how often they did whatever it is "in the last 7 days."

The most serious form that this takes is to ask in a leading fashion and directly about fear. The current BCS specifics suggest that worry is an appropriate attitude to take towards the prospect of victimisation ("Most of us *worry* at some time or other about being the victim of a crime") and that to do so is normal (Jackson, 2006, p. 256). Asking directly about fear is a fatal error. As Garofalo and Laub (1978) claim, "the specification of the problem in terms of the answer is always a specification for failure" (p. 246). They are referring to, as it happens, Leslie Wilkins, who alone, perhaps, has the only evidence that direct questions create the opportunity for socially desirable responses, and for inflated levels of whatever the question is seeking to quantify (but see also Jackson et al., in press). Elsewhere (Wilkins, 1964, pp. 218-219) recounts the telling story of attempts to estimate how many World War II veterans wished to receive awards to which they were entitled. In a small experiment, survey question formats were varied. A single question yielded an estimate that almost 70% of eligible veterans wished to receive medals. Among those responding to a battery of questions that tapped several indirect dimensions associated with the expected behaviour, only 35% were judged likely to pick up their medals, virtually identical to the 34.7% who actually applied for medals.

We will return to this issue later, and suggest how "fear" might better be assessed by asking several indirect questions, themselves derived from a thoughtful conceptual model, but first we address the closely related issue of socially desirable answering in surveys.

The tendency for individuals to respond in socially desirable ways has been known for a long time, and this has been found to affect gender differences in fear. The tools used to assess social desirability are sometimes called "lie scales" because they assess participants' systematic distortion of their attitudes. There are various lie scales, including the Marlowe-Crowne Social Desirability Inventory (Crowne & Marlowe, 1960), Paulhus' Socially Desirable Responding Inventory (Paulhus, 1991), and others that are built into personality inventories. Often questions are asked of participants for which agreement (or disagreement) is socially desirable but highly unlikely to be true (e.g., "I have never been annoyed with an opinionated person" Crowne & Marlowe, 1960). Agreement with items like this may be socially desirable but is almost certainly false, and signifies that participants might be manipulating their responses in order to make a favourable impression. In essence then, such scales capture differences between individuals in the extent to which they *strategically* manipulate their responses. This allows researchers to infer whether differences between individuals on other scales reflect genuine differences in the variable of interest, or instead emerge from the fact that some individuals and groups are more prone to distort their responses.

Sutton and Farrall (2005), using data from the Strathclyde Crime Survey (see Ditton, Bannister, et al., 1999) explored the relationship between gender, the fear of crime, and socially desirable responding. Overall, their data suggest that those men who are most concerned with distorting their responses for self-presentational reasons reported the lowest levels of fear (2005, p. 219). This pattern did not emerge for women in their analyses. These results suggest that masculine identities were to some extent incompatible with admissions of anxiety about crime (see also Bem, 1981; Goodey, 1997). As a result, it would appear that men more than women feel some pressure to suppress their expression of crime-related fears. This suggests two key observations: First, that the widely observed tendency for men to report lower levels of crime fear than women do stemmed from men's reluctance to report their feelings accurately. Second, that when the impact of socially desirable responding is removed, the sex differences disappear, and may even be in the opposite direction to that suggested by much of the literature (i.e., that men, not women, are the more fearful).

WHAT CAN BE DONE TO IMPROVE MEASUREMENT OF THE FEAR OF CRIME?

It is essential to develop more sensitive measures of fear, as reducing it has become a central Key Performance Indicator for the police, the Home Office, and others. Yet fear, as measured in the conventional way, is stubbornly resistant to reduction, even following extensive internal and external environmental improvements (Nair, Ditton, & Phillips, 1993; Ditton, 2000). The out-alone-dark and in-alone-dark "global" questions (bearing in mind our earlier recommendation to move from nominal to interval data) could easily be turned into a scalar variable in the way recommended by Teske and Hazlett (1988) and Brantingham et al. (1986). As part of one of the preparation for a forthcoming longitudinal Trinidadian survey, the following questions have been piloted:

How safe do you feel . . .

1. Walking alone at night *outside* your neighbourhood?

2. Walking with another person at night *outside* your neighbourhood?

3. Walking alone at night *in* your neighbourhood?

4. Walking with another person at night *in* your neighbourhood?

5. Being alone inside your home at night?

6. Being with another person inside your home at night?

Respondents were asked to respond using a 6-point scale with 0 = totally safe through to 6 = totally unsafe. Questions 1 through 4 (the out-of-house ones) intercorrelated at least .59 (Cronbach's alpha of .895), and questions 5 and 6 intercorrelated at .83 (Cronbach's alpha of .908). The out-of house questions only correlated with the in-house ones at between .27 and .58. Teske and Hazlett (1988) recommend checking for unidimensionality and cumulativeness, and this was done successfully manually. The result is a 21-point scale for safe out of house, an 11-point scale for safe in house, and a combined 31-point scale.

People, particularly young people (who do go out alone at night) don't just want safety, they also want its opposite, excitement. Questioning should not assume that safety is a universal goal (Ditton, 2000). A more effective way of thinking about it has been developed by Gibbs and Hanrahan (1993) who suggest the following:

If we separate concern for safety into demand and supply, we have two factors, rather than one, to examine and modify for policy and program purposes. It is one thing to report that people in a certain environment feel unsafe or feel afraid. It is two things to find that demand for safety among inhabitants of a neighborhood is at a certain level and that supply is at a certain level. If demand is average and supply is low, one kind of problem exists. If demand is high and supply is average, another kind of problem exists. The most effective approach to the first problem may not work with the second. (pp. 380, 389)

Redesigning the "specifics" is trickier. Again bearing in mind our earlier recommendation of long rather than short scales for response purposes, and for indirect rather than direct questions (to avoid socially desirable responses), the hypothesised components of fear should be the subject of questions, rather than fear itself. At a logical level, perceived risk of victimisation and perceived harmfulness of victimisation are becoming recognised as constitutive of fear (Chadee, Austen, & Ditton, in press; Ditton & Innes, 2005; Ditton & Chadee, 2006; Jackson, 2004a, 2004b; Jackson, Farrall, et al., 2006).[2]

But what "specifics" should be the subject of questioning? The first Trinidad pilot for the forthcoming survey suggested that rape and murder are significantly outside the acceptable range for skew and kurtosis (i. e., greater than ±1) and were thereafter dropped. A second pilot tested 19 possible victimisations suggested by a trawl of the literature. The following were subsequently dropped for having unacceptable skew and/or kurtosis:

1. Being attacked by someone with a weapon

2. Having someone break into your home when you are there

3. Being beaten up by someone you know

4. Being sold contaminated food

5. Being approached on the street by a beggar

6. Being kidnapped[3]

7. Being overcharged when buying something

8. Being hit by a drunken driver

9. Being mugged.

The following were retained:

1. Having something stolen when you are away from home

2. Having someone break into your house when you are away

- 233 -

3. Having property damaged by vandals

4. Having your car, van, or bicycle stolen

5. Receiving an obscene phone call

6. Having your purse or wallet snatched

7. Having your pocket picked

8. Being conned, cheated, or swindled out of some money

9. Being robbed in the street

10. Having rowdy youths disturbing the peace near your home.

Factor analysis neatly partitioned the acceptable list of 10 into the first 5 (which we broadly consider as a property crime group) and the second 5 (which we see as a personal crime group). Respondents were asked to express how likely they thought each was to happen to them on a 0-5 scale ("certain not to happen" to "certain to happen"), and also how harmful each would be if it did on a 0-5 scale ("no harm" to "maximum harm"). This permits the construction of an additive scale of 0-25 for, separately, property and personal victimisations, and a total scale of 0-50 for all victimisations. This can be done for both risk and harm, allowing a final additive scale of 0-100. Lengthy scales also attend more usefully to the policy agenda than do the usual 4-point Likert-type scales. Long scales such as the one proposed permit changes at the 1% level to be identified, whereas short scales require a change in attitude of more than 25% before an effect can be pinpointed.

A further alternative that attempts to estimate the number of times people have encountered fear-provoking situations has also been developed (Farrall, 2004a; Farrall & Gadd, 2004). Chief amongst the findings that emerged from the BCS, the U.S. NCS, and various other local crime surveys was that rates of fear were quite high. Many surveys reported that in the U.K. and the U.S. anywhere between a quarter and one third of the population were "quite" or "very" worried. However, qualitative data and a general reconsideration of the meanings of such answers led some to question the measurement of the fear of crime. These critiques usually concluded that the questions used to measure the fear of crime routinely produced exaggerated results, due to various undesirable aspects of the questions used. As a way forward, Farrall (2004a) suggested a new set of three questions that were aimed at assessing the frequency with which fearful episodes were encountered.[4] The results suggested that very few people routinely felt fearful. Only around 8% of the total sample interviewed by Farrall and Gadd who had experienced more than five fearful episodes had felt "quite" or "very" fearful on the last occasion. Of course, one cannot know how they had felt on previous occasions – they may have felt less fearful. If we assume, however, that in aggregate the most recent fearful episodes are representative of all fearful events, Only a small proportion of the population felt a high level of fear in the past year (15%) and that for only around half of these people (8% of the total population) was a high level of fear encountered more than once a quarter. Similar findings have been produced with the cooperation of the BCS team as part of the 2003-2004 BCS (see Farrall et al., 2006).

CONCLUSION: LOOKING TO NEW ISSUES

We were asked to comment on the advisability or otherwise of asking questions on terrorism and fraud. We reject the first (although, see Lerner, Gonzalez, Small, & Fischhoff, 2003) as we see no point in creating another fear monster (although this may already have happened; see Lee, 2007). A cautionary tale to this effect can be found in Beck and Willis (1993). They interviewed an opportunity sample of 849 respondents in Leicester, and found that 62% worried "about the possibility of terrorist attack, specifically a bomb explosion" while shopping (p. 1), of whom 32% claimed to have altered their pattern of shopping because of this perceived risk. Note that respondents were not asked what they worried about, but specifically, "Do you ever think about the possibility of bomb explosions while you are shopping?" and if yes, "to what extent are you worried?" and "has this worry changed the way you shop?"

Rather than create new sources of probably exaggerated concern by asking about terrorism, it might be more helpful to seek data on self-reported offending (as the 1982 BCS did) and on attitudes towards non-street-crime victimisation. This is explored in Karstedt and Farrall (2004, 2006) who found a strong relationship between fears about various market crimes and actual experiences of these forms of victimisation. Similarly, those in work appeared to be more fearful than those not working (see also Ditton, 2003). Many studies have found that older people are more likely to report higher levels of the fear of crime. Karstedt and Farrall (2006), however, found a weak, negative relationship suggesting that it was younger people, not older people, who were most likely to be fearful of crimes in the market place. Thus, and unlike many previous studies of the fear of crime, we find that for this type of crime (loosely described as consumer crimes) that it is younger people, not older people, who consistently report the highest fear levels. The typically highly fearful person is aged between 25 and 44, struggling to cope financially despite being a higher earner, employed, but someone who has also been victimised.[5] A further approach comes from combining frequency and standard measures on the fear of crime (see Farrall et al., 2006; Farrall, Gray, & Jackson, 2007; Gray et al., 2006).

Hitherto, the BCS has been more data-driven than theory guided. Some steps towards the development of a coherent testable model were taken initially by Hough (1995) and are currently being explored, with considerable finesse, by Jackson (passim). The moment has finally come, perhaps, when fear of crime is being elaborated by experts on fear, rather than by experts on crime.

Address correspondence to: jasonditton@lineone.net

NOTES

1. Relative chi-square reduces this problem to some extent, but is not widely used.
2. There are, we admit, huge problems involved in asking people to estimate risk (see, inter alia, Jackson, Allum, et al., 2006, para. 51; Ditton & Chadee, 2006; Chadee, et al., forthcoming) and to estimate the probable harm from something they haven't experienced. This does not, however, mean that the two taken together cannot constitute "fear."
3. This is a considerable problem in Trinidad.
4. The questions asked were: "I'd now like to ask you some questions about only the previous year. In the *past year*, have you *ever* felt fearful about becoming a victim of crime?" 1 = yes, 2 = no. If yes, "How frequently have you felt like this in the past year?" (Raw count recorded). "On the last occasion, how fearful did you feel?" 0 = cannot

remember, 1 = not very fearful, 2 = a little bit fearful, 3 = quite fearful, 4 = very fearful.
5. We also feel that identity theft should be covered. See Semmens (2003).

REFERENCES

Beck, A., & Willis, A. (1993). *The terrorist threat to safe shopping*. University of Leicester, Centre for the Study of Public Order.

Bem, S. L. (1981). Gender schema theory: A cognitive account of sex typing. *Psychological Review, 88*, 354-364.

Bilsky, W., & Wetzels, P. (1997). On the relationship between criminal victimisation and fear of crime. *Psychology, Crime & Law, 3*, 309-318.

Brantingham, P., Brantingham, P., & Butcher, D. (1986). Perceived and actual crime risks. In R. Figlio, S. Hakim, & R. Rengert (Eds.), *Metropolitan crime patterns* (pp. 139-159). New York: Criminal Justice Press.

Chadee, D., Austen, L., & Ditton, J. (in press). The relationship between likelihood and fear of criminal victimisation: Evaluating risk sensitivity as a mediating concept. *British Journal of Criminology*.

Chadee, D., Ditton, J., & Virgil, N. (2007). State-trait anxiety and fear of crime: A social psychological perspective. Manuscript submitted for publication.

Clinard, M. (1978). *Cities with little crime: The case of Switzerland*. Cambridge University Press.

Croake, J., & Hinkle, D. (1976). Methodological problems in the study of fears. *Journal of Psychology, 93*, 197-202.

Crowne, D. P., & Marlowe, D. (1960). A new scale of social desirability independent of psychopathology. *Journal of Consulting Psychology, 24*, 349-354.

de Roiste, A. (1996). Sources of worry and happiness in Ireland. *Irish Journal of Psychology, 17*, 193-212.

Ditton, J. (2000). Crime and the city: Public attitudes towards open-street CCTV in Glasgow. *British Journal of Criminology, 40*, 399-413.

Ditton, J. (2003). Worry about housebreaking: Is it affected by employment status? *Scottish Journal of Criminal Justice Studies, 9*, 96-99.

Ditton, J., Bannister, J., Gilchrist, E., & Farrall, S. (1999). Afraid or angry? Recalibrating the "fear" of crime. *International Review of Victimology, 6*, 83-99.

Ditton, J., & Chadee, D. (2006). People's perceptions of their likely future risk of criminal victimisation. *British Journal of Criminology, 46*, 505-518.

Ditton, J., Chadee, D., & Khan, F. (2003). The stability of global and specific measures of the fear of crime: Results from a two wave Trinidadian longitudinal study. *International Review of Victimology, 9*, 49-70.

Ditton, J., & Farrall, S. (2000a). Fear of burglary: Refining national survey questions for use at the local level. *International Journal of Police Science and Management, 3*(1), 9-18.

Ditton, J. & Farrall, S. (Eds.). (2000b). *The Fear of crime*. International Library of Criminology, Criminal Justice and Penology. Aldershot, England: Dartmouth.

Ditton, J., Farrall, S., Bannister, J., & Gilchrist, E. (1998). Measuring fear of crime. *Criminal Justice Matters, 31,* 10-12.

Ditton, J., Farrall, S., Bannister, J., & Gilchrist, E. (2000). Crime surveys and the measurement problem: Fear of crime. In V. Jupp, P. Davies, & P. Francis (Eds.), *Doing criminological research* (pp. 142-156). London: Sage.

Ditton, J., Farrall, S., Bannister, J., Gilchrist, E., &. Pease, K. (1999). Reactions to victimisation: Why has anger been ignored? *Crime Prevention and Community Safety, 1,* 37-54.

Ditton, J., Khan, F., & Chadee, D. (2005). Fear of crime quantitative measurement instability revisited and qualitative consistency added: Results from a three wave Trinidadian longitudinal study. *International Review of Victimology, 12,* 247-271.

Ditton, J., & Innes, M. (2005). The role of perceptual intervention in the management of crime fear. In N. Tilley (Ed.), *Handbook of crime prevention and community safety* (pp. 595-623). Cullompton, England: Willan.

Eve, S. (1985). Criminal victimisation and fear of crime among the non-institutionalised elderly in the United States: A critique of the empirical research literature. *Victimology, 10,* 397-408.

Ewald, U. (2000). Criminal victimisation and social adaptation in modernity: Fear of crime and risk perception in the new Germany. In T. Hope & R. Sparks (Eds.), *Crime, risk and insecurity* (pp. 166-199). London: Routledge.

Farrall, S. (2004a). Revisiting crime surveys: Emotional responses without emotions? – or – Look back at anger. *International Journal of Social Research Methodology, 7,* 157-171.

Farrall, S. (2004b). Can we believe our eyes? A response to Mike Hough. *International Journal of Social Research Methodology, 7,* 177-179.

Farrall, S., Bannister, J., Ditton, J., & Gilchrist, E. (1997a). Questioning the measurement of the "fear of crime": Findings from a major methodological study. *British Journal of Criminology, 37,* 658-679.

Farrall, S., Bannister, J., Ditton, J., & Gilchrist, E. (1997b). Open and closed questions. *Social Research Update,* No. 17.

Farrall, S., Bannister, J., Ditton, J., & Gilchrist, E. (2000). Social psychology and the fear of crime: Re-examining a speculative model. *British Journal of Criminology, 40,* 399-413.

Farrall, S., & Ditton, J. (1999). Improving the measurement of attitudinal responses: An example from a crime survey. *International Journal of Social Research Methodology, 2*(1), 55-68.

Farrall, S., & Ditton, J. (in press). Rethinking how fear of crime is surveyed: Considering social psychological factors. In D. Chadee & J. Young (Eds.), *Current themes in social psychology* (pp. 101-119). University of the West Indies, School of Continuing Studies, Trinidad.

Farrall, S., & Gadd, D. (2004). The frequency of the fear of crime. *British Journal of Criminology, 44,* 127-132.

Farrall, S., Gray, E., & Jackson, J. (2007) *Combining the new and old measures of the fear of crime: Exploring the "worried well."* Working Paper No. 4, ESRC Grant RES 000 23 1108.

Farrall, S., Jackson, J., & Gray, E. (2006). *Everyday emotion and the fear of crime: Preliminary findings from experience & expression.* Working Paper No 1, ESRC Grant RES 000 23 1108.

Fattah, E. (1993). Research on fear of crime: Some common conceptual and measurement problems. In W. Bilsky, C. Pfeiffer, & P. Wetzels (Eds.), *Fear of crime and criminal victimisation* (pp. 45-70). Stuttgart, Germany: Ferdinand Enke Verlag.

Ferraro, K., & LaGrange, R. (1987). The measurement of fear of crime. *Sociological Inquiry, 57*(1), 70-101.

Foa, E., & Kozak, M. (1986). Emotional processing of fear: Exposure to corrective information. *Psychological Bulletin, 99*, 20-35.

Furedi, F. (2005). *Politics of fear: Beyond left and right.* London: Continuum.

Gabriel, U., & Greve, W. (2003). The psychology of fear of crime: Conceptual and methodological perspectives. *British Journal of Criminology, 43*, 600-614.

Garofalo, J. (1981). The fear of crime: Causes and consequences. *Journal of Criminal Law and Criminology, 72*, 839-857.

Garofalo, J., & Laub, J. (1978). The fear of crime: Broadening our perspective. *Victimology, 3*, 242-253.

Gibbs, J., & Hanrahan, K. (1993). Safety demand and supply: An alternative to fear of crime. *Justice Quarterly, 10*, 369-394.

Gilchrist, E., Bannister, J., Ditton, J., & Farrall, S. (1998). Women and the "fear of crime": Challenging the accepted stereotype. *British Journal of Criminology, 38*, 283-298.

Goodey, J. (1997). Boys don't cry: Masculinities, fear of crime and fearlessness. *British Journal of Criminology, 37*, 401-418.

Gray, E., Jackson, J., & Farrall, S. (2006) *Reassessing the fear of crime: Frequencies and correlates of old and new measures.* Working Paper No. 3, ESRC Grant RES 000 23 1108.

Hough, M. (1995). *Anxiety about crime: Findings from the 1994 British Crime Survey.* Home Office Research Study No. 147, Home Office Research and Statistics Directorate.

Hough, M. (2004). Worry about crime: Mental events or mental states? *International Journal of Social Research Methodology, 7*, 173-176.

Jackson, J. (2004a). An analysis of a construct and debate: The fear of crime. In H-J. Albrecht, T. Serassis, & H. Kania (Eds.), *Images of crime II: Representations of crime and the criminal in politics, society, the media and the arts.* Freiburg, Germany: Max-Planck Institut.

Jackson, J. (2004b). Experience and expression: Social and cultural significance in the fear of crime. *British Journal of Criminology, 44*, 946-966.

Jackson, J. (2005). Validating new measures of the fear of crime. *International Journal of Social Research Methodology, 8*, 297-315.

Jackson, J. (2006). Introducing fear of crime to risk research. *Risk Analysis, 26*, 253-264.

Jackson, J., Allum N., & Gaskell, G. (2006). Bridging levels of analysis in risk perception research: The case of the fear of crime. *Forum: Qualitative Social Research, 7*(1) Art. 20.

Jackson, J., Farrall, S., & Gadd, D. (forthcoming. Filtering fear: On the use of filter and frequency questions in crime surveys. Working paper [available from the authors].

Jackson, J., Farrall, S., & Gray, E. (2006). *The provenance of fear.* Working Paper No. 2, ESRC Grant RES 000 23 1108.

Kanner, A., Coyne, J., Schaefer, C., & Lazarus, R. (1981). Comparison of two modes of stress measurement: Daily hassles and uplifts versus major life events. *Journal of Behavioural Medicine, 4*(1), 1-39.

Karstedt, S., & Farrall, S. (2004). The moral maze of the middle class: The predatory society and its emerging regulatory order. In H-J. Albrecht, T. Serassis, & H. Kania (Eds.), *Images of crime II* (pp. 65-93). Freiberg, Germany: Max Plank Institute.

Karstedt, S., & Farrall, S. (2006). The moral economy of everyday crime: Markets, consumers and citizens. *British Journal of Criminology, 46,* 1011-1036.

Kennedy, J. (1992). *Analyzing qualitative data: Log-linear analysis for behavioural research.* New York: Praeger.

Kerner, H-J. (1978). Fear of crime and attitudes towards crime: Comparative criminological reflections. *Annales Internationales de Criminologie, 17,* 83-99.

Kury, H., & Wurger, M. (1993). The influence of the type of data collection method on the results of the victim surveys: A German research project. In A. del Frate, U. Zvekic, & J. van Dijk (Eds.), *Understanding crime: Experiences of crime and crime control* (pp. 137-152). Rome: UNICRI.

Kury, H. (1994). The influence of the specific formulation of questions on the results of victim studies. *European Journal of Criminal Policy and Research, 2*(4), 48-68.

Lee, M. (1999). The fear of crime and self-governance: Towards a genealogy. *Australian and New Zealand Journal of Criminology, 32,* 227-246.

Lee, M. (2001). The genesis of "fear of crime." *Theoretical Criminology, (4),* 467-485.

Lee, M. (2007) *Inventing fear of crime.* Cullomption, England: Willan.

Lerner, J., Gonzalez, R., Small, D., & Fischhoff, B. (2003). Effects of fear and anger on perceived risks of terrorism: A national field experiment. *Psychological Science, 14,* 144-150.

Maxfield, M. (1984). *Fear of crime in England & Wales.* London: HORS 78, HMSO.

Mayhew, P. (2000). Researching the state of crime: Local, national, and international crime surveys. In R. King & E. Wincup (Eds.), *Doing research on crime and justice* (pp. 91-120). Oxford University Press.

Mayhew, P. (1996). Researching crime and victimisation. In P. Davies, P. Francis, & V. Jupp (Eds.), *Understanding victimisation.* Gateshead, England: Northumbria Social Science Press.

Nair, G., Ditton, J., & Phillips, S. (1993). Environmental improvements and the fear of crime: The sad case of the "Pond" area in Glasgow. *British Journal of Criminology, 33,* 555-561.

Paulhus, D. L. (1991). Measurement and control of response bias. In J. Robinson, P. Shaver, & L. Wrightsman (Eds.), *Measures of personality and social psychological attitudes: Measures of social psychological attitudes* (pp. 17-59). San Diego, CA: Academic Press.

Rosenbaum, D. (1987). The theory and research behind neighborhood watch: Is it a sound fear and crime reduction strategy? *Crime & Delinquency, 33*(1), 103-134.

Sarnoff, I., & Zimbardo, P. (1961). Anxiety, fear, and social affiliation. *Journal of Abnormal and Social Psychology, 62,* 356-363.

Schuman, H., & Presser, S. (1996). *Questions and answers in attitude surveys: Experiments on question form, wording, and context.* London: Sage.

Semmens, N. (2003). The fear of plastic card fraud. Unpublished doctoral dissertation. Sheffield University, Faculty of Law.

Semmens, N., Dillane, J., & Ditton, J. (2002). Preliminary findings on seasonality and the fear of crime: A research note. *British Journal of Criminology, 42,* 798-806.

Skogan, W. (1981a). Assessing the behavioral context of victimisation. *Journal of Criminal Law & Criminology, 72,* 727-742.

Skogan, W. (1981b). *Issues in the measurement of victimisation.* Washington, DC: U.S. Government Printing Office.

Sparks, R., Genn, H., & Dodd, D. (1977). *Surveying victims: A study of the measurement of criminal victimisation.* Chichester, England: Wiley.

Sutton, R., & Farrall, S. (2005). Gender, social desirable responding and the fear of crime: Are women really more anxious about crime? *British Journal of Criminology, 45,* 212-224.

Teske, R., & Hazlett, M. (1988). A scale for the measurement of fear of crime. *American Journal of Criminal Justice, 12,* 274-292.

Wilkins, L. (1964). *Social deviance: Social policy, action, and research.* London: Tavistock.

Williams, F., McShane, M., & Akers, R. (2000). Worry about victimisation: An alternative and reliable measure for fear of crime. *Western Criminology Review, 2*(2), http://wcr.sonoma.edu/v2n2/williams.html

Improving National Crime Surveys: With a Focus Upon Strangely Neglected Offenders and Their Offences, Including Fraud, High-Tech Crimes, and Handling Stolen Goods

by

Mike Sutton
Nottingham Centre for Study and Reduction
of Hate Crimes, Bias, and Prejudice
Nottingham Trent University

Abstract: *This chapter proposes new directions for improving the British Crime Survey and other national crime surveys. With more focus upon new and strangely neglected crime types such as fraud and high-tech crimes, these surveys can substantially enhance criminological knowledge and crime prevention policy-making. In this chapter, solutions are proposed to help overcome entrenched and growing criticisms of national crime surveys – particularly the atavistic and tautological relationship between their current criminological focus on the "usual suspects" and its resulting bias in administrative criminology. Therefore, an independent, transparent, less nebulous, and more systematic review process is proposed as a solution to improve decision making about the locations, offences, offenders, and victims to be included in national crime surveys.*

Crime Prevention Studies, volume 22 (2007), pp. 243–261.

What rightfully should be called *policy-oriented* (not administrative) criminology has been at the heart of much Home Office crime reduction policy-making since the pioneering and seminal works of Leslie Wilkins, Ron Clarke, Pat Mayhew, and Mike Hough put it there. Yet those employed by, or who collaborate with, the Home Office in the fields of crime reduction and national crime surveys[1] are collectively and disparagingly known by other members of the academic community as administrative criminologists (Young, 1986). As most U.K. academics will undoubtedly concur, this disdain is currently taught to undergraduate students throughout our universities and is palpable in popular student textbooks. Many critical criminologists portray administrative criminologists to be garnering credibility falsely and selfishly as a small elite group of civil servants or academic crime reduction experts who are the best providers of a realistic and workable school of criminology focused upon criminal justice policy making, crime reduction, and its evaluation (see Hillyard et al., 2004; Walters, 2005). Today, "administrative criminologist" is a label that is applied as a term of abuse to indicate someone as working in a field that lacks credibility in its general aims and outcomes. This harsh criticism of administrative criminology is enduring and needs to be understood if one of the wider goals of criminology is to do something to reduce the harm caused by various types of crime, rather than merely teach, research, write, and present papers about the subject. Because national crime surveys are at the centre of much criticism of administrative criminology, it is particularly useful to examine the background to criticisms aimed against them.

For more than 20 years following its launch, a fundamental requirement in the management of the British Crime Survey (BCS) has been to maintain (1) the routine monitoring of crime rates, (2) measuring and understanding these crime rates, and (3) researching other crimes that are new or strangely neglected. To help prevent the BCS from being reduced to little more than a costly monitoring tool, inevitably at risk of becoming technologically obsolete and intellectually redundant, it is important to maintain these three distinct elements. Most important, the third requirement should not be overshadowed by the short-term administrative gains and political demands of the first two. In the past 5 years. however, this appears to have happened as the original innovative benefits of the BCS are under threat from its new status as a tool used to monitor individual police force performance.

By critically reflecting upon this issue and some other more entrenched criticisms of national crime surveys such as the BCS, this chapter explores several key areas for improvement in their sampling, design, content, and analysis.

Because administrative criminologists currently design and control national crime surveys and then use the findings to shape their work,[2] there is a strong argument to be made for replacing this in-bred administrative criminology with a more widely informed, up-to-date, and comprehensive policy-oriented criminology that has much more external input from expert academics.

To help achieve this goal, greater collaboration between academic and administrative criminologists is required. With that in mind, the label "administrative criminologist" is replaced throughout the remainder of this chapter with an arguably more inspirational and less value-laden description: policy-oriented criminologist.

THE ROLE OF NATIONAL CRIME SURVEYS FOR RESEARCH AND POLICY

Sampling Respondents and Questions Asked

Reliable, accurate, comprehensive, and up-to-date information is required by nations in order to operate effectively and efficiently. The criminal justice system needs information with these four characteristics to ensure that crime problems are adequately identified and resources targeted where most needed. National crime surveys such as the BCS provide some of this information and use robust sampling and design methods to seek to ensure that data are reliable and accurate. Although it is beyond the aims of this chapter to explore complex issues of national crime survey reliability and accuracy, less technical issues of scope and shelf life are examined. To begin with, there is a particularly important need to ask, What robust procedures are followed to ensure that national crime survey questions are comprehensive and up-to-date? This question actually takes quite a lot of answering.

First, in deciding what questions to include, those who manage the BCS are constrained by several factors. There is always a need to ensure that some figures from the latest survey can be compared with previous ones and with police-recorded crime statistics. This continuity requirement has shaped a core set of questions about high-volume crimes such as violence, robbery, burglary, and other thefts, and it facilitates insights into particular crimes that are on the increase, staying about the same, or going down. Using this data, it is possible to compare crime-trend insights with other measures of fear about crime, and also to monitor the relative annual performance of each constabulary in England and Wales.

Cost is another factor affecting what questions to include. For example, the more questions in the BCS, the more it costs to administer. Finally, if there are too many questions, then noncompletion rates will soar as interviews are broken off for a variety of reasons, ranging from respondents' boredom to their need to fetch children from school.

The low incidence of some crime types means that they are unsuitable for inclusion in national crime surveys. Inclusion depends in part upon the calculated prevalence rates of the offence in the general population of England and Wales. This is because if the offence is relatively rare it will not be possible to conduct robust statistical analysis on the attributes of victims or offenders. One problem with selecting in this way, however, is that it is not always possible to know or even guesstimate with any degree of accuracy the proportion of the population that is victim or perpetrator of crimes that are underreported to, or detected by, the police. For example, who could have guessed before the 1994 BCS that 11% of people would have admitted to buying stolen goods in the past 5 years (Sutton, 1998)? Or who could have predicted that 3% of the general population would admit using their mobile phones to threaten and seriously harass people in the past year, and that as many as 12% would have been victims of such behaviour (Allen et al., 2005)?

Social surveys are democratic instruments that collect data on people's fears and experiences of crime and levels of safety in different sectors of our communities (Young, 1992). Yet national crime surveys such as the BCS do not sample data to conduct analysis of separate communities that exist in real geographically defined neighbourhoods.

This is less than ideal because national surveys, even with their small area sampling profiles, can only homogenise all the localised crime problems in England and Wales in order to make robust generalisations about the experiences of particular income groups living in generalised types of housing area. The data cannot be analysed to reveal what goes on within by the actual physical boundaries of real and known problem neighbourhoods.[3] At the community level of analysis, there is an argument then for the superiority of local surveys such as the Islington Crime Survey (Jones et al., 1986) over nationally representative surveys.

One proposed solution is to move forward with a series of independently funded city surveys. Sampling from real geographically defined neighbourhoods, such surveys would provide data for the assessment of levels of fear and victimisation within real neighbourhoods in known cities.[4] Expensive to conduct, yet valuable in their own right, city-level surveys would help to assess the accuracy of national and regional generalisations that arise from BCS findings. This would determine how useful our current national crime surveys are as a genuine barometer of fear, victimisation, and even police performance in the real unhomogenised world – particularly real problem neighbourhoods. Most usefully, known prestigious neighbourhoods should be sampled in the same way. This will enable measurement of comparative levels of fear, victimisation, and self-reported frauds, fiddles, smuggling offences, copyright piracy, online pedophile activity, racist practices, motoring offences, and illegal drug consumption. Such data should also be complemented with ethnographic research in these same neighbourhoods to overcome criminological existing bias towards understanding the more visible, violent, and acquisitive crimes of the usual suspects living in notorious high-crime areas.

THE ROLE OF NEW TECHNOLOGY IN OFFENDING: THE NEED TO SURVEY NEW AND EVOLVING CRIMES

New technologies have:

1. Changed the modus operandi for various types of offending;

2. Increased the incidence of various crime types;

3. Created new crimes;

4. Created or provided additional opportunities for both old and new crime types; and,

5. Created new criminal motivating crime markets.

Of the five technologically influenced crime outcomes outlined above, there are many well-known examples. Drug-taking went through phases from the popularity of the opium dens of 19th century London, chasing the dragon with the aid of aluminum foil on Merseyside in the 1980s (Parker et al., 1988), to the current use of crack cocaine made in microwave ovens. Most recently, the ecstasy dance scene of the 1990s has given way to the current fashion for cocaine and speedballing.[5] The arrival of aerosol paints, Magic Marker pens, and mobile telephones with digital cameras has changed the nature of graffiti, other criminal damage, and gratuitous violence, from something expressive to something now to be recorded, disseminated, and celebrated. File sharing Websites, Internet news groups, and high-quality colour photocopiers and plastic parcel tape[6] are just a few further examples of things that have played roles in creating totally new opportunities for, or ways of, offending and providing more traditional crimes with new MOs.

Designers of national crime surveys should pay closer attention to changes in technologies like the Internet that facilitate offending and other harmful behaviours through rogue Websites, software, and the formation of international high-tech criminal gangs (Mann & Sutton, 1998). New technologies such as the Internet drive new cultural trends and consumption patterns, which can influence crime opportunities, crime scripts (Cornish & Clarke, 1986), and whole new types of harmful behaviour. The need for routine and systematic monitoring of new developments such as these is exactly what the Foresight reports I and II (2000a, 2000b) encourage. Put simply, we need up-to-date data and risk assessments on the offending opportunities that new things bring, with an aim to do something about them before problems escalate.

Strangely Neglected New Crimes and Evolving MOs

The use of the Internet by pornographers and pedophiles required additional legislation in order to tackle new types of obscenity, such as deliberately viewing abusive images of children while online and "making an obscene image of a child," where, for example, it is now illegal to cut and paste an image of the head of a child onto another image of, for instance, a naked woman's body. Other legislation has been drafted to deal with online grooming by pedophiles. Overall, the Internet has facilitated a pedophile plague of previously unforetold and arguably unimaginable proportions in the demand for and supply of abusive images of children.

The Internet has led to other new types of offending such as computer misuse, which includes hacking and virus sending. Online opportunities for music and movie piracy and purchasing counterfeit goods proliferate to such an extent that it is sometimes hard to believe the activity is illegal or harmful to anyone. The advent of chip and pin technology has displaced credit card fraud, although thankfully with a degree of attrition,[7] to the Internet where card-not-present fraud has risen by 21% to £183 million in 2004. Advance fee frauds have similarly escalated because of the advantages of speed, coverage, and reduced cost that e-mail has over traditional postal snail mail. Newspaper reports suggest that various eBay auction frauds, from shill bidding[8] to scams involving dud cheques, are common practice. Race-hate Websites thrive on the Net – distributing a mixture of unmoderated pseudoscience, venomous vitriol, and forging support networks of like-minded individuals (Mann et al., 2003; Sutton, in press). A few Websites encourage suicide among teenagers and certain terrorist Websites encourage adults to become suicide bombers. Bomb and illegal drug-making Websites abound. Online escort agencies are run by what are arguably cyber-pimps. There are many more examples of crimes and otherwise harmful activities that, space and subject matter permitting, could be added to this account of crimes that are strangely neglected by national crime surveys.

In contrast, the traditional offline crime environment is local and in most cases easily understood in terms of the physical presence of offenders, their targets, and victims. Online crimes are quite different. For example, global connectivity transcends time and space, which means that computer-mediated havoc – from viruses, scams or hacking – can escalate rapidly, even occurring simultaneously, over a wide area of the planet (Mann & Sutton, 1998). The Internet provides offenders with the ability to operate anonymously and remotely. This means that commercial security secrets such as hardware and software protection vulnerabilities (e.g., information on how to pirate expensive software or how to break into a particular model of car by exploiting an unusual flaw in its design) can be disseminated in a short time to a worldwide audience before a technical fix can be applied to the problem. Therefore, online banking encryption systems can be widely compromised, and computer viruses and Trojan-horse programmes attached to e-mails or Websites can cause billions of pounds of damage and lost business.

For crime reduction and policing initiatives to be effective, substantially more systematic online research is necessary. Home Office and academic policy-oriented criminologists need to collaborate to monitor and understand better how crimes evolve. Various crimes must be researched in this way to keep new crime waves under control before they get bigger and more costly. Because it seems at least logically feasible that offenders learning new offending techniques – or those new to offending – will fail to succeed in their early criminal attempts, we should ask more about attempts and particularly those that are near-misses. In any new areas that are identified as potentially important, in-depth qualitative interviews with particular types of offenders should, where possible, precede quantitative survey design to determine the extent to which particular types of attempted crimes and new or previously neglected crimes are at least likely to be occurring at a significant enough level to be measurable by national or city level surveys. The emergence, evolution, and surprisingly rapid growth of online fraud provide a particularly powerful example of the need for such systematic monitoring and research.

The Need to Survey Online as Well as Offline Frauds

Only a small proportion of the frauds that take place are recorded by the criminal justice system (Allen et al., 2005). One reason is that many go undetected because perpetrators cover their tracks with crafty accounting. In other cases, the existence and frequency of many frauds is hidden from law enforcement officials and the public to protect the commercial interests of corporate victims seeking to avoid the added expense of having employees' worktime tied up with helping the criminal justice system prosecute offenders. Sometimes businesses fear their share prices will be reduced by market perceptions of losses resulting from inherent security vulnerabilities. Another reason for underreporting is that many frauds are not seen by individual victims as crimes that warrant reporting to the authorities. Examples here might include SMS text frauds, where victims waste only a few pounds dialing a number on their telephone to claim a lottery that they have been informed they won. The lottery never existed, of course, and the phone number is premium rate. Here, the hassle, or culpable embarrassment, of informing the authorities may outweigh the desire to report the scam.

We can know more about frauds, including their impact, dynamics, incidence, prevalence, and underreporting, by conducting self-report victimisation and self-report offending surveys. Although some headway has been made in this area (Allen et al., 2005), a wider programme of research is now required. Those responsible for future national surveys should implement transparent and systematic procedures to ensure that surveys such as the BCS ask questions on the most important and up-to-date subject matter in the right places, asking the right questions of the right people. This might mean, for example, sampling business people to ask whether they have been involved in fraud.

One reason why national crime surveys are not yet particularly sophisticated in their choice of offences, victims, and offenders is that they are a relatively new criminological research method. Further, being so costly to administer, the Home Office national crime surveys have no competitors snapping at their heels. More so, nationally representative fraud surveys of the general public are very new. Not surprisingly then, nationally representative self-report offending surveys of frauds perpetrated by businesses and the public sector have yet to be conducted. To take things forward – to meet the aims of this book – this chapter recommends that the Home Office collaborate with academic experts to adopt a simple, transparent, systematic, and routine scanning of knowable frauds. In such a process, by employing nearsight we can design survey questions to examine routine frauds such as credit card and Internet and mobile-phone-facilitated frauds. With hindsight, we can undertake nationally representative offender and offence surveys to address and redress the past and present official blinkered approach to frauds committed by business and public servants. Using peripheral vision, we can decide whether to survey more obscure areas such as misleading business practices that exploit loopholes in the law and new developments in technology or culture. And with foresight we can anticipate and seek to measure the effects of technology, culture, and policy making on the next fraud problems on the horizon.

Proposing Hybrid Surveys for Internet-facilitated Crimes

High-tech crimes facilitated by the Internet have fueled debates about the merits of using Web-based questionnaires to gather victim and offender data. One of the most prominent criticisms of this method is that findings are representative only of those people visiting a particular Website. Yet a novel way around this problem would be for those administering a national, regional, or city crime survey to take computer assisted personal interviewing (CAPI) one stage further and to ask respondents who use the Internet to connect to a Web-based questionnaire during the face-to-face interview. With modern laptop computers having the ability to connect to the Net via wireless networks and through cell phones, this would utilise the strengths of commercial World Wide Web– based questionnaire programmes such as Survey Monkey over traditional CAPI survey instruments administered only in interviewer-present situations. Using Web-based surveys in this way would be unique in creating two comparable cohorts of respondents for each survey sweep: those who are directed to the Website in the usual way from search engines or through e-mail, other Websites, mass media, specialist press, and poster advertising; and those asked to log on by face-to-face survey interviewers using CAPI. Data from both cohorts can be analysed separately and together, with the results compared and combined accordingly to produce a more cost-effective and representative sample of respondents than could be achieved by either CAPI or Web-based surveys alone. In this way, identifying Web users in a traditional survey to trigger a supplementary online survey is an example of adaptive sampling that could overcome the inherent weaknesses of choosing between traditional and online sampling methods.

THE NEED FOR SURVEYS TO INFORM THEORY AND CRIME REDUCTION INITIATIVES

Despite being used by so many critical criminologists as the only reliable basis for their theorising in the past 25 years (see Hough et al. in this volume), the BCS has been the subject of considerable academic criticism. Most of these criticisms are varied and complex. See, for example, the relatively recent tirades by Hillyard and colleagues (2004), Walters (2005), and Barrett (2006). Although it is beyond the scope of this chapter to rehearse, rehash, and add to the entire list of academic grievances, those aimed specifically at national crime-survey research in the areas of fraud, new and neglected crimes are examined here.

One common criticism of national crime surveys is that they predominantly focus upon crimes committed by the "usual suspects" – poor males between the ages of 15 and 25 (Young, 1986). Although it is reasonable to suggest that the reason young and less affluent males are pursued and processed by the criminal justice system is that so many of them are preying upon so many victims, there is a similar argument to be made for pursuing more affluent middlemen (Sutton, 1995, 1998) and to focus upon other crimes of more powerful members of society, such as business owners, that frequently leads to their greater personal enrichment with less visible yet high levels of victimisation of the rich and poor alike. For example, some reported cases reveal how the so-called super rich have engaged in financial scandals that have had a profound effect upon the quality of life of tens of thousands of shareholders and pensioners (Spalek, 2004).

Looking to criminology to explain crimes of the powerful as well as the poor, Ruggiero (2000) points out some differences between the resources of the poor and the rich and how these resources are factors in their respective offending. Based on his conclusions, Ruggiero tells us how difficult it is for criminology to identify the causes of crime when, for example, (a) lack of available legitimate resources are the cause of the offending of the less wealthy members of society, while (b) an abundance of resources and opportunity are behind the crimes of the rich and powerful.

From a policy-oriented rather than a critical criminology perspective, Ruggiero's argument appears somewhat naïve. For example, the crime dynamics of prolific shoplifters can be used to show why overlooking the importance of what offenders do, and whom they do it with, can mean that the rhetoric of critical criminology is sometimes blind to the reality of offending beyond the written page of textbooks.[9] Shoplifters regularly seek safe and reliable outlets to sell stolen goods. They do, in fact, regularly steal to offer and this is at least as common as stealing to order (Sutton, 2000). Prolific shoplifters are typically problem drug-users, and they seek buyers whom they can identify as a person with money, who is in the business of making a profit, and who is particularly unlikely to be an undercover or off-duty police officer (Klockars, 1974; Steffensmeir, 1986; Langworthy & Lebau, 1992; Sutton, 1998, 2004). In other words, those with less legitimate resources routinely seek out those who have them in order to collaborate in fueling the economy of crime. Therefore, three clearly important causal factors in the crime of theft, for the thief, are opportunity, ability to steal, and finding a safe and ready market for the stolen goods. Although two important causal influences for the buyer of stolen goods are opportunity to deal and having the financial resources to do so, and although the two crimes of stealing and handling stolen goods stem from different causes, they are interrelated. Identifying and understanding such interrelationships helps policy-oriented criminologists tackle important underlying causes of various crimes by developing, implementing, monitoring, fine-tuning, and evaluating promising mechanisms for their reduction.

Understanding the dynamics of each separate crime type and the symbiotic relationship (Felson, 2006) between them presents many opportunities for tackling both, separately or together. Crime surveys have provided the data to further such criminological knowledge and inform new ways to tackle offenders and reduce various crimes. The 1994 BCS, for example, provided a wealth of detail about the extent to which the general public knowingly buys stolen goods and who is most likely to buy (Sutton, 1998). Combined with in-depth interviews with thieves, dealers, and consumers, this informed the development of the market reduction approach (MRA) to theft (Sutton et al., 2001), which is now used by several police forces in England and Wales (Harris et al., 2003). This is one example of the legacy of national crime surveys such as the BCS that we should seek to protect and develop. Clearly then, surveys have the potential to complement in-depth qualitative research to inform criminological theory and systematic studies of different crime types. This potential should be used in more areas to seek to reduce various frauds, high-tech crimes, and other important but relatively neglected offences.

THE NEED TO SURVEY THE ROLE OF THE CRIMEMONGER

Ex-Home Office crime scientist Gloria Laycock (2005) cites Ron Clarke, an ex-Home Office criminologist (Clarke & Eck, 2003), to summarise usefully the concept of what is currently understood to be a *crime facilitator* and explains the difference between three types of crime facilitator – physical, social, and chemical:

1. Physical facilitators – for example, tools used by the burglar, or the gun in an armed robbery, spray paint for vandals, etc.

2. Social facilitators – for example, interactions of young men in a group may encourage rowdyness.

3. Chemical facilitators, which are often disinhibitors such as alcohol, are clearly implicated in many offences, including domestic assault.

Paul Ekblom (1997), yet another ex-Home Office criminologist, uses the term *crime promoters* to refer to people who are in effect social crime facilitators and describes how these individuals provide aid to criminals either unwittingly, carelessly, recklessly, or deliberately.

Social crime facilitators have a role in maintaining and increasing crimes (Sutton, 1998). They can, for example, reinforce criminal behaviour with rewards for stolen property and other illegitimate goods and services and they regularly create an aura of legitimacy around criminal behaviour by merging it in their own minds and blurring it in the minds of other offenders with legal, ethical mercantile practices. All of this plays a role in encouraging early criminal careers and facilitating continuance in criminal activities. As such, some social crime facilitators are in effect traders and dealers in something unpleasant. These dealers continue to trade and hence to profit from facilitating crime while national crime surveys report on – and the criminal justice system incarcerates or otherwise punishes – tens of thousands of young people and the other vulnerable usual suspects every year. An accurate, if somewhat disparaging description, is that these crime facilitators are *crimemongers* (Sutton, 2006) who should be focused upon by national crime surveys so that we can know more details about the day-to-day dynamics of their shady dealings in order to decide how best to seek to curtail the unusual suspects.

Businesses engage in a range of crimemongering activities that include manufacturing and selling speed-detecting cameras and radar-blocking equipment,[10] stealth alcoholic drink containers,[11] electronic lock picks,[12] and cocaine kits that include a mirror, razor blade, and straw that are sold as snuff-taking kits. Other crimemongers legally sell the paraphernalia of marihuana cultivation[13] and use, including seeds, UV lamps, hydroponics kits, and equipment for smoking. So called "evidence eliminator" software can be bought to wipe incriminating data from computer hard drives and is advertised as being so effective that police officers cannot recover the deleted data.[14] And there are crimemongering Websites that facilitate coun-terfeit product sales, software, film, and music piracy. All of these things, though not always illegal, are just a few examples of crimemongers: busi-nesses that knowingly facilitate and encourage crimes.

The important argument being made here is that national crime surveys should conduct regular and systematic reviews of crimemongering. The Home Office has been criticized mercilessly for not doing so (Hillyard et al., 2004).

THE NEED TO ACQUIRE SYSTEMATIC KNOWLEDGE ABOUT THE SEDUCTIONS OF CRIME

Perhaps one potentially useful way to refocus national crime surveys upon the unusual as well as the usual suspects at the root of various crimes is to consider the causes of crimes in terms of Jack Katz's (1988) seductions of crime – that is, the foreground rather than the background factors that precede offending.[15] In looking for new questions to improve national crime surveys, we could begin by asking the following question: In what ways are various type of crime, such as fraud, high-tech crime, drug taking, drug dealing, theft opportunities, crime opportunity hunting, crime readi-ness, and financial rewards for crime, all parts of the *seductions of crime?* These then are interwoven with the seductions inherent in the aura of respect, power, and practices of legitimate businesses that lead many of-fenders to think and talk in terms of committing crimes as a personal "smart" work identity in what is arguably not a straight but a generally "bent" society. Understanding such causal and supportive criminal social dynamics – frequently described by offenders as "just doing the business" (Hobbs, 1989; Foster, 1990) – as well as the dynamics of victimisation, we can know more about who does what with and to whom, where, when, why, how, and with what effect. With rich data of that kind, we can more finely tune policing initiatives and crime- and harm-reduction policy making, to fit better the realities of social systems and interpersonal interactions that motivate and facilitate various crimes.

Before beginning to frame national crime survey questions aimed at unearthing offender and victim dynamics, it is necessary to conduct new qualitative research and also study the results of existing qualitative work. To date, my own ongoing research with offenders into the dynamics of stolen goods markets, to inform the MRA, includes interviews with more than 150 prolific thieves. These interviews reveal some particularly subtle findings about how prolific thieves, and the businesspersons they deal with, are seduced by their respective "outlaw" and "respectable" identities and activities. As well as stealing and selling property to fund their drug use, prolific thieves are seduced by legitimacy, illegitimacy, excitement, usefulness, and reputation – theirs and their buyers. Thieves also seduce otherwise legitimate businesspeople into offending by offering them extra tax-free profits that come from selling stolen goods. And business owners themselves provide motivation for thieves by providing money for stolen goods, information about potential victims, and promises of regular income from crime.

Though findings from national crime surveys currently tell us only about crimes committed by thieves, and sometimes about purchasing patterns of otherwise respectable members of society, to date they tell us nothing about the seductions of crime and where these seductions occur, how they occur, why they occur, how often, and where they are likely to occur in the future. Yet these root-level social seductions – which are undoubtedly relatively subtle compared with other more robust crime predictors such as birth rates, income levels, and state of the economy – are likely to be valuable predictors of the causes of crimes, impending crime waves, and other offending patterns that are crucial determinants as to where scarce resources need to be spent to make society safer and improve the quality of life. Looking at crime in this way involves the type of lateral thinking championed by Pease (2005) and the two Foresight reports (2000a, 2000b). Findings from qualitative research, such as that conducted by Katz, should be used subsequently to shape questions in national crime surveys to provide more in-depth systematic knowledge about various crimes and their causes.

CONCLUSIONS AND THE WAY FORWARD

Criminology – whatever school it belongs to, whether it is, for example, Right or Left realist, critical, cultural or feminist – has a purpose and a design in its ambition. As Walklate (1998) explains, "The desire to work towards the effective implementation of change, whether that be micro policy changes or macro societal change, is deeply embedded in the criminological agenda" (p. 33). The same is true of policy-oriented criminology. For example, Mike Hough and Pat Mayhew designed the first and subsequent British Crime Surveys, at least in part, to put various crimes and the risk of victimisation into a realistic perspective. And Clarke's situational crime prevention approach sets out to explain why crimes occur where they do and to propose realistic and relatively simple and rapid solutions to reduce risk for particular people and places. Further, the market reduction approach proposes both immediate and longer-term solutions to tackle the role of crimemongers and other so-called respectable citizens, in facilitating and providing motivation for theft – something that many critics of so-called administrative criminology failed and continually fail to realise.

National crime survey data can be used better, and better data can be gathered, with an aim to tackle many of the warranted criticisms of power and class bias in their design. In particular, national crime surveys should focus more attention upon crimemongers such as the buyers of stolen goods, Website owners, certain product manufacturers, retailers, and legal loophole exploiters who facilitate and motivate crimes (Sutton, 2006).

Although the Home Office frequently pays or else relies upon the good will of policy-oriented academic criminologists to design questions for national crime surveys, to conduct complex in-depth quantitative analysis, and to write up the findings, such work is increasingly commissioned merely to service the needs of ministers and their advisors in order to comply with short-term and narrowly focused political agendas. Consequently, there is a lot of warranted criticism coming from critical criminologists that published Home Office reports tend to shy away from content, interpretations, and recommendations that do not sit well with current government policies, programmes, or the current party political line on crime and criminality (Walters, 2005). Sometimes huge swathes of work are cut from reports in order to avoid presenting embarrassing challenges to current political thinking. On other occasions, it has been said (Barrett, 2006) that the Home Office will reanalyze figures again and again until a more positive outcome is arrived at. As a former Home Office criminologist with 14 years' standing, I personally witnessed such practices on several occasions. It happens and it should be stopped because it results in junk science and policies doomed to fail from the start. One proposed solution is to ensure a greater diversity of funding sources for crime surveys, enabling more local, independently conducted city-level surveys. This would break what is in effect a Home Office monopoly on crime surveys.

To take forward the proposals in this chapter and to ensure that they can be implemented effectively, given the history of uneasy relations between policy makers, critical criminologists, and other academics, it is important to improve Home Office and academic collaboration. To begin this process, more academic papers could be coauthored by Home Office criminologists and their university counterparts to defend as well as promote policy-oriented criminology.

In order to ensure that the aims and recommendations of the Foresight Committee (2000a, 2000b) on crime are adopted and to tackle criticisms of nebulosity, a visible, routine, and systematic crime scanning process is needed to help determine what crime types and questions are included in national crime surveys and which social groups are sampled.

◆

Address correspondence to: Dr Mike Sutton, Director, Nottingham Trent University, Nottingham Centre for Study and Reduction of Hate Crimes, Bias and Prejudice, School of Social Sciences, Burton Street, Nottingham, NG1 4BU; e-mail: Michael.sutton@ntu.ac.uk

NOTES

1. Either as civil servants or academics working under government research contracts.
2. This chapter does not seek to provide a general critique the past influences of academics on the criminology of the state, or of the politicization of current criminal justice policies – because this has been adequately undertaken elsewhere (Taylor, Walton, & Young, 1973; Lilly, Cullen, & Ball, 1995; Walklate 1998).
3. And notably, in this volume, Tim Hope points out a related potential problem here is that the BCS now samples a smaller proportion of

city areas than before the point when it became a police performance-monitoring tool.

4. To avoid fuelling adverse reputations of certain areas, these neighbourhoods can be made anonymous in the usual way.

5. Mixing injectable cocktails of heroin and cocaine.

6. Used to gain entry to car doors.

7. Chip and pin technology helped cut card fraud overall in 2005 by 13% compared to the 2004 figure of £504m.

8. Bidding on items that you are auctioning yourself in order to raise the price.

9. One could equally have examined drug use, street level prostitution, burglary, car crime, and copyright theft to name only a few.

10. See: www.motaman.co.uk/online catalogue radar detectors 26.html

11. See: www.thebeerbelly.com

12. See: www.devonlocks.com/lock-picking/pick-guns.htm

13. See: www.skunkmarket.com/index.php?cpath=27

14. www.softplatz.com/software/evidence-cleaner/

15. This is also something that Clarke's (1980) Situational Crime Prevention approach and Felson's Routine Activities Theory both do by looking at the immediate situational precursors of crimes rather than the social and psychological attributes of offenders.

REFERENCES

Allen, J., Forrest, S., Levi, M., Roy, H., & Sutton, M. (2005). Fraud and technology crimes: Findings from the 2002/3 British Crime Survey and 2003 Offending, Crime and Justice Survey. London: Home Office Online Report 34/05.

Barrett, D. (2006). Home Office accused of "political bias" in research. *The Scotsman*. Mon 13 Feb. Available online at http://news.scotsman.com/politics.cfm?id=223312006&format=print

Clarke, R. V. (1980). Situational crime prevention: Theory and practice. *British Journal of Criminology, 20,* 136-147.

Clarke, R. V., & Eck, J. (2003). Become a problem-solving crime analyst. London. Jill Dando Institute of Crime Science.

Cornish, D., & Clarke, R. V. (1986). *The reasoning criminal: Rational choice perspectives on offending.* New York: Springer Verlag.

Ekblom, P. (1997). Gearing up against crime: A dynamic framework to help designers keep up with the adaptive criminal in a changing world. *International Journal of Risk, Security and Crime Prevention, 2/4,* 249-265.

Felson, M. (2006). *Crime and nature.* Thousand Oaks, CA: Sage.

Field, S. (1990). *Trends in crime and their interpretation: A study of recorded crime in post-war England and Wales.* Home Office Research Study 119. London: Home Office.

Foresight, I. (2000a). *Turning the corner.* London: Department of Trade and Industry, Crime Prevention Panel.

Foresight II. (2000b). *Just around the corner.* London: Department of Trade and Industry, Crime Prevention Panel.

Foster, J. (1990). *Villains: Crime and community in the inner city.* London: Routledge.

Harris, C., Hale, C., & Uglow, S. (2003). Theory into practice: implementing a market reduction approach to property crime. In K. Bulock & N. Tilley (Eds.), *Crime reduction and problem oriented policing.* Cullompton, England: Willan.

Hillyard, P., Sim, J., Tombs, S., & Whyte, D. (2004). Leaving a "stain upon the silence": Contemporary criminology and the politics of dissent. *British Journal of Criminology, 44,* 369-390.

Hobbs, D. (1989). *Doing the business: Entrepreneurship, the working class and detectives in the East End of London.* Oxford: Oxford University Press.

Jones, T., Maclean, B., & Young, J. (1986). *The Islington Crime Survey.* Aldershot, England: Gower.

Katz, J. (1988). *Seductions of crime: Moral and sensual attractions in doing evil.* New York: Basic Books.

Klockars, C. (1974). *The professional fence.* New York: Free Press.

Langworthy, R., & Lebau, I. (1992). The spatial evolution of sting clientele. *Journal of Criminal Justice, 20,* 135-145.

Laycock, G. (2005). Deciding what to do. In N. Tilley (Ed.), *Handbook of crime prevention and community safety.* Collumpton, England: Willan.

Lilly, J. R., Cullen, F., & Ball, R. (1995). *Criminological theory: Context and consequences.* Thousand Oaks, CA: Sage.

Mann, D., & Sutton, M. (1998). NetCrime: More change in the organisation of thieving. *British Journal of Criminology, 38,*202-229.

Mann, D., Sutton, M., & Tuffin, R. (2003). The evolution of hate: Social dynamics in white racist newsgroups. *Internet Journal of Criminology.* www.internetjournal ofcriminology.com

Parker, H., Bakx, K., & Newcome, R. (1988). *Living with heroin: The impact of a drugs "epidemic" on an English community.* Milton Keynes, UK: Oxford University Press.

Pease, K. (2005). Science in the service of crime reduction. In N. Tilley (Ed.), *Handbook of crime prevention and community safety* (pp. 400-416). Collumpton, England: Willan.

Ruggiero, V. (2000). *Crime and markets: Essays in anti-criminology.* Oxford: Oxford University Press.

Spalek, B. (2004). Policing financial crime: The Financial Services Authority and the myth of the "duped investor." In R. Hopkins Burke (Ed.), *Hard cop, soft cop: Debates and dilemmas in contemporary policing.* Colllumpton, England: Willan.

Steffensmeier, D. (1986). *The fence: In the shadow of two worlds.* Trenton, NJ: Rowman and Littleield.

Sutton, M. (1995). From receiving to thieving: Does the market for second-hand goods play a role in keeping crime figures high. *British Journal of Criminology, 35*(3), 400-416.

Sutton, M. (1998). *Handling stolen goods and theft: A market reduction approach.* Home Office Research Study 178. London: Home Office.

Sutton M. (2004). The market reduction approach is route level situational crime prevention. In R. Hopkins Burke (Ed.), *Hard cop, soft cop: Debates and dilemmas in contemporary policing*. Collumpton, England: Willan.

Sutton, M. (2005). Complicity, trading dynamics and prevalence in stolen goods markets. In N. Tilley (Ed.), *Handbook of crime prevention and community safety*. Collumpton, England: Willan.

Sutton, M. (2006). *Hi-tech crime, crimemongers: Crooked businesses on the internet*. Paper presented at the Policing Transnational Crimes Conference, London. Available at http://www.kcl.ac.uk/depsta/rel/ccjs/sutton-transnational-crimes. ppt

Sutton, M. (in press). Finding the far right online: An exploratory study of white racialist websites. In S. Poynting & J. Wilson (Eds.), *Sticks and stones: Writings and drawings on hatred*. Sydney Institute of Criminology and Federation Press.

Sutton, M., Schneider, J., & Hetherington, S. (2001). *Tackling theft with the market reduction approach*. Home Office Crime Reduction Series Paper 8. London: Home Office.

Taylor, I., Walton, P., & Young, J. (1973). *The new criminology*. London: Routledge and Kegan Paul.

Walklate, S. (1989). *Victimology: The victim and the criminal justice process*. London: Unwin Hyman.

Walklate, S. (1998). *Understanding criminology: Current theoretical debates*. Buckingham, England: Open University Press.

Walters, R. (2005). Boycott, resistance and the role of the deviant voice. *Criminal Justice Matters, 62*, 6-7.

Young, J. (1986). The failure of criminology: The need for a radical realism. In R. Mathews & J. Young (Eds.), *Confronting crime*. London: Sage.

Young, J. (1992). Ten points of realism. In J. Young & R. Mathews (Eds.), *Rethinking criminology: The realist debate*. London: Sage.

Deceptive Evidence: Challenges in Measuring Fraud

by

Jacqueline Hoare
Research Development and Statistics Directorate
U.K. Home Office

Abstract: *The measurement of the scale and costs of fraud is a complex and underinvestigated area. This chapter examines the measurements of fraud in the U.K., covering both surveys and administrative data sources. These different pathways range from victimisation surveys, to police-recorded crime, to central government records based on whistleblowers, to private sector surveys. Each measure is investigated, and the strengths and limitations, are highlighted. The chapter then describes the main findings from each measurement of fraud, before introducing the new concept of identity fraud and some attempts to measure this type of fraud. This emerging crime type has brought more uncertainty to the measurement of fraud, beginning with conceptual difficulties. In summary, it seems clear that although at present there is no way of fully evaluating the nationwide scale and cost of fraud, in the future a combination of improved methods may provide a suitable proxy for these figures.*

The measurement of fraud presents several difficulties from the outset. A legal definition of fraud is described as "the intentional use of deceit, a trick or some dishonest means to deprive another of his/her/its money, property or a legal right." It can cover a wide range of activities, from small-scale deceptions of individuals to large-scale cross-border activities by criminal gangs targeting large financial institutions. No comprehensive measure of the size of the fraud problem exists. However, work on the harm fraud causes to society committed by organised crime has become the third priority of the Serious and Organised Crime Agency in the U.K. (Fraud Review, 2006).

The sources presented here measure fraud in different ways and thus it is difficult to provide an overall cohesive measure.

In law, there was formerly no offence of fraud as such, but instead statutory offences of deception (Hansard, 2005). The recent Fraud Bill creates a statutory offence of fraud, committed in three ways: where a person dishonestly makes a false representation; or wrongfully fails to disclose information; or secretly abuses a position of trust with intent to make a gain or to cause loss or to expose another to the risk of loss. The definition of fraud as an offence will have a positive effect on the measurement of fraud, relieving some of the concerns raised in this chapter.

There are also issues with the measurement of fraud depending on the methodology used. Awareness of fraud through public service campaigns may affect the recorded level of fraud. And as people become familiar with this type of offence, they are more likely to report it to authorities. Similarly, advertisements helping people to protect against fraud may lead to increased awareness and perhaps worry about offences being committed against them.

MEASUREMENT OF FRAUD: DATA SOURCES

In recent years, there has been growing interest in trying to collect information on the level of fraud committed in England and Wales, and surveys have been an important contributor to increasing the knowledge base, adding to the information from administrative sources.

Victimisation and Offending Surveys

Fraud is a complex area and difficult to measure in a self-report *victim* survey such as the British Crime Survey (BCS). On the one hand, some members of the public who have been victims of poor service may perceive themselves to have been defrauded, when this is not the case in law, whereas many of those who had been genuine victims of fraud may not be aware of the fact.

Two victimisation surveys described in this chapter have been commissioned by the Home Office: the BCS and the Commercial Victimisation Survey (CVS). The 2002-2003 BCS was the first nationally representative self-report victimisation survey to cover fraud crimes, providing information on the extent of these activities from the victim's point of view. The BCS covers credit and debit card fraud and more recently this has been expanded to include identity fraud. In addition to this self-report measurement of fraud against the general public, the 2004 CVS measured fraud committed against businesses, both retailers and manufacturers.

The 2003 Offending, Crime and Justice Survey (OCJS) was the first nationally representative self-report *offending* survey to cover fraud crimes, providing information from an offender's perspective. The OCJS covers credit and debit card fraud and also explores benefit fraud, income tax fraud, and insurance fraud.

In the private sector, there are a number of different surveys carried out to estimate the extent and cost of fraud. Ernst & Young, PricewaterhouseCoopers, and Robson Rhodes are probably the best known private surveys, with the first two engaging in global research as well as in the U.K.

Administrative Sources: Police-Recorded Crime

Police-recorded crime provides a count of fraud, based on legal definitions and according to National Crime Recording Standards and Home Office counting rules. Police-recorded statistics of fraud, however, are generally considered to be a poor indication of the real level and trends for reasons that are discussed further on.

Administrative Sources: Central Government

Whereas survey and police-recorded crime figures provide an estimate of the level of fraud taking place (from a victim or offender viewpoint), other administrative sources generally publish data on estimates of the economic cost of fraud.

U.K. central government departments carry out work on detecting fraud to determine losses using a range of methodologies. These include Department for Work and Pensions (DWP), Her Majesty's Revenue and Customs (HMRC), Department of Health (NHS Counter Fraud Service), Her Majesty's Treasury (HMT), Ministry of Defence (MOD) Fraud Analysis Unit, and the Foreign and Commonwealth Office (FCO) (details below from the Fraud Review: Final Report, 2006).

DWP provides estimates on fraud based on customer fraud and error, as well as official error on claims for Income Support, Jobseeker's Allowance and Pension Credit. HMRC provides estimates on the tax losses in the U.K. The NHS Counter Fraud Service (CFS) investigates patient fraud, including patients declaring they have a lower wage or salary in order to receive free or discounted healthcare, or people creating multiple identities in order to receive numerous prescriptions for free. Patient fraud represents a large proportion of the overall figure for NHS fraud. HMT collects data on fraud from other central government departments to produce an annual fraud report. The MOD Fraud Analysis Unit provides estimates based on reports from line management or whistleblowers. The FCO's report is based on information received by them from a variety of countries.

Administrative Sources: Private Sector

The banking and credit card industry itself records a considerable amount of information on fraudulent misuse of its services, which may provide a better indication of the extent and trends in this type of fraud. APACS (the U.K. Payments Association) records information on the financial losses resulting from plastic card fraud in the U.K. Alongside this, information on payment fraud is produced by the British Bankers Association (BBA, 2005).

The Association of British Insurers (ABI) estimates the total amount of fraud suffered by insurers. Where fraud specialists confirm that deliberately dishonest attempts have been made against insurers, it is defined as fraud and it is this total measure of dishonesty that the ABI attempts to capture in its fraud estimate. The ABI has been leading work on tackling fraud in the general insurance industry, including initiatives over data sharing.

In summary, the information previously mentioned describes a wide range of methodologies used to measure fraud – that is, fraud that is carried out by the general public, by employees, and by organised crime. Not only diverse, these administrative sources also generally attempt to estimate value of losses through fraud, rather than count such incidents, and the agencies tend to collect only information that is relevant to their policy area.

LIMITATIONS OF FRAUD MEASUREMENTS

Victimisation and Offending Surveys

Whilst the potential strength of surveys is in measuring fraud at a level that administrative records cannot reach, by their very nature, the surveys of victims and offenders described here are limited to people in private households. It may be that such people who are victims of fraud may not know that the deception is taking place. This is a particular problem facing victim surveys because deception is only one defining feature of fraud. Victims who do become aware that a fraud has been committed may not consider it a crime. On the other hand, some people who have merely been victims of poor service may perceive themselves to have been victims of fraud.

Even if the deception is considered a crime, the people who have been deceived may not consider themselves as victims, but rather assign victim status to the bank or credit card company for example, because quite commonly they will be compensated for their loss. But this may lead to issues of double counting when measuring the deception. In the case of cheque and credit card frauds, the victims are defined as those who are the sellers of goods or services purchased with a stolen card or forged card or cheque, rather than the account holder or the bank or credit card company.

With any survey, question design is a key to obtaining a true measure of the topic under investigation and this is true for both victim and offending surveys. For example, it is difficult to measure fraud offences in the BCS as part of the main offence coding due to the nature of the crime and the overlap with other crime types (notably between theft and fraud). Currently, a credit card (stolen or not) used fraudulently is out of the scope of the BCS. And any amendments to the main offence coding in order to include fraud would affect the crucial ability of the BCS to compare trends over time; hence, the introduction of a specific module in the 2002-2003 BCS to ask respondents about their experiences of fraud.

According to the 2003-2004 BCS, a fifth (20%) of the level of card fraud measured was a direct result of the card(s) being physically stolen or lost from individuals, for example, from a bag or wallet (Wilson, Patterson, Powell, & Hembury, 2006). The BCS, however, only asks if the card fraud was as a result of the card(s) being physically stolen or lost and does not identify other reasons for a person being a victim of card fraud (e.g., skimming).

Evolving crimes, such as Internet fraud, can be difficult to keep up with on a large-scale continuous survey. Questions can be designed to capture specific fraud types, but then require constant updating and checking to ensure continuing relevance, which impacts on comparability over time. Alternatively, broader measures can be used, but specific measurements for new crime may be lost as a result.

The BCS also covers another type of fraud in that it asks about method of entry in cases of burglary, one of which is that the burglar gained access through "false pretences." The Fraud Bill includes "fraud by false representation" within its remit, but this type of burglary is not included within the measure of fraud estimated by the BCS, a result of the difficulties in both measurement and definition of fraud perhaps.

By the very nature of surveys like the BCS, the measurement of crime occurs at one particular point in time. Respondents may be victimised by fraud at the time of interview, but be unaware of the fact. This lag between events and their discovery, and the concerns around the classification of fraud as a crime, contribute to undercounting the prevalence and frequency of fraud.

Even private sector efforts are affected by limitations in survey methodology. For example, the Ernst & Young 9th Global Fraud Survey is the result of interviewing more than 500 corporate leaders representing many of the world's major organisations. This is a valuable insight into the issues of fraud of consideration to large global organisations, particularly in emerging markets, and aims to assist with the development of antifraud measures, but is inherently limited by this focus.

Administrative Sources: Police-Recorded Crime

Police-recorded crime includes deceptions against a range of victims, both personal and commercial. According to police statistics, the level of fraud and forgery offences decreased between 2004 and 2005 and 2005 and 2006 by 17%, including a 28% decrease in the number of cheque and credit card frauds (Walker, Kershaw, & Nicholas, 2006). It is not clear, however, whether this is an indication that the level of fraud is decreasing across England and Wales or whether it reflects a lower level of reporting. It is estimated that the police only receive reports of 5% of fraudulent credit card transactions (Fraud Review, 2006).

Counting rules for fraud were changed in 1998 and thus a continuous time trend only exists from 1998-1999. Many crimes of this type are not reported to the police because either victims are not aware of the incident, or if they are aware, they are more likely to report the offence to the appropriate authority, such as the bank or cardholder company, who may then fail to notify police. According to Shury and colleagues (2005), for example, manufacturers and retailers often felt it was inappropriate to report crimes involving employees, which were most commonly dealt with by disciplinary action.

With the introduction of the Fraud Act of 2006, the way of recording cheque and card fraud by the police has changed. This involves the introduction of a new crime category – economic crime – and also makes the financial institutions the first point of contact for account holders when dealing with fraud. Although this methodology may improve and standardise the recording of card and cheque fraud, this change will affect the trend over time and influence the levels and methods of reporting to the police.

Administrative Sources: Central Government

Measurements of fraud by central government departments employ a range of methodologies. Some use surveys and estimates and have the statistical limitations that come with them. Yet other departments provide a measure of fraud based on reporting, and state that no attempt is made to extrapolate this. Thus, the measure is clearly defined, but may not represent the full picture.

DWP uses a mixture of in-depth rolling programmes that review a large sample of benefits awards each year, and snapshots of fraud and error on other benefits which are up to 6 years old. Results are derived from the analysis of samples and therefore the method is subject to some statistical uncertainties – figures are rounded to the nearest £100 million pounds as a result. DWP began a continuous rolling measurement of Income Support and Job Seeker's Allowance in 1997, recognising their particular vulnerability to fraud loss.

No reliable estimates are available of the total tax loss through non-compliance. Further, there are differences in the way that tax gaps can be estimated for direct and indirect taxes (e.g., VAT and excise duty taxes). For indirect taxes, it is possible to compare actual tax receipts against a theoretical tax yield, calculated from external statistics on consumption. Yet there is no reliable comparable source for direct taxes, and thus there is no single technique for producing the measure of the tax gap in these cases. The estimates that HMRC produce include large confidence intervals because of the level of uncertainty around estimates of consumption used in the analysis. Improvements in the methodology for calculating estimates of the level of HMRC fraud have enabled the routine publication of data. These estimates are believed to be the best possible based on all the information available; however, it is difficult to establish a real level of the value and volume of this type of fraud.

The NHS CFS method involves validating data on a case-by-case basis – decisions are made based on a civil definition as to whether fraud has occurred. Data are analysed and then extrapolated for the whole population. Yet as each area of spend is measured separately, there is no overall estimate of losses.

The report from HMT (2005), collated from central government departments, does not aim to give an overall picture of fraud within government departments, but rather to inform departments of the scale and nature of certain categories of fraud that have been reported to the Treasury.

The MOD report, which is based on fraud information from line management or whistleblowers, whilst proactive, is unclear in scope. The vast majority of the cases relate to theft and it is uncertain whether this consists of deception offences or misappropriation.

The main problem for the FCO is collating information from a wide geographical area and reliance is on information received from others. Many of the frauds they investigate are discovered by overseas staff and relate to standard operation procedures. Published figures relate to the cost of identified fraud relating to the organisation.

Administrative Sources: Private Sector

Perhaps the most reliable source of information from administrative sources is from the banking industry. If the goal is to provide a figure for the economic cost of fraud in society, then the best records are likely to lay with those who incur the losses. (Based on the 2003-2004 BCS, 75% of people who had been victims of card fraud reported the incident to their credit card company or bank). Hence, the APACS figures are frequently referred to in measures of fraud. The limitation here is more that the type of fraud covered is limited – the measurement would seem to be relatively robust.

Fraud Measurement Summary

In summary, self-report surveys measure levels of fraud and have the potential to capture unreported incidents alongside demographic information, but there are conceptual difficulties around the definition and measurement of fraud in surveys. Generally, measurements of crime from the BCS relate to the number of incidents or risk of being a victim of crime, but an important component of fraud is the economic cost, and thus the BCS measures both a count and cost for this crime type.

Police-recorded figures are an accurate data source, but currently are dependent on individuals or companies reporting cases of fraud, so these data are likely to underestimate the problem. Central government agencies produce figures that generally relate to the cost of fraud, are specific to their policy area, and rely on different (not always robust) methodologies. As a measurement of fraud, private sector surveys are limited by their scope and methodology. The figures provided by the banking industry are perhaps the most reliable measure reviewed here, as both levels and cost of fraud can be amalgamated, with high reporting levels, but these cover only limited types of fraud.

The strengths and weaknesses of measurement of fraud through survey and administrative methods, combined with the complexity of the concept of fraud as well as its measurements, could advocate using complementary series to provide the full picture. It is extremely difficult to provide the cost of fraud to the economy, or to persons, and it is important to use the measures that are most suitable and most robust in the area of specific interest.

So far, the strengths and limitations of different sources have been considered. In the remainder of this chapter, the findings from these various sources are presented to provide information on the level of fraud.

MAIN FINDINGS FROM MEASUREMENTS OF FRAUD

Victimisation and Offending Surveys

According to the 2005-2006 BCS, the percentage of card users who had been actual victims of credit or debit card fraud was 4%. This level of victimisation is similar to that disclosed in 2003-2004 (3%). From the BCS, three quarters of people who had been victims of card fraud reported the incident to their credit card company or bank; 25% reported their experience to the police.

In addition to the main findings about people's experience of fraud, information was also collected on the BCS about people's perception of this crime. Results showed that over half of adults (57%) who had used a credit or debit card in the 12 months prior to interview in the 2005-2006 BCS were worried (fairly or very worried) about being a victim of card fraud – someone using their card or their card details in order to buy items or withdraw cash without their permission. This proportion has increased since 2003-2004 (49%). In the 2005-2006 BCS, 19% of adults were very worried about being a victim of card fraud; this is higher than recorded levels of worry about violent crime (17%), car crime (14%), and burglary (13%). According to the 2003-2004 BCS, individuals were slightly more likely to be worried about card fraud when they were using their cards to buy goods over the Internet or over the phone (in both cases 52% were very or fairly worried about this).

The 2004 CVS found that 18% of retailers and 8% of manufacturers had been victims of fraud by outsiders (Shury et al., 2005). Four percent of retailers and 2% of manufacturers had been victims of fraud by employees.

By far the most common type of fraud by outsiders against retailers was card fraud (i.e., credit, debit, or cheque card fraud) with three quarters (74%) of retailers who had experienced fraud by outsiders citing this. Of these, 83% were committed by the customer in the shop, 16% over the telephone, and 3% over the Internet, though this may simply reflect the levels of use of the different transaction methods. The most common types of fraud by employees were fraud using a credit card (35%), fraudulently creating a nonexistent customer (35%), and general fraudulent accounting (29%).

The most common fraud by outsiders against manufacturers was credit card, debit card, and cheque card fraud (32%). One in five (21%) had been the victim of fraud due to dealing with a nonexistent business while 13% had been invoiced by a supplier incorrectly or fraudulently.

The direct financial cost of crime for manufacturing premises was also estimated using the CVS. Looking at the average cost of each type of incident, given as the median amount, fraud by employees (£1,200) and fraud by outsiders (£600) ranked second and third in terms of being the most expensive incidents in terms of direct costs of loss and damage. The maximum cost for any single incident again highlights the potentially serious effects of fraud, particularly by outsiders, with a maximum cost of £1 million, as well as fraud by employees where the maximum was £180,000.

Based on the 2004 OCJS, 1% of those aged from 12 to 25 years reported using someone else's card or card details without the owner's permission in the last 12 months. Levels were similar for males and females and across the age range. Using the comparable age group (aged 18 to 25) the level of card fraud remained stable between 2004 and 2005 (2% in 2003 OCJS and 1% in 2004 OCJS, not a significant difference).

The 2004 OCJS found that among eligible 18- to 25-year-olds, claiming falsified work expenses and committing insurance fraud was relatively common, by 16% and 10% of individuals respectively. Benefit fraud and income tax evasion were less common (each at 2%). Males were more likely than females to report falsifying work expenses; however, females were more likely to report insurance fraud (15%) than males (5%). There were no differences between males and females for reported levels of tax evasion (2%) and benefit fraud (1%).

Administrative Sources: Police-Recorded Crime

Police-recorded crime provides a count of fraud, based on legal definitions and according to National Crime Recording Standards and Home Office counting rules. The number of fraud and forgery offences recorded by the police in 2005-2006 was 233,005, a decrease of 17% from 2004-2005 (Walker et al., 2006). Of these, 87,912 offences were cheque and credit card frauds, a 28% decrease from 121,596 offences recorded in 2004-2005.

Data have been collected by other nonpolice sources to describe the trends, extent, and type of fraud occurring in both the public and private sector.

Administrative Sources: Central Government

• Improvements in protective measures to reduce fraud and improvements to fraud measurement systems have enabled DWP (2005) to produce an estimate of overall losses of £.9 billion for 2004-2005 compared with £1.4 billion for 2003-2004.

• HMRC (2005) estimated a reduction in revenue losses from £6.5 billion-£7.4 billion in 2001-2002 to £4.8 billion-£5.4 billion in 2003-2004.

• Reports from the NHS CFS (2004) indicated that overall patient fraud has been reduced by half (49%) from £171 million in 1998-1999 to £87 million in 2003-2004.

• HMT reported that the value of employee fraud reported by central government bodies for 2004-2005 was £3.1 million (2005).

Administrative Sources: Private Sector

APACS measures a wide range of types of plastic card fraud. Card-not-present (CNP) fraud involves the use of stolen card details in non-face-to-face transactions either on the Internet, by phone, or by mail order.

CNP has been the largest type of card fraud in the U.K. for the past 3 years. Counterfeit card fraud occurs when an illegal copy is made of a genuine credit or debit card. Lost and stolen card fraud is also measured by APACS. Mail nonreceipt fraud involves cards being stolen before they are delivered to the cardholder. Card fraud losses that occur overseas on U.K.-issued cards are also recorded. There are three types of cheque fraud in the U.K.: counterfeit, forged, and fraudulently altered cheque fraud. Losses from online banking fraud are also published by APACS.

- The total losses from plastic card fraud reported by APACS in 2005 were £439.4 million, a decrease of 13% from 2004 (£504.8 million).

- Losses from CNP fraud type were £183.2 million in 2005, up by 21%. In 2005 the amount of CNP fraud that took place over the Internet was estimated at £117.1 million, or 64% of total CNP losses.

- Counterfeit card fraud has fallen since the introduction of chip and PIN in the U.K. Losses were £96.8 million in 2005, a decrease of 25% from 2004, and were at their lowest level since 1999.

- Also related to chip and PIN, lost and stolen card fraud was at its lowest level since 1999; in 2005 losses were £89 million, a 22% decrease from 2004.

- Mail nonreceipt fraud totalled £40 million in 2005, down by 45% from 2004. This decrease is attributable to chip and PIN making it more difficult for fraudsters to use stolen cards, but also because fewer cards were being sent out than at the peak of the chip and PIN rollout.

- Card fraud losses that occur overseas on U.K.-issued cards have decreased for the fourth consecutive year. Fraud abroad now accounts for just under one fifth of fraud (19%) on U.K. cards. Since 2001, fraud abroad has declined by 40%.

- In 2005, cheque fraud in the U.K. amounted to £40.3 million, a 13% decrease from the 2004 total of £46.2 million. Previously, cheque fraud losses had been on the increase, totalling £36 million in 2002 and £45 million in 2003.

- In 2005, total losses from online banking fraud reached £23.2 million, an increase of 90% from the previous year's total of £12.2 million. This fraud is growing from a very small base, which can make losses appear to grow rapidly.

An indication of the extent and trends in fraud according to the banking and credit card industry follows.

* According to Norwich Union (2005), fraud cost the U.K. economy in the region of £16 billion in 2004 and is growing.

* In 2004, commercial insurance fraud was estimated to be over £.5 billion in 2004 by Norwich Union, while ABI estimated that fraudulent insurance claims on motor and household policies total in excess of £1 billion in 2004 (Norwich Union, 2005).

* Losses by U.K. banks from nonplastic-related fraud totalled £107.6 million in 2004 according to figures from the BBA (2005), an increase of 11% from the previous year. Potential losses from fraud increased by 18% during the period to £1.152 billion, but more than 90% of this was prevented by bank staff and security systems.

* The ABI estimates the total amount of fraud suffered by insurers is more than £1 billion per annum. The largest elements of this are personal lines motor and household, with the ABI estimating that around 10% of the total value of personal lines motor and 15% of the total value of household claims are fraudulent.

AN EMERGING ISSUE:
THE MEASUREMENT OF ID THEFT

Although identity theft is sometimes referred to as "Britain's fastest grow-ing crime" by the media, figures collated from the British Crime Survey and APACS don't seem to provide strong evidence to support this claim.

In 2005-2006 a module was added to the BCS asking questions specifi-cally about identity theft and fraud. This is in addition to anything reported in the victim form, where questions are asked of those who say they have been a victim of any crime, and the technology crimes module. It is not possible to classify identity theft or fraud from the offence codes used in the victim form, so analysis is based on the specific questions asked in the identity theft module.

Not all types of identity theft are covered. The module asks specifically whether the respondent's personal details have been used to carry out certain specified activities and later asks about lost or stolen passports, driving licences, and foreign identity cards. For this reason and the inherent problems with measuring ID theft, it is likely that the measure will undercount. It may be more valuable, therefore, to consider looking at the different ways identity is used in different types of fraud, rather than trying to measure all types of identity theft.

As previously mentioned, according to the 2003-2004 BCS, a fifth of card fraud measured was a direct result of the card(s) being physically stolen from or lost by individuals. In these cases, the fraud resulted directly from a known crime, rather than from obtaining someone's identity through deception or manufacturing a false identity. This suggests that considering the use of manufactured identities separately from that of impersonated identities will provide greater understanding of this complex area.

Card ID theft occurs when a criminal uses a fraudulently obtained card or card details, along with stolen personal information, to open or take over a card account in someone else's name. According to APACS (2006), card ID theft has fallen by 17% in the last year, with losses totalling £30.5 million in 2005. Overall, this fraud type accounts for less than 7% of overall card fraud losses. APACS (2006) attributes much of the success in decreasing card fraud to the implementation of chip and PIN and to a specialist police squad that focusses on the recovery of counterfeit cards and compromised card numbers.

Application fraud involves criminals using stolen or false documents to open an account in someone else's name. Criminals steal documents such as utility bills and bank statements to build up usable information. Alternatively, they may use counterfeit documents for identification purposes. Application fraud losses were £12.4 million in 2005, a decrease of 5% (APACS, 2006).

Criminals use fraudulently obtained personal financial information and card details to deceive a bank or card company into believing they are the genuine cardholder. They then take over and start accessing the cardholder's account. In a typical situation, they will also change the address on the account, and ask for new cards and chequebooks to be sent out. Account takeover losses were £18.1 million in 2005, down 24% (APACS, 2006).

The figures from the 2005-2006 BCS show that of those asked about, the most frequent type of identity theft experienced was when a credit or debit card was used to make a purchase without their knowledge, which 4% of people had experienced. One percent of people had experienced criminals applying for and obtaining a credit card and also 1%, obtaining a loan, mortgage, or credit agreement.

Nineteen percent of adults who had ever experienced identity theft reported that they had had a credit or debit card used to make a purchase in the last 12 months. Less than 1% of people had had their identity used to register for a vehicle and none had experienced having their personal details used to apply for a passport, to their knowledge.

Of those who held a U.K. passport, 1% reported that their passport had been lost or stolen in the last 12 months. For U.K. driving licence holders, 2% reported that their licence had been lost or stolen during the same period.

THE WHOLE PICTURE

A cross-government review of the scale and costs of fraud, both direct and indirect, commenced in October 2005. The review includes examination of fraud data-collection systems across different organisations to identify the most appropriate statistical information to inform the government's response to fraud (Fraud Review: Final Report, 2006).

The report concludes that it is not possible to evaluate fully the scale of the problem caused by fraud. There are estimates of some types of fraud (e.g., benefit fraud, credit card fraud, and insurance fraud) as measured by specific organisations. Most measures of fraud, however, have not been carried out according to a robust methodology – they and measure different things – so adding them up to produce an overall total is not possible.

One aim of the Fraud Bill is to introduce fraud as an offence, in order to enable prosecution of fraud in the context of other criminal activity (Hansard, 2005). In doing so, the definition and framework will provide opportunity for effective measurement of fraud. Together with proposed improvements in the Home Office Counting Rules, the bill should make reporting and recording fraud easier.

A common problem with fraud offences is that not all of this type of offence comes to the attention of the authorities, and thus administrative records fail to capture the extent of the problem. Silverstone and Davia (2005) suggest that only 20% of fraud is "exposed and public," with a further 40% of the total "known but not publicised" and an additional 40% "undetected."

Generally, the difficulties with the measurement of fraud through both survey and administrative methods, combined with the complexity of the concept of fraud, could advocate using complementary series to provide a fuller picture of fraud.

When the new legislation and associated counting rules are in place, more emphasis should be placed on the police-recorded measure of fraud. With both individuals and businesses being able to feed into these figures (directly or indirectly) and with standardised methodology, this may prove to be the best method available to provide an estimate of the nationwide level of fraud.

With varying and uncertain methodologies, the other measures of fraud from administrative sources are valuable to their current audience and should be continued to provide measures of trend and evaluation, but their contribution to a nationwide measure of fraud is not key.

The value of survey measurements remains, both from a victim and offender perspective. Surveys can provide an estimate of the unreported hidden incidents of fraud. Also, the demographic, socioeconomic, and attitudinal factors collected provide a much fuller picture of the nature of fraud and will thus be able to contribute to the understanding and policy making that is required to tackle the problem. However, surveys must improve question design and data capture. They should be expanded to include measures of the costs of fraud, in order to better estimate of how much fraud costs the economy.

With identity theft an evolving issue, a combination of data from both the banking industry and information from surveys need to combine to understand this phenomenon better.

✦

Address correspondence to: Jacqueline.Hoare3@homeoffice.gsi.gov.uk

Acknowledgements: Acknowledgements are due to John Flatley (Home Office) and Mike Maxfield (Rutgers, the State University of New Jersey) for their invaluable support and advice.

REFERENCES

APACS. (2006). *Fraud: the facts 2006*. Retrieved December 1, 2006, from http://www.northeastfraudforum.co.uk/documents/Fraud%20the%20Facts%202006.pdf

British Bankers Association. (2005). *Non plastic related fraud increases.* Retrieved December 1, 2006, from http://www.bba.org.uk/bba/jsp/polopoly.jsp?d=145& a=5409

Department for Work and Pensions. (2005). *Reducing fraud in the benefit system: Achievements and ambitions.* Retrieved December 1, 2006, from http:// www.dwp.gov.uk/publications/dwp/2005/fsu/reducingfraud.pdf

Dodd, T., Nicholas, S., Povey, D., & Walker, A. (2004). *Crime in England and Wales 2003/2004.* Home Office Statistical Bulletin 10/04. London: Home Office.

Fraud Review: Final Report. (2006). Retrieved April 10, 2007, from http://www. attorneygeneral.gov.uk/attachments/FraudReview.pdf

Hansard Report. (22 June 2005). Retrieved December 1, 2006, from http:// www.publications.parliament.uk/pa/ld200405/ldhansrd/pdvn/lds05/text/ 50622-04.htm

HM Revenue and Customs. (2005). *Annual report 2004–2005.* Retrieved December 1, 2006, from http://www.hmrc.gov.uk

HM Treasury. (2005). *2004-2005 Fraud report.* Retrieved December 1, 2006 from: http://www.hm-treasury.gov.uk./media/2/8/fraud_report_government_depts_ 04-05.pdf

NHS Counter Fraud and Security Management Service. (2004). *Countering fraud in the NHS: Protecting resources for patients 1999-2004 performance statistics.* Retrieved December 1, 2006, from http://www.mhsc.nhs.uk/pages/About%20the%20 Trust/Departments/Finance/Information/CFSM%20Performance%20Stats% 2099-04.pdf

Nicholas, S., Povey, D., Walker, A., & Kershaw, C. (2005). *Crime in England and Wales 2004/2005.* Home Office Statistical Bulletin 11/05. London: Home Office.

Norwich Union. (2005) *The Fraud Report, shedding light on hidden crime.* Retrieved December 1, 2006, from http://www.aviva.com/csr06/files/fraud_report.pdf

Shury, J., Speed, M., Vivian, D., Kuechel, A., & Nicholas, S. (2005). *Crime against retail and manufacturing premises: Findings from the 2002 commercial victimisation survey.* Home Office OLR 37/05. London: Home Office.

Silverstone, H., & Davia, H. R. (2005). *Fraud 101: Techniques and strategies for detection.* New York: Wiley.

Walker, A., Kershaw, C., & Nicholas, S. (2006). *Crime in England and Wales 2005/ 06.* Home Office Statistical Bulletin 12/06. London: Home Office.

Wilson, D. (2005). *Fraud and technology crimes: Findings from the 2002/03 British Crime Survey and the 2003 Offending, Crime and Justice Survey.* Home Office OLR 34/05. London: Home Office.

Wilson, D., Patterson, A., Powell, G., & Hembury, R. (2006). *Fraud and technology crimes: Findings from the 2003/04 British Crime Survey and the 2004 Offending, Crime and Justice Survey and administrative sources.* Home Office OLR 09/06. London: Home Office.

Addressing the Challenge of Costs and Error in Victimization Surveys: The Potential of New Technologies and Methods

by

David Cantor
Westat, Inc.

and

Joint Program for Survey Methodology
University of Maryland

and

James P. Lynch
Department of Law, Police Science
and Criminal Justice Administration
John Jay College

Abstract: *Over the past 30 years, victimization surveys have evolved from a novelty to a mainstay of crime statistics. This evolution continues, prompted by changes in the technological and social environment of surveys as well as changes in the demand for information on crime. Rising costs, declining response rates, and the fast-moving telecommunications industry pose significant challenges to the quality of information from victim surveys. At the same time, computer-assisted*

*interviewing and the availability of the Internet provide new tools to
address these challenges. Of equal importance in guiding the evolution
of crime surveys is careful consideration of the role of crime surveys
in a system of crime statistics. The information goals of the survey
will dictate how technology can best be used. Setting these information
goals, in turn, should be guided by what we have learned about what
victimization surveys can do well and what would be done better by
other components of a crime statistics system. This chapter discusses
the cost and error tradeoffs as well as the feasibility of employing
various technologies under three different assumptions about the information goals of victimization surveys.*

Victimization surveys are about 30 years old and in that time they have
evolved from a novelty to a mainstay of crime statistics. During this period,
surveys have benefited from technological advances involving computers
and telecommunications. The shift from in-person interviewing to telephone interviewing, for example, allowed surveys to maintain the quality
of the data while keeping costs at an acceptable level (Nathan, 2001). At
the same time computer-assisted interviewing substantially increased the
quality of surveys (Hubble & Wilder, 1988). Although technological
changes have been beneficial to victimization surveys and to the survey
industry generally, victim surveys face new challenges and opportunities
from a changing technological and social environment. On the negative
side, the sampling frame for telephone interviewing is being pressed by
the widespread use of cell phones. It is also becoming more difficult to
enlist the cooperation of the general public in surveys. On the positive
side, further advances in computerization and the wide availability of the
Internet introduce methods that either supplement or totally replace the
need for an interviewer.

Changes in technology and in the public's attitudes toward surveys
coincide with an evolution in the place of victimization surveys as a social
indicator and as a methodology for testing criminological theories. The
need for victim surveys to be a rigorous check on police crime statistics
has waned since the first surveys were fielded in the late 1960s (Lynch &
Addington, 2006; Cantor & Lynch, 2000). There is good evidence that
many of the deficiencies in police information systems that gave rise to
victim surveys have been substantially corrected (Rosenfeld, 2006).

At the same time, there is an increasing demand for surveys to examine
crimes that cannot be investigated easily by omnibus, general population
surveys like the British Crime Survey (BCS) or the National Crime Victimization Survey (NCVS) or by using police records. Changes in technology

have created new categories of crimes, such as cyber theft and corrupting cyber operations. Moreover, the increased sophistication of survey researchers and the public has raised the bar with respect to the quality of information that we have come to expect from victim surveys (Koss, 1996).

This chapter describes the evolution of survey methods and technologies and how the substantive demand for victimization data has changed. It examines the potential for cost and errors following changes in the administration of victimization surveys. Varieties of multimedia and multiple frame surveys are discussed. Finally, we consider the option of abandoning the omnibus crime survey approach in favor of a series of more independent surveys attending to different facets of the crime problem. These methodologies are assessed in terms of their ability to satisfy the changing demand for substantive information on crime.

TECHNOLOGICAL AND SOCIETAL CHANGES AFFECTING SURVEY METHODOLOGY

Technology is used here to refer to methods used to sample respondents, administer the instrument, and process responses. *Societal changes* refer to the evolution of norms affecting responses in surveys as well changes in the demand for information from these surveys. Some of these norms apply directly to behavior in surveys such as the use of answering machines to screen calls, whereas other changes are more general such as the widespread declines in compliance behavior of which nonresponse is just one manifestation.

Technological Changes in Surveys

Advances in the computerization of interviewing are among the major technological innovations in survey research. Other emerging technologies use the Internet to sample populations, to distribute questionnaires, and to administer interviews. Other improvements in old technologies, such as mail surveys, hold promise for achieving appropriate cost/error trade offs.

Computerization

The introduction of computers into the survey process in the 1980s had a tremendous influence on how victimization surveys are conducted. Computer-assisted interviewing has improved the quality of survey responses

– 283 –

(Nicholls & Groves, 1986; Hubble & Wilder, 1988: Biemer & Lyberg, 2003; Cantor & Lynch, 2005), increased the accuracy and speed of data entry, and improved responses to sensitive questioning (Tourangeau & Smith, 1998; Mirrless-Black, 1999; Walby & Allen, 2004; Finney, 2006; Chang & Krosnick, 2003; Taylor, Krane, & Thomas, 2005; Galesic, Tourangeau, & Couper, 2006).

Internet Surveys

The use of the Internet to administer surveys has tremendous potential to change how surveys are conducted and to reduce both cost and error. Internet-based surveys can provide many of the potential cost savings and documented quality enhancements discussed in the previous section. Moreover, Internet surveys could result in additional savings in sampling, mailing costs, and telephone charges. It is not yet clear, however, that access to the Internet and the public's willingness to use it are adequate for general-population surveys.

The major problem in using the Web is its limited population coverage. The National Statistics Omnibus Survey reports that 57% of households in the United Kingdom had access to the Internet in 2006 (Pollard, 2006). In the United States, the Census Bureau estimated that in 2003, 58% of the adult population had access to the Internet in the U.S. A more recent telephone survey estimated that 73% of adults had access (Madden, 2006).[1] More important, particular demographic groups, including minorities, those who are elderly, and those who are poor, are less likely than others to use the Internet. This disparity, sometimes called the "digital divide" (National Telecommunications and Information Agency, 2000; Peters, 2001; Couper, 2000; Pineau & Slotwiner, 2003), could bias any general population sample. Nonetheless, one could argue that at some point in the near future access to the Internet will be more widespread, in much the same way telephone coverage spread in the 20th century. In the U.K., for example, access to the Internet has increased from 46% in 2002 to 57% of households in 2006 (Pollard, 2006).[2]

Even if Internet access were universal, logistical problems must be overcome in drawing an Internet sample. There is no e-mail address directory for the general public, so researchers cannot sample by e-mail addresses the way that they can by postal addresses or telephone numbers. Attempts to recruit respondents for Internet interviews using other interview modes have not been particularly successful. For example, giving respondents the option to use the Internet when making initial contact by mail or by telephone has been found to result in low response rates (Lozar, Vehovar, et al., 2001; Griffin, Fischer, et al., 2001; Cantor et al., 2005). And in many cases, when respondents agree to participate they opt to use the more traditional modes of mail or telephone.

An alternative approach is to recruit a panel of respondents to be part of a continuing series of surveys that would be conducted over the Internet. In this case, respondents are recruited by telephone and other means to participate in a series of self-administered computer-assisted surveys that would be conducted on a regular basis (Saris, 1998; Nyhus, 1996; Pineau & Slotwiner, 2003; Webley & Nyhus, 2005; Keuzenkamp, 2004). Those who agree to be in the panel are asked about their access to a computer (and the Internet), as well as other characteristics about the household. If they do not have Internet access, it is provided for the duration of their participation in the panel. All interviews would be done on the computer. The sample also provides a pool whereby the initial costs of recruitment can be amortized over the subsequent interviews in which respondents participate.

Response rates remain a problem with such recruited panel designs. The Dutch version of this type of panel obtains an initial response rate of about 30% (Saris, 1998). There is additional attrition associated with participation in particular surveys. For example, Nyhus (1996) reports a final response rate of 17.5% for those participating in a study on income. The response rate for the U.S. version of this design is similar. It should also be noted that because the coverage of the surveys is based on a telephone frame (e.g., phone numbers listed in the telephone book; RDD methods), the growing prevalence of mobile phones remains a problem.

Internet surveys work best when the target population can be defined very specifically and a large proportion of the group has Internet access. The most common application has been Internet survey s of businesses, schools, hospitals, or other organizations where access to the Internet is widespread. For example, the United States Bureau of Justice Statistics is currently conducting an Internet survey on the incidence of cybercrime among U.S. businesses. The U.S. National Center for Education Statistics has also implemented a Web-based survey of schools to collect data on incidents of school violence (Couper, 2000).

Changes in the Social Environment of Surveys

The major changes in the social environment of surveys are rooted in the telecommunications industry and the etiquette of phone use. Increased use of cell phones and other means of communication not linked to the residence have made it more complicated to conduct telephone surveys. The extensive use of telephones for marketing and for solicitation has led to a variety of technologies and behaviors that screen calls. All of these factors have reduced the response rate in telephone surveys (Curtin et al., 2005). In addition, the public's willingness to cooperate in surveys of whatever mode has declined (Smith, 1995; Atrostic, Bates, Burt, & Silberstein, 2001). In the U.S., the individual-level response rate for the NCVS, which employs both in-person and telephone interviewing, has dropped from approximately 90% in 1992 to 78% in 2004.[3] It is generally recognized that more effort has to be invested to maintain the same rate from one year to the next. This puts cost pressures on research budgets. Survey administrators are increasingly faced with hard choices related to sacrificing survey quality (e.g., sample cuts, use of inferior modes) to keep the collection of data possible.

In the past, surveys like the BCS and NCVS have dealt with these pressures by moving from in-person to telephone interviewing and using the savings to maintain response rates and the general quality of the data. The use of the telephone in the future is facing significant barriers in addition to the ones mentioned in the foregoing section. One of these is the proliferation of cell phones. In 2005, about 10% of U.S. adults had regular access to a cell phone (Blumberg, Luke, & Cynamon, 2006). In Europe, these numbers are even more dramatic, where the cost of using wireless devices is more competitive with having a landline.

Simply shifting to conduct surveys via mobile phones poses a number of different logistical and statistical problems. It is difficult to sample cell phone users because there is no comprehensive list of cell phone owners and the definitions of the sampling unit is fuzzy, for example, how many people have access to a particular phone? (Dipko, Brick, Brick, & Presser, 2005; Yuan et al., 2005). Moreover, the exclusive reliance on cell phones is not randomly distributed in the population. Age is highly correlated with exclusive use of a cell phone, as are household living arrangements. Random digit dial (RDD) surveys in the U.S., which exclude cell-only households, have not found this to result in significant error in estimates for many health-related indicators (Blumberg et al., 2006). However, this is partly because of the relatively small percentage of households that only have a cell phone. The potential bias in Europe, where cell phones are used more widely, may already make it difficult to use the landline telephone as a primary mode of interview for certain types of surveys.

CHANGES IN THE DEMAND FOR INFORMATION
ON THE CRIME PROBLEM

The import of any change in the technical and social environment of victimization surveys must be assessed with respect to changes in the demand for information on crime. The BCS and NCVS were developed to meet a specific set of demands for information about crime. If these demands have changed, then these changes should be made explicit and be factored into our discussion of future designs. In this section, we argue that the demand for information from victim surveys has evolved to reduce the relative importance of benchmarking police statistics and to increase the goal of expanding our understanding of crime problems. This change in emphasis has implications for the future use of various technologies designed to reduce costs and ensure the quality of the data.

The role of victimization surveys for criminological and criminal justice purposes has evolved from their beginnings in the early 1960s (Biderman, Johnson et al., 1967; Ennis, 1967). At that time, a number of factors encouraged intense interest in using victim reports to estimate the volume of crime. The impetus came largely from the level of crime and urban unrest at the time in the U.S. and resulting efforts of the federal government to improve the criminal justice system. A tangible goal that came out of this was the importance of developing an indicator of crime that was independent of the police (Cantor & Lynch, 2000). As a result, the NCVS was designed to mimic the Uniform Crime Reports (UCR) maintained by the Federal Bureau of Investigation (FBI). So the scope and definition of the crimes covered in the surveys was made to correspond closely to those included in the UCR and less weight was given to the suitability of the crime for measurement within self-report surveys.

The NCVS was also designed to mimic other social indicators in its form, particularly those in the economic and health areas. The social indicators approach emphasizes the production of estimates of level and change in level of a particular phenomenon, in this case crime. This meant that to provide annual estimates of very rare crimes in the UCR, such as rape, the survey would need to be administered to massive samples. More generally, a premium was placed on the stability of the data collection system; series continuity was prized over flexibility.

The BCS was born in a different environment and with different demands. There was less emphasis on the need to take a social indicators approach, and a greater emphasis on the survey's potential as a research instrument designed to shed light on the nature of crime; and in any case, the available resources were very limited, especially at the outset. The outcome was a survey that had smaller sample sizes than its American cousin and less concern for change estimates. As a result, the BCS was much nimbler in its ability to adapt to address more topical issues regarding crime. It became more a complement to the ongoing police statistical system by collecting data that the police statistical system did not. For example, it provided much richer information relevant to emerging opportunity theories of crime and victimization by collecting data on situational crime characteristics (who, what, where, and how).

The maturing of the victim survey method has continued this evolution from the preeminence of the benchmarking and social indicator functions of victim surveys to more of a balance between these goals and the more general goal of understanding crime. This shift in emphasis affects the priority given specific estimates obtained from the survey. First, the scope of crimes covered in surveys need not correspond exactly to the scope of crime in police statistics. There may be overlap, but not absolute correspondence. Second, the emphasis on change estimates could be reduced, which relaxes the requirement of constancy in the design over time. Third, new and different crimes and classifications of crime can be developed that exploit the information richness of victim surveys and take account of the changing nature of crime. Fourth, more attention and resources in the survey can be devoted to the collection of information relevant to understanding why crime occurs and its effect on the public.

The maturing of the victim survey method has also resulted in increased sophistication in the demand for quality in data from these surveys. In the past 30 years, we have learned a great deal about the response process in retrospective surveys (Jabine, Straf, Tanur, & Tourangeau, 1984; Schwarz & Sudman, 1996; Sirken et al., 1999; Tarnai & Dillman, 1992). These advances in theories of response have coincided with intense interest in a particular types of crime to produce particularly telling critiques of victim surveys. Both the research community and sophisticated interest groups have come to realize the strengths and weaknesses of victim surveys. Interest groups demand state-of-the-art data on their crime of choice. When they do not get these data, they attack the surveys that bring the unwanted news. Their attacks are usually focused on a very small and often marginal subject in the survey, for instance, defensive gun use, but have the repercussion of casting doubt on the method more generally.

Often these demands by sophisticated interest groups for higher quality data contain a kernel of truth. Data on a specific type of crime from an omnibus victimization survey is not as good as data from a survey tailored for a specific type of crime because state-of-the-art methodology uniquely applicable to that crime has not been employed. Thanks to the advances in understanding of the response process, we could improve the reporting for any particular type of crime, but only at the cost of decreasing the quality in the reporting of others. The sheer scope of crimes pursued in an omnibus victimization survey almost precludes getting state-of-the-art data on all of them.

The desire to uncouple from omnibus vehicles for surveys on violence against women is one example of this (Tjaden & Thoennes, 2000). Interest groups were convinced that the volume of problems they addressed was much greater than omnibus victimization surveys indicated. They fielded specialized surveys that, for a variety of reasons (some good and some bad), confirmed their suspicions and their support for omnibus surveys waned (Fisher & Cullen, 2000; Lynch, 1996). A similar phenomenon occurred in the debate on the use of guns for defensive purposes (e.g., see McDowall, 2005; Kleck, 1997).

Responding to this demand from the new crop of sophisticated consumers may warrant moving to more specialized surveys rather than a single omnibus victimization survey. It could also involve trimming the scope of omnibus victim surveys to what can be best measured in a victimization survey. Resulting savings could be directed to state-of-the-art methods for measuring a reduced group of crimes.

In fact, these strategies are more complementary than mutually exclusive. Recalling the genesis of victim surveys, the allocation of crimes to the survey was determined by the police (whom the surveys mimicked) rather than by what surveys could do well. The maturity and security of victim surveys may be such that we can reassess the scope of crimes on which they would collect information, with an eye toward improving quality. There may be crimes currently included in victim surveys that should not be there either because household surveys are not the best vehicle for investigating this crime or because it would be easier for other vehicles to collect this information. Thirty years of experience with victim surveys as well as the recent advances in response theory put us in a much better position to make these determinations than was the case in 1970.

Responding in this manner to demands for increasing the quality of data from victim surveys is not without its political risks. Eliminating crimes from the surveys reduces the coalition of persons interested in fielding the survey. It is a question of whether flawed information is better than no information.

FITTING TECHNOLOGY TO DEMANDS
FOR DATA ON CRIME

How advances in technology could or should replace what is currently being used in surveys like the BCS and the NCVS will vary to a great extent according to changes in demand for information on crime. The potential for changes in survey technology depends substantially on how the primary purposes of surveys evolve. If they remain first and foremost an exercise in benchmarking police statistics, one sort of future is implied. There are rather different prospects if they follow the trajectory argued in this chapter, that is, more of a balance between the benchmarking of police statistics, on the one hand, and the pursuit of enlightenment about the nature of crime, on the other.

In this section, we consider three scenarios for employing new technologies in victimization surveys. Each scenario assumes different information goals for the survey and offers a design that uses various combinations of technologies to optimize cost error tradeoffs in achieving those goals. The first scenario assumes the primacy of the benchmarking function, and a cross-sectional and then a panel survey. The second scenario assumes more of a balance between monitoring the construction of police statistics and illuminating the crime problem. The final scenario assumes that illuminating the crime problem takes clear precedence over the monitoring of police statistics.

Traditional Goals

This scenario assumes that the principal purpose of the survey is to monitor the police presentation of the crime problem through their crime statistics. As such, the survey would provide level and changes estimates for those crimes most commonly reported in police statistical series. To do this, the survey will emphasize representative samples of the population, exhaustive screening for eligible crimes, and stability of the methodology and information content of the survey over time.

Under these conditions, the technological advances chosen will emphasize cost reductions and modest quality enhancements. Quality enhancements will come from more universal application of computer assisted interviewing in the surveys including Computer-Assisted Telephone Interviewing (CATI), Audio Computer-Assisted Interviewing (ACASI), and Telephone-audio Computer-Assisted Interviewing (TCASI). We would not expect large cost reductions to result from this application of technology because interviewers will still be required to contact the respondent and deliver the computer hardware. The absence of an Internet sampling frame and gaps in Internet coverage will make large reductions in interviewers impractical.

Some savings can be achieved in general population surveys by using multiple modes of interviewing within the household sample (de Leeuw, 2005). The most economical design starts with a single frame, for example, an address frame, and uses the least expensive mode of interviewing first. Follow-up with more expensive (and intrusive) methods are then implemented to boost response rates. For example, one design would be to draw samples using an address frame, sending letters to respondents asking them to respond to a survey on the Internet. Those that do not respond are then followed up by telephone. This methodology can substantially reduce costs if a significant proportion of the sample uses the cheaper Internet mode. The study cited above by Link and Mokdad (2004) found the public in the U.S. is not quite ready to make the shift. There is evidence that the European public similarly is not leaping on this mode either.

An important constraint on the Internet mode is the difficulty in selecting a respondent within the household. As a practical matter, it is not possible to rely on the initial respondent randomly to select a single person in the house as the primary respondent (Link & Mokdad, 2004). The most promising solution to this is to ask that all adults in the household fill out a questionnaire. This eliminates the need to follow complicated instructions, although it is still clearly not error free.

A more expensive way to use these technologies would be to conduct the survey using both Web/mail and telephone modes. If a common frame exists, a sample of addresses would be selected to which a Web/mail request would be sent. A second sample would be selected for which telephone interviews would be done. By randomly allocating the two modes it will be possible to measure and adjust for errors that may be related to each methodology (de Leeuw, 2005). This would be much harder to do if telephone interviews are only conducted for those who did not respond to the initial Web/mail survey request.

Multimode surveys may be easier to implement in rotating panel designs like the NCVS, where the first contact is done in person. This structure provides a flexible methodology for integrating new technologies in a cost-effective way by using the first interview to determine the mode of interview at subsequent contacts. By moving as many people as possible to the noninterviewer self-administered modes, potentially the survey could save time and money.

Mixing interviewer and self-administered methodologies raises comparability questions (Dillman & Christian, 2005). There is little evidence that when asking about well-defined, nonsensitive, factual, or behavioral data, there are differences between these two methodologies. When asking about sensitive topics, there are significant differences (Mirrless-Black, 1999; Walby & Allen, 2004; Finney, 2006). For subjective, opinion or attitudinal items (e.g., fear of crime, opinions on interventions), interviewer-administered surveys tend to have more context and order effects (e.g., Tarnai & Dillman, 1992; Smyth, Christian, & Dillman, 2006; Chang & Krosnick, 2003). Differences within particular self-administered modes, such as mail versus Web versus T-ACASI, are not as clear. Some studies find no difference (e.g., Lozar et al., 2001; Kerwin et al., 2004), while others do report differences (Link & Mokdad, 2005; Chang & Krosnick, 2003).

It is not clear how these mode differences are reflected when reporting on different forms of victimization. One would expect that there would be significant differences between interviewer- and self-administered methods for events that are subject to strong privacy or sensitivity concerns. It seems unlikely that collection of crimes involving strangers or theft (e.g., larceny, burglary, auto theft) would be similarly affected, though this has not actually been established.

The screening strategies related to defining eligible events and promoting recall have substantial effects on reporting these types of crimes (Kindermann, Lynch, & Cantor, 1997). Self-administered instruments, even if computerized, have constraints. Interviewers are not available to prompt when trying to enhance recall or explain ambiguous terms. As software and methods for programming computers advance, it will also become increasingly possible to simulate the role of the interviewer, detecting signs of confusion by the respondent and taking some action to clarify misunderstandings (Ehlen et al., 2006). Though still in the fairly distant future, it points to a greater reliance on self-administration and decreasing differences between interview modes.

Even if there are substantial mode effects, trends in crime will be unaffected if the mix of modes remains constant over time. In fact, both the BCS and NCVS are subject to a number of effects that differentially affect responses and are correlated with key victim risk factors (e.g., use of CATI, bounded interviewing, supplements). Understanding mode effects would be more important when doing detailed analysis across respondents or measures of change that are systematically associated with different modes.

Benchmarking and Enlightenment Goals as Coequal

In this scenario, the goals of monitoring police statistics and understanding the crime problem would have equal demands on the survey design and resources. The monitoring of the police picture of crime would be restricted to a subset of crimes known to be well reported to the police and in victimization surveys, such as robbery and burglary (Cantor & Lynch, 2005; Kindermann et al., 1997; Rosenfeld, 2006). These crimes would constitute a stable core of the survey and the procedures used to elicit mention of these crimes would be kept constant over time. Because these core crimes have been shown to be relatively easy to identify, the resources devoted to exhaustive cuing in the screening interview could be reduced. The core survey would be supplemented by an aggressive system of one-time and episodic supplements that would be added to the core. The supplements would take various forms such as being administered to the same respondent as the core interview or being administered to other members of the household who are identified during the core interview. Supplements that are administered to the same respondent as the core instrumentation could be conducted during the same session as the core interview or the supplement could be administered in a follow-up interview.

Supplements could be administered more often using Web-based methodologies, in part because the core survey provides the sampling frame. To the extent that the supplements focused on subpopulations that have greater access to the Internet or less reluctance to use the Internet, they will not experience the undercoverage that plagues general population surveys.

The core and supplement design would not necessarily reduce costs nor would it address the problem of nonresponse in the surveys. It would increase the ability of the survey to serve multiple information needs by reducing the scope and complexity of the police monitoring task and applying those resources to crimes and tasks that are uniquely suited to the strengths of self-report surveys. So the reductions in the length of the screening interview that would occur as a result of the elimination of hard-to-measure crimes like sexual assault could be applied to screening for other crimes or to collecting more information on the context of the victimization event.

New Goals and a System of Specialized Surveys

This scenario assumes that the demands for information on crime and the goals of victim surveys change completely from that of benchmarking monitoring police performance to illuminating the crime problem. The scope of crime to be addressed in the survey would be independent of the crimes addressed in statistical series maintained by the police. Indeed, the crimes chosen would be those that are measured poorly by police data and well measured in victim surveys. Emphasis would be on describing and understanding why crimes occur, rather than estimating the level and change in level of these crimes. As a result, the content of the information collected in the survey would change considerably over time, and the information collected on events and on victims would go well beyond the information necessary to classify these events in the police type of crime categories.

These changes in the goals and objectives of the survey make more attractive the idea of a system of surveys to replace the omnibus household surveys like the NCVS and the BCS. This approach would allow victim surveys to pursue wholeheartedly types of crime that are not well monitored by police statistics but that are very salient to the public. It would also allow the surveys to provide the high-quality information that sophisticated special interest consumers are demanding. This approach may permit greater use of technologies discussed in previous sections that could reduce costs and increase the quality of victim surveys. Finally, a more flexible "family" of surveys would be more readily adapted to measure nontraditional crimes or victims.

The requirement that victim surveys imitate police-administrative series wastes resources that could be used to monitor crimes not well captured in police record systems. If domestic violence and sexual assault, for example, are not well reported to the police, then they should be the focus of victim surveys. If these types of crime have been shown to be not well reported in omnibus "crime" surveys, then perhaps they should be monitored in specialized surveys where victim reporting may be more complete. Similarly, if crimes against students in schools are better measured by surveys conducted in schools, then that is the type of survey that should be used. These specialized surveys in schools and in the workplace may afford greater coverage of the target populations and greater access to the Internet.

The key to this dramatic break with the past is developing a crime classification system that departs from police statistics on crime. Once this is established, then it will be easier to allocate the responsibility of collecting data on these crimes to the appropriate survey vehicles, that is, those vehicles that provide the highest quality data on that type of crime.

Building an alternative to the current crime classification would take a good deal of thought, but we can illustrate what such an alternative crime classification would look like. The general principles behind this crime classification are that (1) the crime is important in its impact on persons or groups, (2) the crime is well measured by a survey method, (3) it is not well measured by other methods, and (4) it exploits the information available in the survey. Other routinely published crime rates should emphasize the social context of the crime, rather than simply the attributes of the criminal act itself.

The public is concerned about crimes among strangers and crimes among intimates so that this attribute of the crime should figure prominently in a crime classification. Commercial and noncommercial crimes are also distinctions that crime classifications should make. The former are crimes in which a business or commercial entity was the victim and the latter are crimes where a private citizen was a victim. These distinctions are not made consistently in current crime classifications. Crime classifications that emphasize the activity of the victim at the time of the incident would also be useful for understanding the risk of victimization. So, crime rates at school or at work would be informative for citizens who want a realistic picture of their victimization risks.

With a new crime classification system in place, we can begin to allocate responsibility for obtaining the information necessary to estimate these indicators to different survey vehicles. These vehicles, in turn, may be able to make greater or lesser use of the advances in technology discussed earlier.

One component of the system would be a survey for estimating crimes among intimates. Police statistics are notoriously bad at estimating the level and change in this type of crime. Crime surveys may be better but only if expensive, labor-intensive methods are used. One alternative here is to use a very sophisticated household survey to obtain information on this type of crime. Another would be to estimate the volume of crime with a supplement to a health-centered survey on injury or use of the medical system. A third alternative could be some sort of composite or dual frame estimate, with one frame being the household frame from a victimization survey and the other frame coming from the health survey frame that could be households or emergency rooms.

Commercial, workplace, and school crime rates are good candidates for self-report Internet surveys. There is some evidence that access to the Internet would be higher for these establishments and that recall within the context may be more exhaustive than in household surveys.

CONCLUSION

This discussion of a radically different approach to victim surveys and its implications for the use of technologies in these surveys is a little glib. Much more thought and specific information must be brought to bear on these issues. It is important, however, at least to engage in the exercise of rethinking substantially the role and goals of the victim surveys before considering the future role of technology in these surveys. We have learned a great deal about the victim survey method in the last 30 years, about what it can do and what it cannot do. This knowledge should be brought to bear in thinking about what the surveys *should* do and how technology can be used to help them do it.

The first generation of victim surveys was driven by a specific set of information demands that differed somewhat in the U.S. and the U.K. These information demands have changed over time and our approach to meeting these demands may need to change as well. Our consideration of the relative importance of different information demands on victim surveys should draw upon what we have learned from the first generation of surveys. Specifically, we know that there are certain things that omnibus household surveys of victimization do not do well and we should not ask them to do these things. At the same time, there are things that they do very well and these things should figure more prominently in the role allocated to victim surveys.

Another lesson from the first generation is that the role of victim surveys should be viewed in the context of a system of crime statistics that may include not only an omnibus victimization survey but other more specialized surveys as well as administrative record data from criminal justice and health care agencies. Responsibility for serving the information needs of the public regarding crime should be allocated among these vehicles, with each addressing that part of the crime problem that it is best equipped to address. Just because a need for information can be addressed by an omnibus household survey of victims does not mean it should be.

Finally, the first generation of victim surveys, at least in the United States, has been driven by the technological demands of surveys and led by survey statisticians. In assessing the future of the victim survey method, it is important for criminologists and substantive area experts to take a more aggressive role in presenting alternative conceptualizations of the crime problem and the measurement of same. Only when these substantive issues have been thoroughly addressed can survey methodologists consider the technological changes in the survey that can best serve these goals.

Address correspondence to: David Cantor, Associate Director, Westat Inc., 1650 Research Blvd., Rockville, MD.

Acknowledgments: The authors would like to thank Michael Maxfield and Mike Hough for organizing the very enlightening meeting on the 25th anniversary of the British Crime Survey that prompted the article on which this chapter is based and for commenting on earlier drafts.

NOTES

1. Unlike the Census Bureau data, the Pew data are based on a random digit dial telephone survey that does not cover households without a telephone or those with only a cell phone. In addition, the response rate for these surveys was relatively low (around 30%), compared to the Census Bureau study, which has a response rate in the low to mid 90s.
2. Pineau and Slotwiner (2003) report similar increases in the U.S. but that the size of these increases are decreasing over time.
3. Rates are at the person level and are across all rotation groups for the data collection year.

REFERENCES

Atrostic, B. K., Bates, N., Burt, G., & Silberstein, A. (2001). Nonresponse in U.S. government surveys: Consistent measures, recent trends and new insights. *Journal of Official Statistics, 2*, 209-226.
Biderman, A. D., Johnson, L. A., McIntyre, J., & Weir, A. W. (1967). *Report on a pilot study in the District of Columbia on victimization and attitudes toward law*

enforcement. Field Surveys No. 1. President's Commission on Law Enforcement and Administration of Justice. Washington, DC: Government Printing Office.

Biderman, A. D., & Lynch, J. P. (1991). *Understanding crime incidence statistics: Why the UCR diverges from the NCS.* New York: Springer Verlag.

Biemer, P., & Lyberg, L. E. (2003). *Introduction to survey quality.* Hoboken, NJ: Wiley-Inter-science.

Blumberg, S., Luke, J. V., & Cynamon, M. (2006). Telephone coverage and health survey estimates: Evaluating the need for concern about wireless substitution. *American Journal of Public Health, 96,* 926-931.

Cantor, D., & Lynch, J. P. (2000). Self-report surveys as measures of crime and victimization. *Criminal justice 2000: Measurement and analysis of crime and justice,* Vol. 4. Washington, DC: National Institute of Justice.

Cantor, D., & Lynch, J. P. (2005). Exploring the effects of changes in design on the analytical uses of the NCVS data. *Journal of Quantitative Criminology, 30,* 23-40.

Cantor, D., Schiffrin, H., Park, I., Davis, T., & Hesse, B. (2005). *An experiment giving respondents the option to complete on the Web a random digit dial health communications survey.* Paper presented at the Conference on Critical Issues in eHealth Research, Bethesda, MD.

Caspar, R. (2004). *Census 2000 testing, experimentation and evaluation program synthesis, Report No. 18, TR-18, results from the Response Mode and Incentive Experiment 2000.* Washington, DC: U.S. Bureau of Census.

Chang, L. C., & Krosnick, J. A. (2003). *National surveys via RDD telephone interviewing versus the internet: Comparing sample representativeness and response quality.* Retrieved August 30, 2006 from http://communication.stanford.edu/faculty/ Krosnick/Tel%20Int%20Mode%20Experiment.pdf

Conrad, F. G., & Schober, M. F. (2000). Clarifying question meaning in a household telephone survey. *Public Opinion Quarterly, 64,* 1-28.

Cook, P. J. (1985). The case of the missing victims: Gunshot wounds in the National Crime Survey. *Journal of Quantitative Criminology, 1,* 91-102.

Couper, M. P. (2000). Web surveys: A review of issues and approaches. *Public Opinion Quarterly, 64,* 464-494.

Couper, M. P., & Nicholls, W. L. (1998). The history and development of computer assisted survey information collection. In M. P. Couper et al. (Eds.), *Computer assisted survey information collection.* New York: Wiley.

Curtin, R., Presser, S., & Singer, E. (2005). Changes in telephone survey nonresponse over the past quarter century. *Public Opinion Quarterly, 69,* 87-98.

Currivan, D. B., Nyman, A. L., Turner, C. F., & Biener, L. (2004). Does telephone audio computer-assisted self-interviewing improve the accuracy of prevalence estimates of youth smoking?: Evidence from the UMass tobacco study. *Public Opinion Quarterly, 68,* 542-564.

de Leeuw, E. D. (1992). *Data quality in mail, telephone, and face-to-face surveys.* Amsterdam: TT-Publicaties.

de Leeuw, E. D. (2005). To mix or not to mix data collection modes in surveys. *Journal of Official Statistics, 21,* 233-255.

de Leeuw, E., & Van der Zouwen, J. (1988). Data quality in telephone and face-to-face surveys: A comparative meta-analysis. In R. Groves, P. Biemer, L. Lyberg, J.

Massey, W. Nicholls II, & J. Waksberg (Eds.), *Telephone survey methodology.* New York: Wiley.

Dillman, D., & Christian, L. M. (2005). Survey mode as a source of instability in responses across surveys. *Field Methods, 17,* 30-52.

Dipko, S., Brick, P. D., Brick, M., & Presser, S. (2005, May). *An investigation of response differences between cell phone and landline interviews.* Paper presented at the 2005 Annual Meeting of the American Association for Public Opinion Research, Miami Beach, FL.

Ehlen, P., Schober, M. F., & Conrad, F. G. (2006). *Modeling response times for old and young respondents to improve their understanding of survey questions.* Paper presented at the 2006 Annual Meeting of the American Association for Public Opinion Research, Montreal, May 18-21.

Ennis, P. H. (1967). *Criminal victimization in the United States: A report from a national survey.* Presidents Commission on Law Enforcement and the Administration of Justice. Field Surveys Two. Washington, DC: U.S. Government Printing Office.

Finney, A. (2006). *Domestic violence, sexual assault and stalking: Findings from the 2004/05 British Crime Survey.* London: Home Office.

Fisher, B. S., & Cullen, F. T. (2000). Measuring the sexual victimization of women: Evolution, current controversies and future research. *Criminal justice 2000: Measurement and analysis of crime and justice,* Vol. 4. Washington, DC: National Institute of Justice.

Galesic, M., Tourangeau, R., & Couper, M. P. (2006). Complementing random-digit-dial telephone surveys with other approaches to collecting sensitive data. *American Journal of Preventive Medicine, 31,* 437-443.

Griffin, D. H., Fischer, D. P., & Morgan, M. T. (2001). *Testing and internet response option for the American community survey.* Paper presented to the American Association for Public Opinion Research, Montreal, Quebec.

Hauser, R. M. (2005). Survey response in the long run: The Wisconsin longitudinal study. *Field Methods, 17,* 3-29.

Hochstim, J. R. (1967). A critical comparison of three strategies of collecting data from households. *Journal of the American Statistical Association, 62,* 976-989.

Holbrook, A., Green, H., & Krosnick, J. (2003). Telephone versus face-to-face interviewing of national probability samples with long questionnaires: Comparisons of respondent satisficing and social desirability response bias. *Public Opinion Quarterly, 67,* 79-125.

Hubble, D., & Wilder, B. E. (1988, August). *Preliminary results from the National Crime Survey CATI experiment.* Proceedings of the American Statistical Association: Survey Methods Section, New Orleans, LA.

Jabine, T., Straf, M., Tanur, J., & Tourangeau, R. (Eds.). (1984). *Cognitive aspects of survey methodology: Building a bridge between disciplines.* Washington, DC: National Academy Press.

Kerwin, J., Brick, P. D., Levin, K., Cantor, D., O'Brien, J., Wang, A., et al. (2004). *Surveying R&D professionals by web and mail: An experiment.* Paper presented to the American Statistical Association, Toronto, Canada.

Keuzenkamp, S. (2004, October). *Attitudes on violence against women.* Working paper No. 24, presented at Conference of European Statisticians, Geneva, Switzerland.

Kindermann, C., Lynch, J. P., & Cantor, D. (1997). *Effects of the redesign on victimization estimates.* Washington, DC: U.S. Department of Justice, Bureau of Justice Statistics.

Kleck, G. (1997). *Targeting guns: Firearms and their control.* New York: Aldine De Gruyter.

Koss, M. (1996). The measurement of rape victimization in crime surveys. *Criminal Justice and Behavior, 23,* 55-69.

Link, M. W., & Mokdad, A. (2004). Are web and mail modes feasible options for the behavioral risk factor surveillance survey? In S. B. Cohen & J. M. Lepkowski (Eds.), *Eighth conference on health survey research methods* (pp. 149-154). Hyattsville, MD: National Center for Health Statistics.

Link, M., & Mokdad, A. (2005). Effects of survey mode on self-reports of adult alcohol consumption: Comparison of web, mail and telephone. *Journal of Studies on Alcohol, 66,* 239-245.

Lozar Manfreda, K., Vehovar, V., & Batagelj, Z. (2001). Web versus mail questionnaire for an institutional survey. Accessed on September 9, 2006 at http://www.or.zumamannheim.de/gaeste/klm2001/lozar%20manfreda_vehovar_batagelj%202001.pdf

Lynch, J. P. (1996). Clarifying divergent estimates of the incidence of rape from three national surveys. *Public Opinion Quarterly, 60,* 410-430.

Lynch, J. P., & Addington, L. A. (2006). *Understanding crime incidence statistics: Revisiting the divergence of the UCR and the NCVS.* New York: Cambridge University Press.

Madden, M. (2006). *Internet penetration and impact.* Data Memo, Pew Internet and American Life Project. Accessed at www.pewinternet.org on September 8, 2006.

McDowall, D. (2005). John R. Lott, Jr.'s defensive gun use brandishing estimates. *Public Opinion Quarterly, 69,* 246-263.

McDowall, D., & Loftin, C. (2006). What is divergence and what do we know about it? In J. P. Lynch & L. A. Addington (Eds.), *Understanding crime statistics: Revisiting the divergence of the NCVS and the UCR.* New York: Cambridge University Press.

Mirrlees-Black, C. (1999). *Domestic violence: Findings from a new British crime survey Self-completion questionnaire.* Home Office Research Study 191. London: Home Office.

Nathan, G. (2001). Telesurvey methodologies for household surveys-A review and some thoughts for the Future. *Survey Methodology, 27,* 7-31.

National Telecommunications and Information Agency. (2000). *Falling through the net: Toward digital inclusion. A report on Americans' access to technology tools.* Washington, DC: Author.

Nicholls, W. L., II, & Groves, R. M. (1986). The status of computer assisted telephone interviewing, Part I: Introduction, cost and timeliness, *Journal of Official Statistics, 2,* 93-115.

Nyhus, E. K. (1996). *The VSB-center savings project: Data collection methods, questionnaires and sampling procedures.* Center for Economic Research, Progress Report 42. Retrieved September 5, 2006 from www.center.kub.nl/pub/vsbpr2.html

Peters, L. (2001). Respondent panel and face-to-face interview compared: The cultural changes in the Netherlands 2000 survey. The Hague. Accessed at http://

www.scp.nl/english/data/respondent/respondent-panel-facetoface-interview-compared.pdf on September 9, 2006.

Pollard, M. (2006). *First release: Internet access households and individuals*. National Statistics, London. Retrieved August 28, 2006 from http://www.statistics.gov.uk/pdfdir/inta0806.pdf

Pineau, V., & Slotwiner, D. (2003). *Probability samples v. volunteer respondents in InternetResearch*. Knowledge Networks, Inc. Retrieved September 25, 2006 from www.knowledgenetworks.com/info/press/papers/Volunteer%white%20paper%201119-03.pdf

Ramos, M., Sedivi, B. M., & Sweet, E. M. (1998). Computerized self-administered questionnaires (CSAQ). In M. P. Couper et al. (Eds.), *Computer assisted survey information collection*. New York: Wiley.

Rand, M., Lynch, J. P., & Cantor, D. (1997). *Long term trends in crime victimization*. Washington, DC: U.S. Bureau of Justice Statistics.

Rosenfeld, R. (2006). Explaining the divergence between UCR and NCVS aggravated assault trends. In J. P. Lynch & L. A. Addington (Eds.), *Understanding crime incidence statistics: Revisiting the divergence of the UCR and the NCVS* (pp. 277-299). New York: Cambridge University Press.

Saris, W. E. (1998). Ten years of interviewing without interviewers: The telepanel. In M. P. Couper et al. (Eds.), *Computer assisted survey information collection* (pp. 409-429). New York: Wiley.

Schaeffer, N. C., & Maynard, D. W. (2006, May). *Sounds of silence: Structure of response latency*. Paper presented at the 2006 Annual Meeting of the American Association for Public Opinion Research, Montreal, Canada.

Schwarz, N., & Sudman, S. (Eds.). (1996). *Answering questions: Methodology for determining cognitive and communicative processes in survey research*. San Francisco: Jossey-Bass.

Sirken, M. G., Hermann, D. J., Schechter, S., Schwarz, N., Tanur, J., & Tourangeau, R. (Eds.). (1999). *Cognition and survey research*. New York: Wiley.

Smith, T. W. (1995). Trends in Nonresponse rates. *International Journal of Public Opinion Research, 7*, 157-171.

Smyth, J. D., Christian, L. M., & Dillman, D. A. (2006, January). *Does yes or no on the telephone mean the same as check-all-that-apply on the web?* Paper presented at the 21st International Conference on Telephone Survey Methodology, Miami, FL.

Tarnai, J., & Dillman, D. A. (1992). Questionnaire context as a source of response differences in mail versus telephone surveys. In N. Schwarz & S. Sudman (Eds.), *Context effects in social and psychological research*. New York: Springer Verlag.

Taylor, H., Krane, D., & Thomas, R. K. (2005, May). *How does social desirability affect responses? Differences in telephone and online surveys*. Paper presented at the Annual Meetings of the American Association for Public Opinion Research, Miami Beach, FL.

Tjaden, P., & Thoennes, N. (2000) *The prevalence, incidence, and consequences of violence against women*. Washington, DC: U.S. National Institute of Justice.

Tourangeau, R., Miller Steiger, D., & Wilson, D. (2002). Self-administered questions by telephone: Evaluating interactive voice response. *Public Opinion Quarterly, 66*, 265-278.

Tourangeau, R., & Smith, T. W. (1998). Collecting sensitive information with different modes of data collection. In M. P. Couper et al. (Eds.), *Computer assisted survey information collection*. New York: Wiley.

van Hattum, M. J. C., & de Leeuw, E. D. (1999). A disk by mail survey of pupils in primary schools: Data quality and logistics. *Journal of Official Statistics, 15,* 413-429.

Villarroel, M. A., et al. (2006). Same-gender sex in the United States: Impact of T-Acasi on prevalence estimates. *Public Opinion Quarterly, 70,* 166-196.

Walby, S., & Allen, J. (2004). *Domestic violence, sexual assault and stalking: Findings from the British crime survey*. Home Office Research Study 276. London: Home Office.

Webley, P., & Nyhus, E. K. (2005). Parents influence on children's future orientation and saving. *Journal of Economic Psychology, 27,* 140-164.

Yuan, Y. A., et al. (2005, May). *Surveying cell phone households – Results and lessons?* Paper presented at the 2005 annual meeting of the American Association for Public Opinion Research, Miami Beach, FL.

Surveying Crime in the 21st Century: Summary and Recommendations

by

Mike Maxfield
School of Criminal Justice
Rutgers University, Newark

Mike Hough
Institute for Criminal Policy Research
King's College London

and

Pat Mayhew
Crime and Justice Research Center
Victoria University of Wellington

Chapters in this volume have described many of the important contributions to criminological theory and justice policy produced by crime surveys
generally, and the British Crime Survey (BCS) in particular. Much has
been learned, especially since the BCS was first launched in 1982. However,
a recurring theme throughout the book is that many crimes and types of
victims are poorly represented in traditional crime surveys. Some authors
have posed the question whether large-scale crime surveys as they have
been conducted for more than 30 years can or should continue into the
future.

Crime Prevention Studies, volume 22 (2007), pp. 303–316.

This concluding chapter pulls together some of these themes. It looks at the factors that limit the ability of crime surveys to represent crime problems faithfully, then lays out possible directions for producing better data. Our consideration of problems and future directions draws on conference discussion as well as chapters in this volume.

What does the future hold for large-scale national surveys of crime – and indeed, for supranational surveys such as the International Crime Victimization Survey (ICVS)? The answer depends on where you look. Some countries, such as Australia, New Zealand, France, and Scotland are fielding or developing revised national surveys with some enthusiasm. We have seen how the British Crime Survey has now become deeply embedded in the British government's approach to performance management in criminal justice. On the other hand, the future of the U.S. National Crime Victimization Survey is uncertain, and some would see the conventional large-scale national crime survey as approaching obsolescence. Certainly there are pressures on surveys to adapt and evolve, both to meet the growing technical challenges in mounting large sample surveys, and to reflect new demands for information in a changing political context.

TECHNICAL CHALLENGES

Sample surveys are becoming more difficult to mount. They are labor-intensive, especially when conducted face-to-face, and this makes them very expensive in developed countries. The population is also becoming less compliant to the demands of interviews, and response rates are declining for many surveys. On the one hand, this probably reflects a sort of survey saturation, with increasing competition from market researchers and public surveyors for the finite attention and commitment of respondents. On the other hand, there is probably less of a sense of obligation to participate in government surveys than there was 25 years ago. The British Crime Survey has actually managed to stave off declines in response rates over the last 7 years, routinely achieving figures of 75%. Most would agree, however, that the long-term prospects for retaining high response rates are discouraging. There may be some point below which response rates are so low as to make national sample surveys unusable.

Two decades ago, random-digit-dialing (RDD) phone surveys promised to be a cheaper alternative to the face-to-face survey. These now face equal or larger problems with response rates, however, as chapters by van Dijk, Rand, and Cantor and Lynch point out. There are also some intractable problems in sampling that reflect the growing variety of phone modalities – what Cantor and Lynch call changes in the social environment of surveys. The proportion of households served only by a fixed landline is fast shrinking; the proportion served only by mobile phones is growing. Internet-based voice services are also rapidly increasing. RDD surveys cannot rely any longer solely on landline samples, as this would fatally underrepresent the groups most at risk of crime.[1] It is questionable, however, whether viable RDD samples can be assembled from the new patchwork-quilt of phone provision. These problems – of low response rates and problematic sampling frames – seem to have been particularly acute for the 2005 ICVS. Response rates that often fell below 50% for individual countries and a failure to reach the growing proportion of young "mobile only" respondents point to a pressing need to solve these problems if this particular survey vehicle is to retain any credibility in the future (van Dijk et al., 2007). It is also worth noting the failure of the 2005 Scottish Crime Survey, which failed to yield credible results using RDD and an incomplete sampling frame that excluded the mobile-only population (Hope, 2005).

Other changes in the social environment of surveys also threaten the viability of the household-based approach. Twenty-five years ago, the vast majority of the populations of developed countries lived in conventional single-dwelling households. Now, it is much more common for people to have a second home – either for leisure time, or because they have to work away from their main home. Some institutional populations have also grown, most notably students. When the BCS started, it seemed reasonable to ignore the fact that students living away from home were omitted from the sample; after all, they accounted for less than half a percent of the population. Now they account for around 2%, and we know that students are amongst the most heavily victimized groups. The population of older people living in institutions is also growing, and most developed countries have a significant population of homeless people – those who do not maintain a permanent residence in a single household, and those who otherwise do not wish to be counted among a household's residents (Martin, 1999). As the Smith Review argued, it is increasingly hard for crime surveys to ignore these nonhousehold populations (Smith, 2006). Equally, as the scale of crime committed against teenagers is becoming clearer, the typical lower age limits to survey samples look hard to justify.

Finally, the nature of crime is changing, and surveys have to adapt to capture new phenomena properly. Sometimes the necessary adjustments to survey instruments are simple. For example, over the life of the BCS, the checklist of items stolen from crime victims has expanded to include video equipment, DVD players, camcorders, mobile phones, computers, and laptops. Other new forms of crime are more challenging to capture in surveys, as discussed in chapters by van Dijk, Hoare, and Sutton. E-fraud and e-theft, for example, are much harder to locate in space and time than burglary or car theft. They have more opaque boundaries than conventional forms of theft, if indeed they can be conceptualized as events. These forms of crime, however, obviously need to be included in crime surveys. Recognizing this, the BCS has added items asking about card fraud, and the NCVS has covered identity-related fraud (Wilson, Patterson, Powell, & Hembury, 2006; Baum, 2006).

NEW DEMANDS FOR INFORMATION

In parallel with these technical challenges, there have been changes in the nature of political demands for crime-related information. These changes reflect long-run shifts in the governance of industrialized countries. Some of the changes serve to institutionalize crime surveys and others work to reduce their value. Giddens (1990, 1991) has drawn attention to the way in which, under conditions of late modernity, democratic governments give decreasing weight to the voice of professional expertise in the management of state institutions and correspondingly greater weight to public opinion. In Britain, responsiveness to public opinion is one of the hallmarks of New Public Management, the other being the use of quantitative performance measures. It is little surprise, therefore, to find that the expense of the BCS is now substantially justified by its ability to yield performance indicators on people's experience of, and attitudes towards, crime, policing, and justice.

Whether other national surveys, and the supranational ICVS, take on this role remains to be seen. With respect to Europe, our prediction is that over the coming two decades governments will increasingly appreciate the importance of information about the perceived legitimacy of institutions of justice, to set beside information about crime trends. Governments will need to know whether people trust their police and court systems, and whether they think these are effectively managed. It is unclear if national sample surveys will be the most efficient means of collecting such information. If it proves possible to stabilize survey response rates and to contain problems of sample bias, we think that surveys have an important future in discharging this function.

The more general question is whether crime surveys can "earn their keep" by providing a national index of crime, which in turn could depend on whether crime control remains a significant political responsibility at the national (or federal) level. One form of political future for industrialized democracies in the 21st century involves radical devolution of political decision-making to neighborhood – or at least city – level. The Smith Review of crime statistics in England and Wales clearly nailed its banner to the mast of localism, and stressed the importance of making fine-grained local crime statistics more readily available to the general public (Smith, 2006), so that local people could hold local agencies to account. In this particular future, surveys like the BCS and NCVS will only prove useful as a very general – and episodic – sort of check against police measures. No survey could conceivably be mounted on a scale that would allow genuinely local benchmarking of police statistics across any country.

Finally, the broader crime landscape is changing, and this change brings a different mix of informational needs for government. Arguably, crime surveys have tended to place in the policy foreground those crimes committed against individuals and their private property. This probably reflected with some accuracy the policy priority attached to these crimes in the 1980s and 1990s. Our 21st century preoccupations are different.

Crimes against the environment are in no sense new, but our sensitivity to their importance is growing rapidly. Similarly, terrorist crimes are not new,[2] but the scale of some of them, coupled with the use of suicide tactics, is distinctively new, and poses a threat that makes significant demands on the criminal justice system. Van Dijk's chapter reminds us how various other forms of organized and transnational crime are increasing to a point that constitutes a significant threat to order in some countries. Crimes committed against businesses and other organizations are also taking on increased visibility – arguably as a consequence of effective prevention of crimes against individuals and their private property. And, of course, none of these forms of crime are well captured by conventional crime survey methods.

BEYOND HOUSEHOLDS AND INDIVIDUALS

It is time to reconsider the role of victims in crime surveys. Whilst crime surveys never claimed to measure "total crime," one can see a tendency for crime surveys to reify "victim" in such a way as to divert attention from other kinds of offenses, or from victims who cannot be measured with household-based samples. The focus on personal victims resulted from the recognition that surveying victims was the key to measuring unreported and unrecorded crimes. This remains of interest and importance to governments across the industrialized world. Various countries continue to develop and expand their programmes of crime surveys. The original purposes of crime surveys, however, no longer seem quite as compelling as they did 20 or 30 years ago. The big questions about the shape and scale of unreported and unrecorded crime have been answered, and it seems unlikely that future household surveys of crime will achieve the sort of fundamental reorientation towards crime that crime surveys triggered three decade ago. It is probably high time that empirical criminology broadened its focus to embrace crimes poorly measured by both police and victim reports.

Precisely how this is best done is one of the major criminological questions for the 21st century. An approach with considerable attractions is the one that has been developed by the British Home Office, with support from reviews of crime statistics carried out by the Statistics Commission (2006) and Smith Review (2006). This involves the development of a growing matrix of surveys that in combination cover as much of the terrain of crime measurement as possible. Thus the BCS estimates can now be read alongside those from the Offending and Criminal Justice Survey (a survey of young people's experience as victims and offenders), the Commercial Victimization Survey, and the Citizenship Survey. Ways are being examined for covering the crime experience of teenagers aged under 16 and that of institutional populations such as students. Some of these surveys are planned to be repeated on a regular basis, whilst others are likely to be episodic.

Of course, there is nothing new about the principle of this "portfolio" approach to surveying crime, even if the scale of the British approach is unusually large. Rand notes that commercial establishments were included in city surveys conducted in the U.S., but were discontinued in 1977 when it was found that most incidents of any significance were reported to the police. Surveys of retail and manufacturing premises were conducted in England and Wales in 1994 and 2002 (Mirrlees-Black & Ross, 1995; Shury, Speed, Vivian, Kuechel, & Nicholas, 2005). Scotland has also made inroads into commercial victimization (Hopkins & Ingram, 2001) and Australia has looked at this (Taylor & Mayhew, 2002) and at farms (Anderson & McCall, 2005). Commercial and industrial establishments form only some of the nonhousehold targets of crime – there are also hospitals, schools, government offices, and so forth. Some crimes against businesses will also be hard to measure. Companies could be particularly resistant to saying much about fraud, for instance, and it will be hard to capture many of the offenses that van Dijk attributes to organized crime and official corruption. Another challenge for victim surveys is how they can cover illegal-market crimes like prostitution and drug dealing. Such offenses are customarily termed victimless crimes, a misconception that ignores how illegal markets affect the businesses and communities in which they operate.[3]

SURVEYING CRIME IN THE 21st CENTURY: A BRIEF AGENDA

In predicting the future use of surveys for criminal policy and criminology, it makes sense to recognise the tension between governmental need for information, and the practical constraints on what can be bought, in terms of cost and public compliance. So long as the technical quality of surveys can be retained at affordable levels, we expect governments to make growing use of surveys of some sort. But what will become of the traditional household surveys of victimization that have dominated empirical criminology in the last quarter of the 20th century?

It is useful to keep in mind the seemingly trite point that general-purpose surveys serve general purposes. As research tools, surveys frequently offer preliminary answers to questions that are either exploratory or descriptive (or both); they are less appropriate for revealing causal explanations or understanding complex sequences of events or specialized problems that affect more narrowly defined subsets of the general population.

The general approach is to parse large-scale national crime surveys into smaller chunks that fulfill better two broad purposes: (1) routine monitoring of core offenses and attitudes; and (2) conducting research into new and specialized topics that might affect specialized populations.

Retain Scaled-back Crime Surveys as Social Indicators

Several chapters describe the role of crime surveys as key parts of a statistical system to measure victimization and its impact. The need to monitor police recording practices may no longer be as central as it was, but annual estimates of victimization for core offenses are important social indicators. However, one must question whether surveys on the scale of the NCVS, or even the BCS, are needed. There is probably a sensible compromise to be struck between the very large sample sizes of these national surveys and the very much smaller samples – averaging 2,000 per country – of the ICVS. Indeed the limiting factor of the ICVS is probably sample bias, rather than sampling error. Sweeps of the survey prior to 2005 have demonstrated that meaningful estimates can be derived at a country level. As a general principle, it is better to invest first in the quality of samples, and second in their precision: imprecise survey estimates from a small, unbiased sample are more valuable than precisely wrong ones from larger but biased samples.[4]

Scaling back crime surveys to estimate a subset of crimes offers potential cost savings in two related ways. First, crimes such as burglary and thefts involving vehicles are numerous enough to be estimated with smaller sample sizes. Second, the goal of national crime surveys can be redefined to estimate prevalence for a subset of key offenses. As a result, the larger samples needed to provide detailed information about incidents would no longer be necessary.[5] One rationale for gathering details on incidents was largely to understand better the nature of victimization. After decades of research, we have learned a great deal about this and are unlikely to discover new dimensions by continuing in the same way with general crime surveys. Without the need to gather details on incidents, much of the lengthy victim forms can be eliminated, reducing the length of interviews. Whatever resources can be freed by trimming sample sizes and questionnaire detail can be reinvested in fuller analysis of the data that *are* collected, and in other surveys in the crime "portfolio."

Because distribution of attitudes to crime and justice is less skewed than victimization, smaller sample sizes can yield reliable information at the national level. Criminal justice policy is not a prominent national issue in the U.S., but a set of core items could be retained in a system of social indicators.

To some extent, the need to maintain a consistent series to monitor trends has constrained the NCVS. This is complicated by the fact that the U.S. Census Bureau conducts the survey for the Bureau of Justice Statistics, a sometimes uneasy partnership that complicates the task of modifying the NCVS. A leaner, more specialized survey for monitoring core offenses and attitudes would be more appropriately administered by a national statistical agency more distanced from crime policy, such as the Census Bureau in the U.S. When the BCS was initiated in Britain, it was determined to keep the survey out of the hands of the equivalent body – the Office of Population Censuses and Surveys – precisely because that organisaton was seen at that time (at least within the Home Office) as imposing a dead hand on good ideas. More recently the Statistics Commission (2006) has suggested that the BCS might be moved from the Home Office to the Office of National Statistics (the successor to OPCS) to ensure greater independence and thus credibility. It is hard to say whether the resulting gains in independence will actually offset the distancing from policy interests.

Conduct Supplementary Surveys on Specific Targets

From its first sweep in 1982, the BCS built in supplementary modules of questions on special topics. These changed from year to year and were administered to a subset of survey respondents, because large sample sizes were not always needed for the behavioral and attitudinal questions included in the supplements. A great deal of what has been learned from the BCS stemmed from these supplementary modules, which were usually developed through consultation with academic and other outside researchers. To a lesser extent, the NCVS adopted occasional supplements to standard core items to assess special topics.

This model offers promise for future crime surveys. Many of the data and information needs described by authors in this volume might be addressed by fielding more focused sample surveys of individuals and of other target populations. Similarly, sampling techniques can be tested on nontraditional target populations through supplementary surveys, some complementing the BCS.

Supplementary surveys might center on specific types of offenses or types of victims. For example, it should be possible to learn more about the process and circumstances of repeat victimization through specialized interviews with samples of repeat victims. Similarly, the seductions of crime (Sutton) or the victimization and offending nexus (Lauritsen & Laub) could be examined more closely with focused interviews and samples.

Other chapters offer suggestions on approaches to learning about nontraditional crime. Van Dijk suggests interviewing people most likely to be affected by or knowledgeable about corruption, and considering proxy measures for corruption or organized crime. Additional research to develop families of new measures could lead to better systems for monitoring.

Research has shown that trafficking in stolen goods operates in loosely organized networks of people connected to legitimate businesses. Theft of vehicles and parts, for example, involves people working in vehicle sales and repair industries in some capacity; illegal activity is readily screened by the large volume of legal transactions. Yet because particular business sectors are involved, these may be appropriate subjects for more systematic research involving surveys of businesses. These would target neither victims nor offenders, but rather participation in illegal markets in an effort to learn more about how these networks operate (Brown & Clarke, 2004; Tremblay, Talon, & Hurley, 2001).

Experiment with Segmented Samples and Survey Administration

If the stable monitoring function of crime surveys can be separated from focused research on special topics, then the latter can use different kinds of sampling strategies. For example, uneven access to Internet resources is commonly cited as a reason why general population surveys cannot use Web-based sampling and survey administration. On the other hand, Web-based samples might be ideal for studying Internet-facilitated fraud. Coupled with Web-based questionnaires, such studies might be conducted very economically.

It is also worthwhile to explore mixed-mode surveys and samples. Sutton offers a useful example of Web-based questionnaires for survey respondents who meet some screening criterion for Internet access. Screening might be determined through initial telephone or mail contact, reserving in-person interviews for those lacking Internet access. Split-half and other methodological experiments could be conducted as they were in testing various forms of computer-assisted interviewing. Surveys of businesses are most likely the best candidates for Web-based probability sampling and survey administration.

Experiments with samples and survey administration recognize that surveys can be representative in different ways. It is not always necessary to strive for strict statistical representativeness to provide useful information for understanding crime problems. This is especially the case for nontraditional, nonvolume crimes, where more exploratory or descriptive research is needed. The concern about obtaining traditional representative samples stemmed from the focus on counting. Although that is important, counting can be restricted to a particular sample or to a particular crime experience (and even noncrime experience) where prevalence rates are better known. We should also think about using survey techniques to understand the mechanisms of nontraditional crimes. Just as problem-oriented policing uses interviews with nonrepresentative samples of offenders to understand how cars are stolen or homes burgled, interviews with nontraditional samples of victims and offenders can reveal information about how volume frauds such as phishing (sending fraudulent e-mails to obtain identification and account numbers from individuals) are perpetrated. This might then lead to narrowing a target population that can then be more precisely defined for the purpose of producing better counts. Such approaches are not without their own problems. Sampling frames for Web-based surveys would have to be specified. Monitoring software raises serious ethical and privacy questions. These and other obstacles preclude such experimentation for general-purpose crime surveys, but are better viewed as possible problems to be solved in supplementary surveys that focus more on basic research than on precise estimates of population parameters.

Launch a Series of Subnational Surveys

National crime surveys assume something meaningful can be learned from national-level estimates of victimization and other related issues. This is likely to be more true for the more narrow routine monitoring function of crime surveys described in this chapter. Yet problems of crime and disorder, and their impact on people's lives, vary substantially across communities and neighborhoods. Modern policing stresses the importance of understanding local problems in context.

To some extent, the expansion of the BCS sample size to represent police force areas recognizes the need to monitor local problems. Yet the relatively small sample sizes for relatively large force areas allow only the most general monitoring. A program of national-level monitoring and periodic specialized surveys should also address the need for more localized, detailed information about crime and justice policy. It may not be necessary to launch a bundle of surveys in all areas of England and Wales, or other countries. Instead, local crime surveys could combine a package of standard items with efforts to understand better the problems specific to individual communities. Such surveys need not be conducted annually, though in some areas they might. The general purpose is to better understand local problems and devise appropriate actions based on that information.

Collaborate More Closely with Academic and Other Researchers

With respect to the BCS, several chapters call for closer collaboration between Home Office researchers and the academic community. It is generally felt that more secondary analysis of BCS and other surveys should be supported. More important, Home Office staff should work more closely with academics in developing supplementary surveys and samples. This was done in earlier sweeps of the BCS, and to some extent it still happens. Even greater collaboration would be needed if recommendations for shifting the focus of crime surveys are followed.

CONCLUSION

Much of what we recommend in this chapter is not new. Earlier sweeps of the BCS combined standard items asked of a large sample with more specialized spin-off questionnaires. The Offending, Crime and Justice Survey has adopted creative sampling and panel methods to understand better offending among the general population and cohorts at higher risk of offending. Commercial victim surveys have been conducted twice in England and Wales, combining probability and purposive sampling methods. Hough and Roberts describe supplementary questions to understand public knowledge and perceptions of crime and justice better. The Smith Review (2006) presents a collection of recommendations similar to many topics discussed here, including greater involvement of academic criminologists. Michael Rand's chapter concludes that the NCVS will probably have to abandon past goals of continuity and stability, becoming more flexible in efforts to understand new crime problems in a tighter fiscal climate.

In considering the accomplishments of crime surveys in the past and the directions they might take in the future, it is helpful to keep in mind that surveys of victims were launched 40 years ago to measure crimes not well represented in police reports. To a great extent, this volume represents a realization that we may again need to develop new techniques for understanding crime and related problems for which large national surveys are less appropriate.

Address correspondence to: maxfield@rutgers.edu or
mike.hough@kcl.ac.uk

NOTES

1. Blumberg, Luke, and Julian (2006) report that among respondents to the U.S. National Health Interview Survey in 2004-2005, households headed by younger persons were more likely to report mobile-only phone service, and social routines that placed them at greater risk of injury.
2. At least not new to countries such as Britain and Spain, both of which have long histories of grappling with terrorist attacks.
3. Interestingly, the U.S. FBI has moved beyond traditional victim categories to include "government" and "society" in the evolving incident-based police data system, a data series that also attempts to capture a broader range of offenses including fraud, embezzlement, and bribery. Results from 2002 data, submitted by agencies that represent about 20% of the nation's population, suggest that despite these efforts few such offenses are being captured and reasonably coded by police. Only 121 bribery incidents were coded among more than 3.7 million incidents recorded in 2002; and only 17 of those 121 incidents involved government victims (author tabulations).
4. Of course, samples that are both large and unbiased are best in the best of all possible worlds.
5. In the case of the BCS, the sample sizes are driven by the need for precision in performance measures at a subnational (police force area) level. Smaller samples would threaten this function.

REFERENCES

Alvazzi del Frate, A. (2004). The International Crime Business Survey: Findings from nine central-Eastern European cities. *European Journal on Criminal Policy and Research, 10*, 137-161.

Anderson, K., & McCall, M. (2005). *Farm crime in Australia.* Canberra: Australian Government Attorney-General's Department.

Baum, K. (2006, April). *Identity theft, 2004.* BJS Bulletin. Washington, DC: U.S. Department of Justice, Office of Justice Programs, Bureau of Justice Statistics.

Blumberg, S. J., Luke, J. V., & Cynamon, M. L. (2006, June). Telephone coverage and health survey estimates: Evaluating the need for concern about wireless substitution. *American Journal of Public Health, 96*, 926-931.

Brown, R., & Clarke, R. V. (2004). Police intelligence and theft of vehicles for export: Recent U.K. Experience. In M. G. Maxfield & R. V. Clarke (Eds.), *Understanding and preventing car theft.* Crime prevention studies, vol. 17. Monsey, NY: Criminal Justice Press.

Giddens, A. (1990). *The consequences of modernity*. Cambridge, England: Polity Press.

Giddens, A. (1991). *Modernity and self-identity*. Cambridge, England: Polity Press.

Hope, S. (2005). *Scottish crime and victimisation survey: Calibration exercise – A comparison of survey methodologies*. Research report for the Scottish Executive. Available at http://www.scotland.gov.uk/Resource/Doc/47121/0020932.pdf

Hopkins, M., & Ingram, M. (2001), Crimes against business: The first Scottish business crime survey. *Security Journal, 14*(3), 43-59.

Lynch, J. P., & Addington, L. A. (Eds.). (2007). *Understanding crime statistics: Revisiting the divergence of the NCVS and the UCR*. New York: Cambridge University Press.

Martin, E. (1999). Who knows who lives here? Within-household disagreements as a source of survey coverage error. *Public Opinion Quarterly, 63*, 220-236.

Mirrlees-Black, C., & Ross, A. (1995). *Crime against retail and manufacturing premises: Findings from the 1994 commercial victimization survey*. Home Office Research Study, 146. London: Her Majesty's Stationery Office.

Shury, J., Speed, M., Vivian, D., Kuechel, A., & Nicholas, S. (2005). *Crime against retail and manufacturing premises: Findings from the 2002 commercial victimization survey*. Online Report 37/05. London: Research, Development and Statistics Directorate, Home Office. Available at Http://www.homeoffice.gov.uk/rds/onlinepubs1.html

Smith, A. (2006). *Crime statistics: An independent review*. (Carried out by the Crime Statistics Review Group for the Secretary of State for the Home Department, November 2006). London: Home Office Office. Available at http://www.homeoffice.gov.uk/rds/pdfs06/crime-statistics-independent-review-06.pdf

Smith, S. K., Steadman, G. W., Minton, T. D., & Townsend, M. (1999, June). *Criminal victimization and perceptions of community safety in 12 cities, 1998*. Washington, DC: U.S. Department of Justice, Office of Justice Programs, Bureau of Justice Statistics and Office of Community Oriented Police Services.

Statistics Commission. (2006). *Crime statistics: User perspectives* (Matrix Research Consultancy, T. Hope) [Report by the Statistics Commission] (Rep. No. 30). London: Author. Available at http://www.statscom.org.uk

Taylor, N., & Mayhew, P. (2002, March). *Patterns of victimisation among small retail businesses*. (Trends and Issues, no. 221). Canberra, Australia: Australian Institute of Criminology.

Tremblay, P., Talon, B., & Hurley, D. (2001). Body switching and related adaptations in the resale of stolen vehicles. *British Journal of Criminology, 41*, 561-579.

van Dijk, J., Manchin, R., Van Kesteren, J., Nevala, S., & Hideg, G. (2007). *The burden of crime in the EU: A comparative analysis of the European survey of crime and safety (EU ICS) 2005*. Brussels, Belgium: Gallup Europe.

Wilson, D., Patterson, A., Powell, G., & Hembury, R. (2006). *Fraud and technology crimes: Findings from the 2003/04 British Crime Survey, the 2004 offending, crime and justice survey and administrative sources*. Online Report 09/06. London: Research, Development and Statistics Directorate, Home Office. Available at http://www.homeoffice.gov.uk/rds/offending_survey.html

---

Appendix
The British Crime Survey –
Past and Future
16–17 October 2006

CONFERENCE PARTICIPANTS

Jonathan Allen	Home Office RDS[1]
Penny Babb	Home Office RDS
Keith Bolling	BMRB
David Cantor	Westat
Prof. Ron Clarke	Rutgers University
Prof. Jason Ditton	University of Sheffield
Jan van Dijk	University of Tilburg
Stephen Farrall	Keele University
Graham Farrell	Loughborough University
John Flatley	Home Office RDS
Brian French	Northern Ireland Office
Prof. Chris Hale	University of Kent at Canterbury
Jacqueline Hoare	Home Office RDS
Prof. Tim Hope	Keele University
Prof. Mike Hough	ICPR, King's College London
Krista Jansson	Home Office RDS
Maya Kara	Home Office RDS

Chris Kershaw	Home Office RDS
Prof. Janet Lauritsen	University of Missouri-St. Louis
Jorgen Lovbakke	Home Office RDS
Prof. James Lynch	John Jay College
Dr. Heather McCraken	National Centre for Social Research
Beth McMaster	Scottish Executive
Susan McVie	University of Edinburgh
Prof. Mike Maguire	University of Wales at Cardiff
Prof. Michael Maxfield	Rutgers University
David Matz	Home Office RDS
Pat Mayhew	Victoria University of Wellington
Catriona Mirrlees-Black	Metropolitan Police Service
Bob Morris	Formerly Assistant Under Secretary of State, Home Office
Rachel Murphy	Home Office RDS
Helen Murray	Home Office
Camilla Nevill	National Centre for Social Research
Sian Nicholas	Home Office RDS
Juan Carlos Oyanedel	King's College London
David Povey	Home Office RDS
Michael Rand	U.S. Department of Justice
Jon Simmons	Home Office RDS
Prof. Wesley Skogan	Northwestern University
Barry Stalker	Scottish Executive
Prof. Mike Sutton	Nottingham Trent University
Katharine Thorpe	Home Office RDS
Prof. Jackie Tombs	Sterling University
Andromachi Tseloni	Nottingham Trent University

Alison Walker	Home Office RDS
Prof. Paul Wiles	Home Office
Frances Wilkinson	Economic and Social Research Council
Charlotte Wood	Home Office RDS

NOTE

1. RDS is the Research Development and Statistics Directorate of the U.K. Home Office.